Roman Drama

ROMAN DRAMA

A Reader

Gesine Manuwald

Duckworth

First published in 2010 by
Gerald Duckworth & Co. Ltd.
90-93 Cowcross Street
London EC1M 6BF
Tel: 020 7490 7300
Fax: 020 7490 0080
info@duckworth-publishers.co.uk
www.ducknet.co.uk

A catalogue record for this book is available
from the British Library

ISBN 978 0 7156 3869 9

Typeset by Ray Davies
Printed and bound in Great Britain by
CPI Antony Rowe, Chippenham and Eastbourne

Contents

Contents

Dramatic Texts

Nachleben of Roman Drama

Preface

The study of Roman drama has been largely confined to the completely surviving works of Plautus, Terence and Seneca. Interesting and important as these are, the understanding and appreciation of Roman drama and its development over the centuries of its existence will increase when these plays are seen in context. Facilitating this and returning Roman drama as a whole to a wider audience is the purpose of this anthology.

It provides a basic introduction to the essentials of Roman drama as well as a selection of representative dramatic texts, including extracts from tragedy (crepidata), comedy (palliata), praetexta, togata and mime from both the Republican and imperial periods. Additionally, there is a selection of key testimonia to the background of Roman theatre with particular reference to the Republican period, since in the absence of complete texts for some dramatic genres and of other contemporary evidence, these testimonia acquire great significance, but are all too often neglected or inaccessible. A final (very selective) section on the reception of Roman drama by poets in England, from 'the first English comedy' to the twentieth century, allows glimpses into how Roman drama continues to influence the European dramatic tradition. All texts are provided in the original language and in English translation; technical discussions are omitted. Therefore the book should be particularly useful for students and teachers (ways of exploring the topic further are indicated in the bibliography).

So it remains to hope that this book will be as enjoyable for readers using it as it has been for the author writing it and that it will contribute to making an interesting and important area of Roman literature more widely known. Warmest thanks are due to Matthew Robinson, Niall Slater and Kathryn Tempest, who all took the time during busy periods to read through an entire draft of the book and saved me from a number of embarrassing errors and infelicities. Deborah Blake at Duckworth has enthusiastically supported this project from the beginning and ensured its timely and beautiful production; individuals, publishers and institutions have kindly granted permission for reprints or reproductions: I am grateful to everyone involved.

London, September 2009   G.M.

Notes for the Reader

Introduction

Since the introduction is intended to convey basic background information necessary for reading and understanding the texts that form the body of this book, it does not have footnotes or numerous references to primary and secondary sources. Further details can be found with the help the bibliography (at the end of the volume), which is divided into thematic sections. There are, however, references to passages to primary texts included in this anthology if these illustrate or provide evidence for a particular issue (for the format see below on 'References').

Latin texts

The Latin texts printed in this anthology are based on the standard editions in the Oxford Classical Texts or Bibliotheca Teubneriana series for authors whose writings have been preserved in their entirety (with slight modifications where necessary). The text of the dramatic fragments is based on the third edition of Otto Ribbeck's collections of the comic and tragic fragments (1897/98), still the only comprehensive edition of all dramatic fragments; this has been compared with more recent editions where they are available (and adapted where appropriate). The numbering of the fragments in Ribbeck's third edition [R.³] and in Warmington's Loeb edition [W.] is given for the convenience of readers; more recent editions (see bibliography) typically include concordances. For these references the various dramatic genres are indicated by the abbreviations of their names (*Trag*[*oedia*], *Praet*[*exta*], *Com*[*oedia*], *Tog*[*ata*], *Mim*[*us*]); fragments not explicitly attributed to a specific author and/or work in the transmission are designated as *Incerta* (*Inc.* or *Inc. inc.*), even if here they may be assigned to a particular play for other reasons.

Although establishing the text is notoriously difficult in the case of fragments, the generally accepted and/or most plausible version of the Latin has been printed and a textual apparatus has been omitted, since the purpose of this book is to facilitate reading and appreciating these dramatic texts rather than the discussion of technical questions, which can be found elsewhere. Where major changes to the transmitted texts have been adopted, these are marked in the Latin (by [ ] for deletions and

< > for additions); deleted words have not been translated, supplemented ones have been included in the English version without any indication. Where problems in the Latin texts have been suspected and no satisfactory solutions have been proposed so far, this has also been indicated (by † for uncertain text and * for possible lacunae); an approximate sense is rendered in the English version.

English translations

All English translations are new translations by the author. They aim at being sufficiently idiomatic to be read on their own, but still sufficiently close to the original text to provide guidance to understanding the Latin.

Commentary

There is no separate section of commentary on the texts assembled in this book, but the brief introductions to each extract provide the necessary background. And a few factual clarifications (short ones included within square brackets in the English translations and longer ones placed below the Latin or English texts as notes) and identifications of quotations (included within square brackets in the Latin texts) should provide enough information on details.

Bibliography

The bibliography is not an exhaustive list of literature on Roman drama, but rather a selection of books and articles (mainly in English) that are useful starting points for readers who would like to explore the subject beyond the material given in this anthology. Hence the bibliography mainly lists editions, commentaries, translations and surveys as well as introductions to dramatic poets and genres and to the background of Roman drama. The entries are arranged in thematic sections and include brief comments where necessary.

References

The texts presented are divided into Testimonia (T), Dramatic texts (D) and *Nachleben* (N); the passages in each section are numbered consecutively. Together with the letter symbol for each section texts can be identified and referred to easily and concisely (e.g. T 1; D 1; N 1). The same is true for the Introduction (I) and its sections (e.g. I 1).

Notes for the Reader

Illustrations

The figures can be found at the end of the Introduction, on pp. 31-3.

Sources and acknowledgements: Figs 1, 2, 4, 5: from F. Sear, *Roman Theatres. An Architectural Study*, Oxford 2006 (Oxford Monographs on Classical Archaeology), figs 1, 3, 30a, plan 25, reproduced by kind permission of the author. Fig. 3: Photograph: Gesine Manuwald. Fig. 6: © Trustees of the British Museum.

Introduction:
Overview of Roman Drama

I 1. Background and evolution

According to the prevailing Roman tradition (adopted by modern scholars) Roman 'literary' drama emerged in 240 BCE, one year after the end of the First Punic War (264-241 BCE), when the magistrates in charge commissioned the poet Livius Andronicus to produce a play (or plays) in Greek style for the annual public festival. Later Roman writers, who applied the literary standards of their own time and regarded the development in Rome against the background of Greece, thought that Rome acquired poetry rather late (cf. e.g. T 5). By the mid-third century BCE Greek drama, for instance, had existed for centuries and already gone through several phases: notably the classical period in the fifth century BCE, when Aeschylus (525/24-456/55 BCE), Sophocles (497/96-406/05 BCE) and Euripides (485/84-407/06 BCE) produced tragedies and Aristophanes (c. 445-385 BCE) was active in the area of Old Comedy; followed by the Hellenistic period, best known for Menander (342/41-293/92 BCE), who wrote New Comedy. Dramatic performances in Italy prior to 240 BCE consisted of various indigenous, pre-literary forms as well as productions of classical and Hellenistic Greek dramas in the Hellenized southern regions.

This specific historical situation influenced what was to become 'Roman drama'. By the middle of the third century BCE Romans had been in contact with other nations in Italy and elsewhere in the Mediterranean for centuries, including Etruscans, Oscans and other Italic peoples, Greeks in mainland Greece and in the Greek colonies and also Carthaginians. Romans had trade links with all these inhabitants of the Mediterranean and were exposed to various aspects of their cultures. For instance, Romans will have seen a variety of dramatic performances and experienced different performance conventions, besides having access to written scripts where they existed. Hence, when the Romans started to produce their own dramatic poetry in Latin, their poets did not develop it from scratch, but could build upon sophisticated dramatic forms that had been established elsewhere. The major dramatic genres in Rome, therefore, did not undergo a gradual and independent development from simple to more refined forms; instead shadowy beginnings were immediately followed by a relatively advanced literary stage.

1

Above all, Greek drama exerted a major influence. Greek drama was open to being taken over by non-Greeks, since, besides catering for Athenian audiences, it had the potential for universality and adaptability as it dealt with general issues of human behaviour and society. Besides, the Romans in particular are said to have been highly receptive, flexible and ready to appropriate whatever suited them; hence they were able to adopt and adapt convenient dramatic structures and elements. So it may not be a coincidence that it was the Romans who took the step of developing something new and tailored to their own situation out of the existing forms of Greek literary drama.

With the transposition of Greek tragedies and comedies into Latin, the art of 'literary translation' is said to have been introduced as an artistic method to Europe. This type of translation does not consist in word-for-word literal rendering, but in transposing the meaning and structure of texts to a different environment; this process leads to genuine literary works based on models in a foreign language, but arranged for another culture with its own traditions. Thereby the Romans became the first cultural community in Europe to appropriate and adapt literary models from another European culture.

Since early Roman playwrights worked on the basis of existing literature, they were confronted with a wide variety of models; their choices as to what to select from this range of possibilities and how to reuse this material constitute their first independent artistic decisions. They apparently favoured stories and themes relevant to contemporary Roman audiences and adapted dramatic structures to the requirements of the Latin language and to the emerging conventions of the Roman stage. Soon after their first experiences with Greek-style serious and light drama (tragedy and comedy), early Roman playwrights additionally developed Roman variants on this basis: Roman-style serious and light drama, i.e. dramas on events from Roman history (praetexta) and comedies set in Rome and Italy and dealing with family affairs (togata). The range of dramatic genres in Rome was enriched further when pre-literary dramatic forms in Italy became literary in the first century BCE.

I 2. Dramatic genres

Ancient Rome eventually saw a wider variety of dramatic genres than classical Greece: there were dramatic forms taken over from the Greeks (tragedy and comedy), Roman variants of these dramatic genres developed on the basis of the Greek precedent (praetexta and togata) as well as indigenous varieties that became literary and more sophisticated (Atellana, mime, pantomime). These dramatic genres with their typical characteristics were distinguished from each other from the beginning, even though specific generic terms are only attested later in some cases. By the late Republican/early Augustan period the appropriate terminology had been developed in Rome, and ancient scholars discussed the relationships between and the characteristics of the various dramatic genres (in addition to what dramatic poets themselves had done in some of their plays). Results of these considerations survive as well-structured systems (more or less complete) in late-antique grammarians, commentators and scholiasts (cf. T 12).

According to these, the main dramatic genres are divided into their Greek and their Roman varieties and into four corresponding types for each side. In the system outlined by the grammarian Diomedes (writing in the fourth century CE) these are *tragica* (*tragoedia*, also called *crepidata* by other writers), *comica* (*comoedia*), *satyrica, mimica* for the Greek side and *praetextata* (called *praetexta* by earlier writers), *tabernaria* (called *togata* by other writers), *Atellana, planipes* (called *mimus* by other writers) for the Roman side. Greek dramatic genres are distinguished from Roman ones by their setting; the various dramatic forms on each side differ in protagonists, mood and subject matter, while Greek and Roman versions in the same position correspond in type; distinctions between dramatic genres based on formal features such as dramatic structure, metrical form or language are not made. This organization of dramatic genres and also empirical evidence indicate that Greece only had the dramatic forms and terms of tragedy, comedy, satyr-play and mime; further distinctions were partly unnecessary and partly not attempted. In Rome, however, more specific terms were coined, probably owing to the greater variety of dramatic forms and perhaps also to a greater generic awareness of a later period. The new terms were often derived from characteristic pieces of the protagonists' clothing.

The most common form of serious drama in Rome was **tragoedia**, also called **fabula crepidata** in technical discourse (after the tragic shoe: Gr. κρηπίς, Lat. *crepida*) and usually referred to as 'tragedy' in modern scholarship. This is Roman tragedy of Greek type, i.e. dramas in Latin on sections of Greek myth in an elevated style, based on existing Greek plays on the same myth (mainly those by the three great Greek tragic poets of the classical period) or on mythographical or even other literary sources. This form of drama was introduced to Rome by her first poet Livius Andronicus; the only fully preserved examples of Roman tragedy are dramas composed by the imperial playwright Seneca. Although no connection of individual tragedies to specific events in Roman history can be demonstrated, Roman poets seem to have chosen myths that were relevant to Roman audiences on a general level, for instance when they involved discussions of the legitimacy of power or of the relationship between victors and the conquered; they not only presented these stories in Latin, but also used Roman concepts and reference points relevant to Roman audiences. The subject matter for a sizeable number of Roman tragedies was taken from the Trojan cycle, though other mythical cycles were also present from the start; the last Republican tragedian Accius even seems to have made an attempt to cover as wide a range of myths as possible (cf. D 1-5; 14).

Fabula praetexta or *praetextata* (in a later variant) is a genuine Roman form of serious drama (cf. Hor. *Ars P.* 285-8), which dramatizes scenes from Rome's early (almost mythical) history as well as significant events from the more recent past or contemporary incidents (e.g. Romulus and Remus; Brutus and the foundation of the Republic; military victories); historical drama was not recognized as a separate dramatic genre in Greece. The protagonists in these historical dramas are Roman magistrates, generals and other public figures. This explains the Latin name for this dramatic genre, derived from a quintessentially Roman garment, the *toga praetexta*, worn by curule magistrates as a symbol of their position. Despite their different subject matter, these historical dramas seem to have been close to Roman tragedies in form and style. The genre of praetexta was inaugurated by Naevius, Rome's second poet, who apparently made the fledgling literary genres in Rome 'more Roman'. Nowadays, few remains of praetextae survive (merely some titles and fragments); a single example of this dramatic genre is completely extant, the imperial pseudo-Senecan *Octavia* (cf. D 6; 15).

Fabula palliata refers to light drama of Greek type in Rome (*comoedia*). Initially these dramas were simply called *comoediae*; later they acquired the generic description of *fabulae palliatae*, presumably in order to distinguish them from comedies in Roman setting, called *fabulae togatae*, the two varieties being named after a typical Greek and a typical Roman outer garment. Palliatae were based on works of Hellenistic New Comedy, particularly those by Menander. They often presented love affairs in a private setting, frequently following a standard plot: a young man is in love with a girl, who is in the possession of a pimp or a wealthier rival; hence the young man needs money, which he finds with the help of a clever slave, often by tricking his father and by using all means of deception. In the end the girl is revealed as the daughter of a respected citizen, abducted in her youth, recognized by means of various tokens; therefore a marriage becomes possible, and the negative characters are punished. However, there are also a number of variations of this basic plot (cf. T 13), including some unexpected varieties, such as Plautus' *Amphitruo*, which the poet himself defines as 'tragi-comedy' (cf. T 13a; D 7). Such comedies discuss general moral and ethical questions relevant to Roman audiences. Greek-style comedy in Rome came into being at about the same time as Greek-style tragedy, both forms being introduced by Livius Andronicus. The most famous representatives are the mid-Republican playwrights Plautus and Terence; a number of their plays survive complete (cf. D 7-11).

The Roman form of comedy, ***fabula togata***, named after the characteristic Roman garment, the *toga*, is a complement to *fabula palliata*. While the expression *fabula togata* seems to have been the term commonly used for Roman comedy, it functioned as the overall description of all Roman types of drama in some grammatical systems: in these Roman comedy was called (*fabula*) *tabernaria* (derived from *taberna*, 'wooden hut'). In any case *fabula tabernaria* or *fabula togata* (in the sense of 'Roman comedy') completes the set-up that allows for a four-fold division of major dramatic genres with two different types of pairings (serious and light or Greek and Roman). The two forms of light drama in Rome correspond to each other in types of plot and rank of characters while they are distinguished by their respective Greek or Roman settings and personages; both forms of light drama differ from the serious dramatic genres by the lowliness of the protagonists and the private subject matter. The emergence of togatae probably in the early second century BCE is likely to be a result of differentiation: it was possible and desirable to create a Roman comic form when palliatae were becoming more Hellenic, but had provided precedents for plot-based light drama in Latin. Togatae differ from palliatae beyond the setting, even though poets of togatae seem to have continued to look to Greek New Comedy as a dramatic model in terms of structure and possible plots. Togatae were apparently more serious and solemn, and they seem to have dealt with more 'normal' love relationships within the family: there is a marked focus on marriages, discussions of projected matches, preparations and consequences of marriages, unfaithfulness and divorce. Togatae only survive in fragments from the Republican period (cf. D 12).

Fabula Atellana is a distinct form of light drama, named after the Oscan town of Atella in Campania, where it is said to have been first performed. It may have been brought to Rome by Oscan workmen, where it was Romanized. Later, this dramatic genre acquired literary status, when it came to be more regular and to be based on written scripts. Quintessentially, Atellanae featured a fixed number of stock characters with invariable features, the 'Oscan characters' (*Oscae personae*). Extant titles and fragments of literary Atellanae as well as testimonia point to at least four stock figures, who share a certain degree of gluttony, clownishness and foolishness and who bear simple, speaking names: Maccus, the fool and stupid clown; Bucco, the foolish braggart; Pappus, the foolish old man; Dossennus, the cunning trickster and/or glutton. However, there were various types of Atellanae, including mythical dramas and palliata-like stories. Fragments of literary Atellanae from the

5

early first century BCE remain; in this period Atellanae could be given as 'after-pieces' after performances of dramas of other genres.

The Greek *mimus* is called *planipes* in Latin, after the bare feet of its performers (or the humbleness of its plot or its performance in the orchestra). But both *mimus* and *planipes* are used as terms for the Roman type by Latin authors; *mimus* seems to be the more common form, with *planipes* found mainly in technical contexts. Ancient grammarians define *planipes/mimus* as a simple and humble form analogous to the Greek mime. In Rome mimes are similar to Atellanae in that they had gone through a pre-literary phase in Italy before they became literary. Both genres tend to be given a minor role in systems of dramatic genres, as they are regarded as less sophisticated than Greek and Roman versions of 'tragedy' and 'comedy'. Mimes turned literary only at the very end of the Republican period, when they might be given as 'after-pieces'; fragments of mimes from this period have been preserved. Although mimes were regarded as low, crude and vulgar, they could include serious (philosophical or moral) messages and comments on topical issues (cf. D 13).

The Roman *pantomimus* was a type of dance by a single performer, who, by his movement and gestures, interpreted a text, which was sung by a chorus accompanied by a variety of musical instruments. The stories presented in pantomimes were based on famous mythical and historical characters, on the analogy of serious drama; in contrast to performances of those dramatic genres, where different characters could appear on stage together and interact, the characters and their actions could only be portrayed successively in a pantomime. Although ancient sources date the introduction of pantomime to Rome to 22 BCE, it is likely to have emerged already in the late 40s BCE, marking the final stages of developments on the Roman stage during the Republican period. The genre was popular and promoted under emperors from Augustus until late antiquity. In pantomimes music, dance, costumes and props were paramount, and audiences were not required to understand the words fully in order to follow the story or to enjoy the performance.

I 3. Dramatic poets

The early poets in Rome, who established Latin as a literary language and initiated the creation of literary works in Latin in the Republican period, did not come from Rome, but from other parts of Italy or even from outside Italy. All these regions of the Mediterranean, particularly Campania and the area around Tarentum, were heavily influenced by Greek culture. Hence these poets brought knowledge of their local customs and language, along with familiarity with Greek traditions, to

6

Rome. Yet despite their diverse origins they all used the Latin language when they started their literary careers in Rome. Moreover, in contrast to practitioners of other literary genres, the early dramatists were of low social status, being slaves, freedmen or foreigners. Only towards the end of the Republic, when dramas were no longer necessarily composed for full-scale stage productions, did educated noblemen start writing dramatic poetry. The early dramatists were in touch with influential noblemen and may have accepted individual commissions, but it is unlikely that they were generally dependent on individuals as 'client poets' and therefore had to compromise their poetry. They probably just had to make sure that their plays were successful with the audience at large so as to win further contracts, since they received payment for their plays, which presumably constituted at least part of their living.

The Republican comic poets Plautus and Terence as well as the imperial tragic poet Seneca are the only Roman playwrights by whom complete dramas survive. However a number of further dramatists are known at least by name (besides *c.* 120 lines from light drama, mostly palliatae, and *c.* 260 lines from tragedies transmitted without indication of playwright or work), and several are represented by a sizeable number of titles and fragments (though the reading of titles and the attribution of fragments are not always certain). Those who are regarded as the major representatives of Roman drama today, because a significant portion of their works survive and because they are mentioned by later writers, had already come to be regarded as the more important poets in antiquity, which in turn influenced the attention given to their works. The mere existence of further writers, however, proves that writing plays was a more widespread activity than the usual focus on the major representatives might suggest (cf. T 4-6).

The more prominent playwrights in the Republican period are distributed over genres and periods as follows: writers of tragedies (crepidatae) and comedies (palliatae) are spread over the period from the beginnings of Roman drama to the early first century BCE; for tragedy five major poets are attested (Livius Andronicus, Naevius, Ennius, Pacuvius, Accius), for comedy there are at least eight well-known poets (Livius Andronicus, Naevius, Ennius, Plautus, Caecilius Statius, Luscius Lanuvinus, Terence, Turpilius). The series for praetexta and togata have fewer representatives, but end about the same time; the known poets for praetextae are Naevius, Ennius, Pacuvius, Accius, for togatae there are Titinius, Afranius, Atta. For literary Atellana, literary mime and pantomime, which flourished throughout much shorter periods, fewer poets are attested, and their dates are closer together: for literary Atellana there are Pomponius and Novius in the early first century; literary mimes were written by Decimus Laberius and Publilius Syrus in the mid-first century; and for pantomime Pylades from Cilicia and Bathyllos from Alexandria are credited with 'developing the Italian style of dance' in the mid to late first century BCE (cf. Appendix 1; 2).

Rome's first known playwright was **Lucius Livius Andronicus** (*c.* 280/70-200 BCE); according to the prevailing Roman tradition he introduced several literary genres to Rome and was instrumental in lifting Roman performance culture to a 'literary' level (cf. T 1; 3). He produced a Latin version of Homer's *Odyssey* and thus the first epic in Latin (*Odusia*). This achievement probably established his poetic credentials and made him an ideal candidate when the magistrates decided to introduce Greek-style drama at the public festival of 240 BCE. Livius Andronicus provided a play (or plays) for this festival and continued to write Greek-style comedies and tragedies throughout his career. The extant remains of his poetry in all literary genres are meagre: titles of between eight and ten tragedies (and about 40, partly incomplete, verses) and of two or three comedies (and a few fragments), about 40 verses from the *Odusia* and testimonia on a ritual song.

His immediate successor and contemporary **Gnaeus Naevius** (*c.* 280/60-200 BCE) continued to be active in a variety of literary genres. He also wrote an epic, tragedies and comedies, but he took the step of increasing the 'Roman' element in these literary genres and of adding a genuinely Roman dramatic form: his epic was not an adaptation of a Greek mythical story, it rather narrated an event from Roman history, the First Punic War (*Bellum Poenicum*); Naevius also inaugurated serious drama on Roman subjects (praetexta) as he wrote plays about events from early Roman history and recent incidents. His works of Greek-style dramatic genres feature allusions to Roman reality too. Because of this and due to some questionable biographical notices Naevius has often been regarded as particularly outspoken and as even having run into trouble with the authorities on this account. However, the evidence is doubtful, and he might just have been a well-informed individual, closely following contemporary developments. All works of Naevius have only been transmitted in fragments: there are titles of about 35 comedies and about 140 (partly incomplete) comic verses, titles of six tragedies and about 60 (partly incomplete) tragic verses, titles of two praetextae with a few lines each and about 60 fragments of the epic *Bellum Poenicum*. Naevius' tragedies took up some of the stories dramatized by Livius Andronicus, while he also introduced new topics, for instance by presenting a god on stage in his tragedy *Lycurgus*. In antiquity Naevius was mainly known as a comic poet; and the fragments of his prolific output foreshadow characteristics later found in Plautus.

Livius Andronicus and Naevius were followed by **Quintus Ennius** (239-169 BCE), who was about a generation younger than the two pioneers.

Ennius was arguably the most versatile early Latin poet and made important contributions to the establishment of Roman literature and national identity (cf. Hor. *Epist.* 1.19.7: *pater Ennius* – 'father Ennius'). His epic *Annales* was the first comprehensive narrative of Roman history in Latin verse (and the first Roman epic written in hexameters). Ennius' reputation in later periods largely rests on this epic and on his tragedies; his comedies and praetextae only play a minor role. The poet's versatility and his experiments with content and form are demonstrated also by his so-called *opera minora*, his other works besides epic and drama, particularly by the new literary genre of *satura* and philosophical writings. What remains from Ennius' works are about 24 titles of dramas and more than 400 (partly incomplete) verses, including two praetextae and two comedies, more than 600 verses of *Annales* and about 200 verses and passages in prose from the *opera minora*. In addition to developing Latin poetic technique further and presenting himself as a self-confident poet, Ennius' works display a significant 'Roman' character, since characteristic values and forms of behaviour (such as virtue, bravery, loyalty or support of the community) come to the fore (cf. D 1-2).

Marcus Pacuvius (*c.* 220-130 BCE) belongs to a later generation of Republican dramatists. He was the first Roman playwright to concentrate on serious drama only (besides being a painter); after Ennius a distinction between poets of various light dramatic genres and poets of serious drama became established. Of Pacuvius' dramatic output, about thirteen titles of tragedies (and about 430, partly incomplete, lines) as well as four verses of the praetexta *Paulus* survive. Pacuvius, who was regarded as 'learned' (*doctus*) by later ancient authorities (cf. T 5; 6), seems to have preferred less famous versions or sections of well-known myths for his tragedies, which allowed him to focus on particular themes (such as family relationships, struggles for power or philosophical discussions) and to create effective drama (cf. D 3-4).

Lucius Accius (170-*c.* 80 BCE), the last major tragic poet in Republican times, wrote dramas as well as works of other literary genres. As a dramatist, he focused on serious genres like his predecessor Pacuvius, but far more dramas are known for Accius. Titles of about 45 tragedies and two praetextae survive, along with almost 700 (partly incomplete) verses. In addition Accius was a literary critic and grammarian influenced by Hellenistic scholarship; he wrote treatises on grammatical, theatrical and literary questions (*Didascalica*, *Pragmatica*), an epic *Annales* and some other poetry, poorly attested. Even though Ennius provides a precedent for a versatile poet who went beyond drama and epic and was active in a variety of literary genres, Accius is the only Republican playwright who also composed separate works on literary questions and theatre history and thereby engaged with the subject of drama in both theory and practice. This academic interest agrees with developments in the late second and the first centuries BCE, when scholars, who were not dramatic poets themselves, started to discuss aspects of literary history. The number and distribution of preserved titles for his tragedies suggest that Accius explored the full range of mythical cycles and a corresponding breadth of sources. Like Pacuvius, he strove for dramatic effects; at the same time he seems to have chosen myths or versions and sections of myths that allowed him to discuss questions relevant to Roman audiences (such as ancestry, genealogies of families or the consequences of deeds done in the past on later generations). Such topics become connected with another important aspect, the theme of proper rule, when someone's descent and membership in a house or family function as legitimizing factors (cf. D 5-6).

Titus Maccius Plautus (*c.* 250-184 BCE) is the earliest Roman dramatist by whom complete plays survive, and he is also the one for whom the largest number of plays is extant. Plautus was the first Roman playwright to concentrate on one dramatic genre only (palliata). He seems to have been active in Rome as a successful dramatist for more than two decades around 200 BCE and to have been a prolific poet. Later 130 'Plautine' comedies circulated under his name; therefore Plautus was one of the earliest Republican playwrights to become the object of scholarly discussion, when ancient critics tried to distinguish between genuine and spurious plays. Various attempts were made until Varro identified a core of 21 comedies that were accepted as genuine by everyone. These were called *fabulae Varronianae* ('Varro's plays'); and it is virtually certain that these are the 21 (almost complete) comedies in the extant Plautine manuscripts (besides, there are further titles and fragments, which may or may not be genuine). In antiquity already Plautus was known for his metrical variety, linguistic exuberance and inventiveness. The characters in his plays remain in constant contact with the audience in awareness of the performance situation ('metatheatre'). Plots may seem to be full of meaningless comic banter and to be governed by chance and unforeseen events, but they go beyond that in telling coherent and well-structured stories. Within this framework Plautus presents, for instance, a wide range of human temperaments and emotions in a variety of situations, tensions between young lovers and the conventions of society, arguments between members of different generations, demonstrations of the power of chance, comments on social customs, different ways of love, the problem of justice and punishment, moral considerations governing human behaviour, faithfulness and loyalty, ways of dealing with foreigners as well as other social and moral issues (cf. T 13a-b; D 7-8).

Caecilius Statius (*c.* 230/20-168/7 BCE) was a palliata poet active between Plautus and Terence. Caecilius' palliatae, however, have only been transmitted in fragments. What remains are 42 titles of comedies, almost 300 (partly incomplete) lines quoted in later writers and, what is unique for Roman drama, a papyrus fragment (originally containing 550 lines) of the play *Obolostates sive Faenerator* ('*Money-lender*'). Caecilius is often seen as an intermediate or transitional poet. Indeed he seems to have followed the Plautine tradition of his predecessors in aspects such as metre, style, linguistic features, use of puns and comic effects, while in other areas such as themes, elements of dramatic technique and involvement in literary discussions he looks forward to Terence. Issues and values prominent in Caecilius are mostly related to family life, the corresponding relationships and the impact on one's position in society (cf. D 9).

Publius Terentius Afer (*c.* 195/4-159 BCE) is the second writer of preserved palliatae after Plautus. Terence is also the only Republican dramatist whose output seems to have been preserved in its entirety and the only one for whom production notices (*didascaliae*) survive, which give information about dates and occasions for the plays and about individuals involved in the original performances. Terence's plays are often regarded as more restrained and more 'Hellenic' than those of Plautus, since they have prologues dealing with metaliterary questions, and there is less linguistic and metrical exuberance, less explicit metatheatre, less slapstick comedy and less overt allusion to a Roman context. However, his plays do have a specific significance for contemporary audiences, since, within the framework of the standard comic plot, they address general human problems, presented within a bourgeois world, for instance various relationships between siblings, friends or parents and children, love affairs as well as problems of education. According to Terence's prologues, some of his plays experienced problems getting a hearing when they were produced for the first time; yet the descriptions in the prologues point to opposition from contemporary playwrights, who tried to oust Terence from the stage because of his success, as the reason for these difficulties rather than poor audience response (cf. T 13c-d; 14; D 10-11).

Sextus Turpilius is the last known writer of palliatae within the Republican period; he died in old age in Sinuessa in 104/3 BCE. Thirteen titles and just over 200 (partly incomplete) lines of his plays have been preserved. While Turpilius appears to have followed Terence's (and Caecilius') more restrained and 'Hellenized' version of palliata in titles, themes and choice of Greek models, he seems to have been closer to Plautus (and Naevius) in language, use of stylistic features and scene structures, besides appropriating elements of contemporary developments in other dramatic genres.

Titinius (*fl. c.* 200 BCE) is probably the oldest known writer of genuinely Roman comedies (togatae). Virtually nothing is known about his biography, and his dates are therefore disputed. The general consensus of modern scholars seems to favour placing Titinius before Terence and close to Plautus, and he is widely thought to have been active in the years just after the Second Punic War. The evidence from approximately fifteen titles and about 180 (partly incomplete) lines indeed suggests that Titinius is an early representative of togata: there is a noticeable similarity to both Atellana and Plautine palliata, which might point to a dramatic genre that is evolving and looking for its own distinctive position within the framework of light dramatic genres. Although Titinius' plays display features similar to palliatae, they exhibit characteristics different from them, in particular the prominence of more 'normal' family relationships (e.g. love affairs and marriage arrangements within the family) or the notable presence of Roman and Italic places and institutions. Beyond the standard comic plots Titinius seems to have used stories that allowed him to comment upon issues of topical relevance in his time.

Lucius Afranius (*fl. c.* 160-120 BCE) is the second known representative of togata. Although the ancients regarded Afranius as the most important togata poet, and hence the largest number of extant togata fragments comes from his works, almost nothing is known about his dates and biography. Statements by ancient writers and internal evidence place his poetic activity in the second half of the second century BCE, in the period after Terence. Forty-three titles and about 430 (partly incomplete) lines have been preserved, which reveal some of Afranius' characteristics and preferred topics. On the basis established by Titinius, Afranius seems to have developed the dramatic genre of togata further and given it a distinctive form in relation to contemporary palliata: palliata was becoming more 'Hellenic' by the period of Terence, and togata underwent a similar development by Afranius' time, led by Terence's precedent. Also, Afranius' plays include metaliterary statements and display the influence of other literary genres. This is combined with entertaining plots typical of this dramatic genre, including issues such as marriages, dowries or difficult relationships between husbands and wives. The family seems to have been a major focus, Afranius enlarging the spectrum of family members involved to the extended family (cf. D 12).

Titus Quinctius Atta is the last of the triad of clearly attested togata poets; he died in Rome in 77 BCE. All that survives of his dramatic output are twelve titles and nearly 25 (partly incomplete) verses. Atta seems to have engaged with Roman issues, while indications of standard comic plots are not lacking. The plays cover Roman games and their organization, lascivious life in a spa, sacrifices and religious customs, mercenaries or a discussion of the first month of the year. These details confirm the Roman outlook of this dramatic genre and exemplify the general trend towards both spectacle and erudition in Atta's time.

Lucius Pomponius from Bononia (modern Bologna) was active in 89 BCE. He is described as a writer of Atellanae and is even credited with having invented a new genre (cf. Vell. Pat. 2.9.6). However, Novius seems to have been a contemporary of his, and at least a pre-literary Atellana was previously in existence. Hence this description most likely recognizes that Pomponius turned Atellana into a literary dramatic genre. Of his dramatic output about 70 titles of Atellanae and almost 200 (partly incomplete) lines remain. Titles and fragments feature the stock characters of Atellanae, who could apparently experience various (unusual) situations for additional comic effects. Another well-represented area is the world of craftsmen, such as fullers, and of farmers. A number of sometimes rather mundane details of rural affairs or of running a farm are mentioned. Beyond these specific Atellana themes, some titles of Pomponius overlap with those of palliatae and togatae; additionally there are mythical titles, some of which are identical with those of tragedies. There are references to contemporary society and (meta-)literary matters.

Like Pomponius, **Novius** was a writer of Atellanae; he was a contemporary of Pomponius, the two of them representing the literary Atellana in the early first century BCE. Since it is Pomponius rather than Novius who is credited with having invented this dramatic genre, Novius is generally assumed to have been active slightly later or to have been less prominent (*fl. c.* 85 BCE). Fewer titles and fragments are known for him: just over 40 titles and just over 100 (partly incomplete) lines have been preserved. Novius' titles cover some of the same areas as those of Pomponius, namely experiences of Atellana stock characters, the world of tradesmen and farmers, such as fullers and vintners, as well as mythical topics, although the range is not as wide. Novius shares some titles with Roman tragedies, and his remakes of mythical stories seem to have been parodic. In other plays the usual topics of Atellana and light drama surface, such as love affairs and their typical difficulties or problems with inheritance and wives with dowries.

Decimus Laberius (*c.* 106-43 BCE) was a writer of literary mimes in the late Republic. He composed mimes for the stage, although he came from an equestrian family; this social status sets him apart from other Republican playwrights. What remains of Laberius' mimes are just over 40 titles and about 150 (partly incomplete) lines; the verses spoken when challenged by the dictator Caesar constitute the longest piece extant from the Roman mime. Later writers acknowledged Laberius' wittiness, critical irony and elegant thoughts, but disapproved of his diction, which they regarded as crude and unpolished, condemning colloquialisms and neologisms. The remaining titles and fragments feature frequent comic characters, such as wives, courtesans, slaves and masters, as well as typical motifs, such as conflicts between family members, discussions about inheritance and prodigal sons, marriages and festivals, business on farms, tradesmen and, of course, love affairs. Despite this atmosphere, Laberius' mimes were also a means of literary comment, 'philosophical discussion' as well as political and social polemic (cf. D 13).

Publilius Syrus, an actor and writer of mimes, is probably the youngest of the well-known Republican playwrights. After he had started to produce mimes with great success in the towns of Italy, he was fetched to Rome for games organized by the dictator Caesar and produced as star of the show, whence the contest between himself and the older equestrian poet Decimus Laberius followed. Of Publilius Syrus' output only two titles and a few fragments remain, besides a collection of so-called *sententiae*. Apparently his style was sententious and therefore invited to culling and collecting one-liners with proverbial meaning from his writings (cf. D 13).

Towards the end of the Republic changes in the number of new plays produced, in the social status of playwrights and in performance conventions started to take place: while performances of old plays and other entertainment continued, only a few new plays were written for the stage. Instead, from the late first century BCE onwards, noblemen turned to writing poetry as a spare-time activity and intellectual pursuit; they composed dramas to be read, recited and sent to friends, but not necessarily to be performed on stage in full-scale productions. These noblemen focussed on serious drama, composing mainly tragedies and occasionally praetextae; yet no substantial remains survive.

The names of more than thirty writers of tragedy are known for the first centuries BCE and CE; some of these writers are obscure, while a significant number are prominent figures, better known for their political or military activities or their work in other literary genres. These men include, for instance, Cicero's brother Quintus, who is said to have written four tragedies during a sixteen-day leave in the middle of a military campaign, and C. Asinius Pollio, politician, general, orator and historian in the second half of the first century BCE. In the Augustan period L. Varius Rufus wrote a *Thyestes* and Ovid a *Medea*, both praised by Quintilian (cf. T 6). An older contemporary of Seneca was P. Pomponius Secundus (also mentioned by Quintilian), who produced an *Aeneas* and debated tragic diction with Seneca. Tacitus' *Dialogus* portrays Curiatius Maternus, who is credited with *Cato, Domitius, Thyestes* and *Medea*.

Seneca (*c.* 1 BCE-65 CE) is the only imperial dramatist and the only Roman tragic poet by whom complete plays survive. Seneca enjoyed a thorough rhetorical and philosophical education before obtaining various positions at the imperial court (interrupted by exile); his most prominent role was that of tutor and later adviser to the emperor Nero (reigned: 54-

68 CE). The corpus of Senecan drama consists of ten plays. One of those is the praetexta *Octavia*, which is now generally regarded as spurious. It deals with Nero's divorce from his wife Octavia, Claudius' daughter, and his marriage with his beloved Poppaea and was probably written soon after these events some time in the last third of the first century CE. This drama is the only completely preserved example of a praetexta (cf. D 15). Of the remaining nine tragedies, *Hercules Oetaeus* too is often suspected of being spurious, which leaves a corpus of eight genuine tragedies, written presumably during the latter part of Seneca's life. Their exact dates are unknown, and it is also unclear whether they were ever given full-scale productions in public theatres. Seneca's tragedies take up well-known Greek myths, and their form comes closer to classical Greek tragedies than Republican tragedies seem to have done, since they adopt the alternation of episodes and choral odes and have a more regular metrical structure. What is characteristic of them is their sophisticated rhetorical set-up and their highly emotional and expressive atmosphere. The precise meaning and purpose of the tragedies are disputed; various readings, including moral, political and philosophical ones, have been suggested by scholars (cf. D 14).

I 4. Occasions and venues

In Republican times dramatic performances were part of public festivals organized by the magistrates in charge (curule aediles, plebeian aediles or praetor); these were political and religious events, lasting for several days and consisting of sacrifices as well as of a variety of entertainments. Originally there was only one festival, *Ludi Romani*, which dates back to regal times. In 364 BCE scenic performances (*ludi scaenici*) are said to have been added to the festival, which previously had only offered shows in the circus. In 240 BCE, when magistrates commissioned Rome's first poet Livius Andronicus, scenic performances at the Roman games moved to Greek-style drama (cf. T 1). This new form of performances did not remain a single event, but soon developed into a standard feature of Roman festivals.

In the period between the eve of the Second Punic War and the successful completion of this war and of those against eastern kingdoms (c. 220-170 BCE), five further regular festivals were added (*Ludi plebeii*, *Ludi Ceriales*, *Ludi Apollinares*, *Ludi Megalenses*, *Ludi Florales*). In addition, there were individual public or private festivals on special occasions, such as a military victory, the dedication of a temple or the funeral of an eminent personality. In the late Republic two more regular public festivals were added: *Ludi Victoriae (Sullanae)* and *Ludi Victoriae Caesaris*.

Each of the public festivals had a fixed number of days reserved for dramatic performances, but it is not known how many plays were performed at each festival or on any one day, what the respective proportions for different dramatic genres were or even whether there were any rules for the distribution of dramatic genres. At any rate from the late third/early second century BCE onwards there was a significant number of opportunities for producing and watching plays throughout the year.

Magistrates or noblemen running a festival were given some public funding, which they could supplement by their own means; these funds were used to create venues for shows in the circus and on stage and to buy the entertainment given in those locations, i.e. animals for circus games and plays for dramatic performances.

Initially, different performance venues were used for the various festivals in Rome. All of those were not specifically set up as theatres throughout the year, but were turned into theatrical spaces for a limited time by temporary structures. In the beginning dramas seem to have been staged in the circus, in the Forum or in front of the temple of the god of the respective festival. Temporary stages were erected; and the auditorium was provisional, spectators using the tiers of the circus, the steps of the temple or other convenient structures for seating. And while the site of the Circus Maximus, where circensic games took place, was improved throughout the second century BCE, there was no comparable building activity for venues of scenic performances.

This results in the paradoxical situation that during the most creative period of Roman stage drama there was no permanent stone theatre; instead, plays were acted on temporary stages till the end of the Republic. Yet the absence of a permanent theatre in Rome throughout most of the Republican period is not due to an inability on the part of the Romans to build such structures, but is rather the consequence of a decision against erecting them. Several attempts to construct permanent theatres in Rome were made by various officials throughout the second century BCE, when numerous dramas were composed and produced, but they all failed due to opposition from within the nobility. A number of reasons for this attitude have been proposed; the most likely one is perhaps that a permanent theatre would have interfered with religious traditions, since it would have prevented holding performances in front of the temple of the respective god honoured by a festival; and it would also have prevented performances in the Forum at the heart of the community. Resistance to a permanent structure therefore could be seen as an attempt to preserve traditional civic and religious customs. However, although theatre structures in Rome remained temporary almost till the end of the Republican period, they became more and more ornate and luxurious: the development towards spectacle affected both the physical appearance of theatre buildings and the preference for pageants, spectacular effects or more sensational dramatic genres (cf. T 8; 11).

In 55 BCE Pompey dedicated the first permanent stone theatre in Rome, a monument that had been built after his triumph in 61 BCE (cf. T 7b; 11a). Pompey's theatre was soon followed by the theatre of Balbus (13 BCE) and the theatre of Marcellus, begun by Caesar and completed and inaugurated by Augustus (13/11 BCE). Pompey's building was a huge complex on the Campus Martius, including a full theatre and a temple of Venus (Victrix) on top of the auditorium, its central wedge forming a monumental staircase leading up to the temple. In the mid-first century BCE, in the run-up to the establishment of the Principate, it had apparently become easier for individuals to erect permanent structures of display, while traditional customs still had to be observed (cf. Figs 1-6).

Due to the peculiar history of theatre buildings at Rome, there is no unambiguous evidence for their shape in the Republican period. Hence, the origins of what was to become the typical layout of a Roman theatre are not entirely certain. It seems, however, that in southern and central Italy elements of the Hellenistic Greek theatre (as common in the western Greek provinces) and local traditions were fused to create a distinctive performance space adapted to the requirements of Roman dramatic performances.

At any rate fully developed Roman theatres differ from Greek ones in a number of significant features (cf. T 7a): whereas Greek theatre buildings tend to make use of a natural hill for the rising auditorium and to give the audience a view into the distance, Roman ones form compact, freestanding, purpose-built units on flat surfaces. The Romans created a self-contained, coherent architectural unit out of a simple stage and a rounded auditorium (with its substructures). Because of the theatre's overall composition, the outline of the stage and its relationship to the spectator area are different in Rome: the auditorium has the size of about a half-circle only, the stage is lower and deeper (to allow for all stage action) and is terminated by the vertical façade of the stage building, directing the audience's view to the inside of the theatre. This façade with its three doors, elaborately decorated in later stone theatres, forms the permanent back wall of the stage; yet the decoration is not related to the setting of particular plays. The area between stage and auditorium (the orchestra, reserved for the chorus in Greek theatres) was used for seats for distinguished spectators. The side-entrances (between auditorium and stage on either side) were vaulted, and there were boxes for the organizers above them. Since, therefore, the Roman stage was framed on all sides, audiences were made to watch as onlookers from a distance.

The impressive remains of Roman theatres that can be found all over the empire date from early imperial times: the majority of surviving theatre structures belong to the period between the late Republic and the middle of the first century CE. At the same time it is not certain whether new plays written in early imperial times were necessarily designed for full-stage productions in large public theatres; at any rate theatre buildings in those days could be used for all sorts of entertainments. Additionally, there were small private venues for performances or recitations in front of select audiences. Dramatic productions were no longer restricted to public festivals.

I 5. Actors and productions

Whereas in Greece all participants in a dramatic production came from the citizenry, in Rome theatre business was the domain of professionals. In Republican times magistrates bought plays (i.e. presumably scripts) from playwrights (perhaps on the recommendation of professional producers) or from professional producers, who had previously acquired them from poets. It is not entirely clear what information magistrates may have received about plays prior to purchasing them and what their criteria for selection were, but they are likely to have aimed at plays that were bound to be successful with audiences and supportive of Roman ideology.

When the magistrates had chosen a play, they delegated all further arrangements for bringing it on stage to a professional producer/impresario/actor-manager, who had a group of theatre people as well as some equipment at his disposal. The most famous man in this capacity was perhaps Ambivius Turpio, who worked for the comic poets Caecilius Statius and Terence and also originally delivered the prologues to some of Terence's comedies (cf. T 14).

Appearing on stage for payment was looked down upon in Roman society, which prevented members of higher classes from taking up this profession. Hence most actors were of low social status; many were foreigners, freedmen or slaves; and they were denied basic citizen rights. However, successful actors could gain appreciation, win actors' contests and even become 'stars' in the late Republic, such as Q. Roscius Gallus and Clodius Aesopus in Cicero's time (cf. T 10b; 11a). In the first century BCE important public figures such as Sulla or Mark Antony began to socialize with actors, which was a target of reproach for their opponents.

Actors tended to specialize in either serious or light drama, yet they were not confined to one form exclusively. In almost all dramatic genres men played all roles; only mimes had actresses, and this was one reason why this dramatic genre was regarded as licentious. Although the number of players engaged in a performance as well as the number of speaking actors simultaneously present on stage was not limited to three as in classical Greece, actors' troupes in Rome still seem to have been rather small, for mere economic reasons. Most Roman comedies (the only dramatic genre for which inferences can be made) can be performed by a small number of actors (especially if one assumes a doubling of roles); they could have been supplemented by hired extras on occasion.

Each troupe of actors may have had their own musician, who was probably the composer as well as the performer of the music and arranged, presumably in consultation with the poet, the producer and/or the actors, how the set of various metres as prescribed by the dramatic script should be turned into music, since the majority of metres in Republican drama was accompanied by music and their delivery rather resembled modern arias or recitatives. The musician was called *tibicen*, since he played the *tibia*, a woodwind instrument with reeds. This instrument was virtually always played in pairs, one pipe fingered by each hand; the two parts of the pair (right and left) might be either equal or unequal in length. This allowed for a variety of tones and pitches, from which the musician could choose the version appropriate for each play or each section of a play.

For all venues and dramatic performances, set and scenery were broadly similar: the stage and its back wall represented an open area, frequently a street, in front of the doors to several buildings, with exits to the further distance (typically the countryside and the harbour) and to the nearer distance (typically the city centre) on either side of the stage. Sometimes there was an altar on the stage, but generally additional stage equipment was scarce. The performance had to rely on the imagination of audiences, to whom the particular meaning of buildings and locations in each drama would be made clear by information given in the plays themselves, primarily in the prologue or the initial scenes. Clarity was increased further by the announcement of entrances and exits of characters, the use of gestures and stage action underlining what was being said. Events that could not or did not take place in the open space represented by the stage area could not be shown and had to be narrated by 'messengers', i.e. characters who had watched these incidents taking place in the house or elsewhere and then informed other characters (on stage) about them. Only towards the end of the Republican period and the beginning of the imperial era did stage equipment become more sophisticated, for instance by the use of machines with revolving sides, which could indicate different kinds of background (cf. T 7a). During the final decades of the Republic, when more and more funds were spent on providing dramatic entertainment, the construction of theatres and the materials used became more and more lavish and elaborate (cf. T 8).

Prior to the late-antique period there is little definite evidence on actors' costumes and masks; details can only be inferred from the plays themselves and from a few references in contemporary or near-contemporary writers. Generally, dress seems to be referred to in the dramatic scripts mainly when there is something special and it is exploited to characterize someone or to enable the plot; characters shown in particular situations may have had the appropriate attire or at least a few props. People in palliatae wear (the tunic and) the *pallium*, which characterizes them as Greeks. In drama set in Roman surroundings actors must have worn Roman dress: in praetextae characters such as consuls might have had a *toga praetexta*; the fragments of the togata mention togas, tunics and shoes.

A further important part of the attire of actors of all dramatic genres consists of masks. Unfortunately, the question of when masks were introduced in Rome is vexed and controversial, since the evidence of the sources is contradictory. However, it would be strange if the Romans dispensed with this device used by all other theatre cultures they experienced, yet adopted and adapted all the other main elements of theatrical practice. Hence the existence of masks in the Roman theatre from early times onwards is generally assumed although their use will have differed across the various dramatic genres; it is clear that masks were known in the imperial period.

I 6. Audiences

Dramatic performances were a 'business' run by a particular group of people specialized in the theatre and paid for by the authorities. Therefore audiences enjoyed performances as entertainment provided by officials and professionals.

Since dramatic performances in Republican Rome were part of public festivals, they could potentially attract a large and diverse crowd of spectators, drawn from all groups of the local populace and visitors from elsewhere. Even though at least some early venues seem not to have been able to seat more than a few thousand spectators, this is already a sizeable number of people; and there are indications that excuses for repetitions of performances might have been sought, which increased the size of the overall audience of an individual production.

As festivals were funded by public money and contributions of the presiding magistrates (or wealthy families), there was no entrance fee. The various groups in the audience must have represented a range of varying degrees of education and experience. Yet plays can obviously be enjoyed on several levels. Some comic prologues suggest that there was noise and unruliness among the audience before the start of a performance, but this does not imply that Roman audiences were

20

generally unsophisticated or not interested in proper dramatic performances.

By the time of the surviving Republican comedies audiences had gained some experience of watching Greek-style plays in Rome; and judging from the kind of familiarity with Greek culture or dramatic conventions presupposed by Roman dramatic scripts, audiences seem to have become more sophisticated over time. Later dramatists dealt with Greek models more self-confidently, which became possible by the refinement of literary techniques and presumably also by the increased receptiveness of audiences: metaliterary, self-referential comments on dramatic genres and their conventions indicate that playwrights assumed audiences to be familiar with the standard set-up and generic conventions for each dramatic form. Poets would not have included such remarks if there had been no response from audiences. Besides, Cicero highlights the musical and rhythmical sensibility of average audiences (cf. e.g. Cic. *De or.* 3.196; *Parad.* 26; *Orat.* 173).

Audience reactions at revivals of old plays in the late Republican period indicate that spectators were familiar with the music and the verses of particular dramas (cf. e.g. Cic. *Acad.* 2.20; Hor. *Sat.* 2.3.60-2a). They were also able to relate individual lines to the contemporary political situation (cf. T 10). When existing dramatic scripts started to become available beyond the confines of the theatre in the late Republic and recitations of old and new dramas (as of other literary genres) also developed, there were new ways of engaging with dramatic poetry, and new types of audiences with specific interests emerged. The availability of scripts, for instance, enabled close reading and scholarly discussions of all sorts of questions concerning the plays (cf. I 10).

I 7. Poetry and performance

Greek-style tragedies and comedies in Rome were set in Greece and based on Greek dramas with similar plots or at least on Greek myths narrated elsewhere. Roman playwrights apparently did not translate or transpose word for word the Greek dramas they had chosen as models. Instead, they used a method often called 'free translation': they transferred plays according to the conventions of the Latin language and Roman thinking, transposing the plot and the main ideas of the Greek models, while adapting, altering, replacing, cutting and adding points of detail (cf. T 15). Even if Roman poets started off by using existing Greek dramas as the basis for their own plays and might therefore be thought to display little 'originality' in the modern sense, the poets' choices of what to transpose and how to do it are signs of their own poetic individuality. Their independence is also suggested by the so-called technique of 'contamination', when Roman playwrights combined elements from different Greek dramas into one new play.

For plots and subject matter of Greek-style dramas Republican playwrights seem to have looked back to the 'classics' as their main models: writers of tragedies to the classical Greek tragic poets, Euripides in particular, and writers of comedies to the poets of Hellenistic New Comedy. Both of these main groups of models had a potential for transferability, which, for instance, the Old Comedy of Aristophanes (just as Roman praetextae) did not have to the same extent, due to clear references to particular events in a specific people's history. Contemporary Hellenistic drama is more likely to have been one of the vehicles by which Roman poets got to know Greek 'classics' and to have demonstrated aspects of dramatic technique and ways of presentation.

The fact that from the start Roman poets could build on a fully developed literature in Greek, complete with literary criticism and early commentaries, as well as on indigenous traditions is perhaps one of the reasons why from the outset Roman poets seem to have been aware of literary techniques and literary history. This is obvious from numerous explicit metatheatrical references in light dramatic genres (as serious dramatic genres tend to limit these), which refer to the fact that what is going on is a performance (in which the actors take part), play with characteristics of the respective dramatic genre, allude to other dramatic genres or even discuss other poets (cf. T 13-14). Poets also take the work of predecessors into account in that they refer to it (seriously or parodically) or avoid overlap. The same is true for writers of serious dramatic genres, who, exploring connections in more indirect ways, might allude to lines of earlier playwrights, pass over topics and plots already dramatized by predecessors or prefer to present those in different ways (cf. e.g. the story of Medea: D 2; 3; 5; 14).

This awareness, along with specialization and differentiation among dramatic genres, means that a genuine Roman literary tradition, in addition to the Greek one, emerged from a relatively early stage in the development of drama at Rome. This led to intertextual relationships among Roman plays of the same and of different dramatic genres (on top of similar connections to Greek texts). At the same time the proliferation of poets and their restrictions to specific dramatic genres may have been a cause for rivalry between playwrights in Republican times, as suggested by Terence's prologues, since competition for being the foremost poet in any one dramatic genre and arguments about keeping to the rules arose (cf. T 13-14).

Although all that remains of Roman dramas today are texts (many of them in fragmentary state), dramatic scripts were only one element contributing to full-scale events (at least while dramas continued to be performed in large public theatres): these originally were comprehensive performances including all sorts of visual, acoustic and situational effects, while stage actions may have been designed with a view to the possibilities offered by the layout of the venues. And if one is to believe intellectuals of the late Republican period, the spectacular aspects of dramatic performances became more and more dominant over time at the expense of meaningful dialogue and presentations of entire dramas (cf. T 11). In early imperial times this seems to have led eventually to a split between impressive performances and the composition of complete serious dramas not necessarily designed for full-scale performances.

I 8. Form and style

Early Roman poets were active in a variety of literary genres. And while they observed a basic generic distinction between epic and drama from the start (for instance by using different metres), they developed a broadly similar form for both tragedy and comedy when they first adapted it from the Greeks, though distinctions in style and vocabulary between serious and light dramatic genres were present from the outset.

For the Republican period definite descriptions of formal elements, especially in the area of dramatic structure, can hardly be given, since the comedies by Plautus and Terence are the only examples to survive as complete scripts. Nevertheless, it can be inferred tentatively that dramatic structures were broadly similar across all Roman dramatic genres common in the Republican period, particularly tragedy, praetexta, comedy and togata: plays consisted of a prologue (not obligatory) and a subsequent series of monologues and dialogues, which could express a variety of different thoughts and feelings. In contrast to Greek drama, Roman Republican dramas did not have choral interludes; hence there was no separation of scenes by choral odes; instead the dramatic action ran through continuously (without act-division).

There was, however, a strong musical element, extended (in comparison with Greece) and transferred to individual actors: as extant scripts show, only a limited number of lines were in spoken metre (iambic senarius); a large proportion of verses was accompanied by music from the instrumentalist and therefore rather 'sung' or 'recited' (in longer iambic or trochaic metres or lyric metres). Almost all plays in the light dramatic genres seem not to have had a chorus; choruses did, however, feature in tragedies and praetextae, where they were integrated into the action, just as another actor. It is only in the imperial dramas by Seneca (the only extant examples from this period) that there is a return to the structure of Greek dramas as it were, since his plays consist of an alternation of episodes and choral odes, sung by a chorus whose relation to the action may be tenuous. Also, his iambic lines allow for less resolution and therefore come closer to the form of the Greek trimeter.

The language of Republican drama belongs to what is called 'archaic Latin', which indicates an earlier level of language in comparison with the 'classical Latin' of the Ciceronian period. Hence the plays exhibit linguistic features that had become obsolete by classical times, particularly in the area of morphology and syntax. The dramas also display stylistic elements typical of archaic poetry, such as a penchant for alliteration, assonance and other sound effects; word plays and puns are employed, as well as neologisms and complex compounds. Later writers sometimes regarded the language of the early poets as unsophisticated or artificial, while it was admired by archaists in the second century CE. Plays adapted from the Greek included Greek names and also some Greek terms, but equally Roman terms and references to Roman institutions, their number naturally being higher in dramatic genres set in Rome.

The style of Seneca, writing after the classical period and having enjoyed a rhetorical education like all young men of his age, is influenced by what was taught in contemporary declamation schools. His dramas have therefore been called 'rhetorical', often in a negative sense, but the epithet should rather be used more neutrally to describe the use of succinct expressions, set speeches and figures of speech common in his time.

I 9. Characteristics and developments

Each dramatic genre and each playwright as well as original performances and revivals have their own individual characteristics. Within the conventions of their chosen dramatic genre, poets could give their pieces a particular shape by choosing and emphasizing particular topics, themes and styles of presentation. Despite the scattered evidence, it is therefore possible to some extent to establish specific characteristics of individual playwrights.

At the same time one can identify elements that Republican playwrights seem to have had in common and that therefore characterize (early) Roman drama. The fact that proper Roman drama started with the adaptation of Greek plays and stories contributed to creating a distance between the immediate experiences of audiences and the world presented on stage; consequently audiences will have felt less directly involved and could therefore both be entertained and be encouraged to reflect on the issues presented; due to general human problems addressed even dramas based on Greek stories could interest Roman audiences.

Roman adaptations of Greek drama privileged topics that were particularly important to Roman society (by means of choices and changes made by poets), such as questions of adequate moral conduct, social behaviour, the relationship between family members, issues of government, the role of a major political power, dealing with conquered people, treatment of foreigners, influx of foreign (Greek) customs or incoming new religious and philosophical ideas. Dramatic forms based on Greek precedents as well as dramatic genres later developed in Rome therefore played a role in defining and confirming Roman self-understanding and confidence against the background of political and social changes. The dramatic action on stage also allowed the presentation of ideas new to Roman audiences (e.g. Greek philosophy).

Still, Roman dramas were not entirely dominated by material which could be seen as 'educational' or by topical references to the contemporary situation. So, while praetextae naturally alluded to specific events in Roman history, which might be recent incidents, the remaining dramatic genres typically avoided explicit allusions to topical issues of contemporary politics. Plays were prevented from becoming too serious as a result of the issues touched upon by combining those with entertaining features. This is obvious for light dramatic genres, which contained all sorts of jokes, farce and slapstick, ridiculous characters and weird actions, although the Roman light dramatic genre of togata remained more sober than the Greek-based palliata. Increasingly, tragedies included stunning scenes, spectacular scenic effects, sudden reversals and the presentation of ordinary figures or noble characters in reduced circumstances. The only dramatic genre rather immune to these developments was perhaps praetexta, since it might have been difficult to mix events from Roman history with humorous scenes; the only sensational element in praetextae may have consisted in a tendency towards spectacular battle scenes.

Hence, over the course of the Republican period, Greek-style tragedy and comedy gradually came closer together since they adopted features of one another and exploited similar structures and motifs: tragedy employed effective comic motifs, and comedy addressed general problems of society. Additional dramatic genres that appeared (in literary form) from the late second century onwards and throughout the first century BCE (especially Atellana, mime, pantomime) proceeded along similar lines. All new forms of performances continued tendencies observable in late Republican comedies and tragedies: they presented ordinary, rather simple characters, stunning scenic effects and elaborate stage-business and a large amount of pageantry on stage, while conveying moral messages (perhaps in simplified form) and some comment on the contemporary situation.

What characterizes Roman drama overall, therefore, is a mixture of these two aspects: presenting themes that concern the life of individuals

25

or society in Rome on the one hand and the provision of enjoyable entertainment and spectacle on the other hand, in other words, Horace's *prodesse* and *delectare* or *utile* and *dulce* (cf. Hor. *Ars P.* 333-4; 343-4).

While the combination of these two features formed a unified whole at the beginning, in the early imperial period the element of pageant apparently had become so dominant (cf. T 11) that it was no longer possible to have serious content of equal weight and impact; this is where the stories of burlesque entertaining performances and of proper drama started to diverge. Only few genuine full-length performances of traditional serious or light dramatic genres are attested for the imperial period; theatre events seem to have consisted mainly of mimes and pantomimes, dances, musicals or individual celebrated pieces from old plays.

What continued into the imperial period was the use of dramatic plays as a vehicle for the other aspect of Roman drama, the conveying of serious messages. Yet these plays were no longer performed to a mixed audience in big public theatres as a matter of course, but could also be read or recited and were therefore stripped of most elements needed to satisfy a desire for entertainment. This reduction of characteristics in comparison with Republican dramas suggests that dramatic genres that had always been more sober and serious and relied less on effective stage-business had a higher chance of being taken up under the changed circumstances.

While the connection with full-scale performances in the theatre and the corresponding stage-business had become loose, works of those dramatic genres that were taken up in the imperial period continued the developments observable in revivals, new dramatic genres and the few examples of traditional dramatic genres being written at the end of the Republic: plays composed in the imperial period can be understood to have a topical political aspect, which is no longer supportive as in the early days of Roman drama, but critical instead. Even under changed conditions for production and reception Roman drama remained a literary genre that was rooted in Roman society and engaged with issues concerning it.

I 10. Reception and transmission

Originally, in Republican Rome (as in classical Greece) dramas were typically composed for a single performance at a particular festival; however, the organization of the theatre business was different. It is thought that in Republican Rome the dramatic script remained in the possession of the theatre company, which enabled them to put it on again (possibly in adapted form) if there was demand. This might be the case soon after the original performance if a so-called *instauratio* was deemed necessary, i.e. the repetition of a festival as a whole or in part when a religious mistake had been noted (or caused or alleged for particular reasons).

Apparently, an awareness of the early dramatists as 'classics' was developing around the middle of the second century BCE; and this date coincides with the beginnings of philological, literary-historical and editorial activity at Rome. From this period onwards there seems to have been an interest in revival performances of old plays. An indication of the possibility of revivals can perhaps be seen already in the fact that Terence's prologues, in contrast to those of Plautus, highlight the novelty of the plays. Clear proof of revivals follows for the middle of the second century BCE: the extant prologue to Plautus' *Casina* belongs to a revival performance about a generation after the play's first performance; according to this text audiences asked for performances of the popular plays of 'old poets' (cf. T 9). An increasing prominence of revivals around the middle of the second century BCE would agree with the dates for revivals of Terence's comedies, which can be inferred from details given in the surviving production notices.

More information on a flourishing culture of revivals is available for the time of Cicero. Those revivals seem to have concentrated on a limited canon of established writers, or, in other words, contributed to setting it up; for all identifiable revivals concern plays of those poets who came to be regarded as the great Republican tragic and comic playwrights, and those plays for which revivals are known or inferred are those that are cited or referred to most frequently in Cicero and other writers of the period.

By then changes in the audience's reception of dramas seem to have occurred: if one is to believe intellectuals of the middle to late Republic, and also in view of the dramatic genres produced, audiences apparently preferred increasingly impressive staging, stunning effects, violent utterances and actions, magnificent costumes and elaborate stage properties over meaningful dialogue (cf. T 11). Further, even though plays were originally free of direct comments on contemporary events, it seems to have become common practice by Cicero's time to read allusions to the contemporary situation into old plays, on the part of organizing magistrates, actors or audiences, and possibly to exploit the occasion as a whole for political statements (cf. T 10).

Initially, dramatic scripts would have been used by the respective theatre companies, but not have been generally available. Distribution was only facilitated in the second century BCE, when revivals also started. For when scholars first approached questions of literary history in the second half of the second century BCE, they obviously had access to written texts. Hence the beginning of reading dramatic scripts coincides with the beginning of philological work on them, which led to an appreciation of the 'literary' potential of drama. Scholars discussed issues such as establishing a canon of major writers in any one dramatic genre, the genuineness of plays transmitted under one playwright's name, the chronology of poets or principles of translation (cf. T 4-6; 15; D 9). Cicero went beyond philological questions: he also voiced his assessment of poets and discussed the contents of plays, the ways of presentation and the relevance to present-day audiences.

In the area of literature, early drama, particularly tragedy and comedy, started to exert an influence on other poetic genres, as the works of Catullus, Lucretius and Vergil, for instance, demonstrate. In Horace's *Ars poetica* drama is the main example used to exemplify a variety of literary techniques and principles. Quintilian includes an assessment of Roman dramatists up to his time in his overview of literature (cf. T 6) and makes extensive use of comparisons between orators and actors in order to illustrate what is required of orators and what they should avoid. By then the dramatic scripts of some playwrights had become standard texts in schools.

The works of those authors that continued to be read were transmitted and preserved. All six plays of Terence survive; and for Plautus twenty-one plays that were singled out as genuine by scholars of the first century BCE are extant, while other plays, which may or may not be genuine, have only been transmitted in fragments or have been lost. For Seneca too all known plays survive, supplemented by two possibly spurious ones.

The works of other poets however, who apparently failed to win lasting interest and a sustained readership, were not transmitted beyond a certain point in time; all that remains therefore are bits and pieces quoted by later Latin writers. Some fragments survive in the literary tradition, in authors such as Cicero or the Author to Herennius, who quote fragments in their own texts when they want to make a point or discuss the contents of a passage, the behaviour of a character or the plot of a play; others verses survive in grammarians, scholiasts and commentators, who quote individual lines to illustrate unusual words, certain grammatical forms or tropes.

Reception beyond antiquity naturally focuses on the completely surviving plays by Plautus, Terence and Seneca, who have exerted an enormous influence on later poets since the Middle Ages, particularly during the Renaissance. Terence was widely read in schools from antiquity onwards; his dramas were preferred over those of Plautus due to their greater restraint, humane attitude and more elegant Latin. After the complete works of Plautus were rediscovered in the fifteenth century, his comedies were performed, and attempts at supplementing missing scenes were made. Seneca continued to be mentioned (and therefore read) by other writers from the start, but his dramatic works only gained real prominence from the fourteenth century onwards and then became an influential model for a pathetic and tragic style. In the early modern period classical plays were a fixed item in the educational syllabus, and schools and universities regularly staged performances of classical plays in the original languages.

Close engagement with ancient dramatic works prompted early humanist scholars in the fourteenth to sixteenth centuries (with times varying in the different European countries) not only to produce commentaries and translations into vernacular languages, but also to compose their own plays, originally still written in Latin, on the model of these exemplars in classical Latin. The Italian statesman and writer Albertino Mussato (1261-1329), for instance, produced a commentary on Seneca's tragedies and wrote one of the first Roman-style dramas in the modern period, *Ecerinis* (*c.* 1315). This play deals with an almost contemporary national subject, the fate and actions of the tyrannical ruler Ezzelino III da Romano (1194-1259). It follows the Senecan corpus as a model in theme, style and metre; and the dramatic presentation of contemporary politics and history as well as aspects of dramaturgy are reminiscent of the praetexta *Octavia*. In fact the pseudo-Senecan *Octavia* provided the only surviving model for a dramatic presentation of events from Roman history and became the typological ancestor of all history plays and even the thematic model for a number of later dramas and operas on Nero. One of the first history plays in England was Matthew Gwinne's (*c.* 1558-1627) *Nero* (1603), a university drama and a 'tragoedia nova' written in Latin (cf. N 3). The most famous version of the topic was to be the Italian opera *L'incoronazione di Poppea* (1642/3; libretto by Giovanni Francesco Busenello [1598-1659] and music attributed to Claudio Monteverdi [1567-1643]).

What has been called the first regular comedy in English, Nicholas Udall's *Roister Doister* (1552), was modelled on the structure of Roman comedy and of two plays by Plautus and Terence, *Miles gloriosus* and *Eunuchus*, in particular (cf. N 1). Well-known other adaptations of famous Plautine and Terentian comedies include in Italy Lodovico Ariosto's (1474-1533) *La Cassaria* (1508/1531) and *I suppositi* (1509/28-1531), in France Jean de Rotrou's (1609-1650) *Les Ménechmes* (1636) as well as Molière's (1622-1673) *L'Avare ou l'École du mensonge* (1668), in England Charles Sedley's (1639-1701) *Bellamira; or: The Mistress* (1687; modelled on Terence's *Eunuchus*), John Dryden's (1631-1700) *Amphitryon; or The Two Sosias* (1690; cf. N 4), Henry Fielding's (1707-1754) *The Miser* (1733; 'A Comedy. Taken from Plautus and Molière') and *The Fathers: or, The Good-Natur'd Man* (1778; modelled on Terence's *Adelphoe*) and in the United States Thornton Wilder's (1897-1975) *The Woman of Andros* (1930). This novel by Thornton Wilder demonstrates, just as the works

29

Kassandra (1983) and *Medea: Stimmen* (1996) by the German novelist Christa Wolf (b. 1929) or the British writer Tony Harrison's (b. 1937) *Medea: a sex-war opera* (1985; cf. N 5), that poetic adaptation of classical dramatic plots with obvious references to Greek and/or Roman models continues to the present day.

Apart from those works that refer back directly to one or two specific classical plays by their titles and/or plots, there are numerous plays, especially from the early modern period, that take up individual structural elements, motifs and characters from ancient dramas, such as some of Shakespeare's plays (cf. N 2).

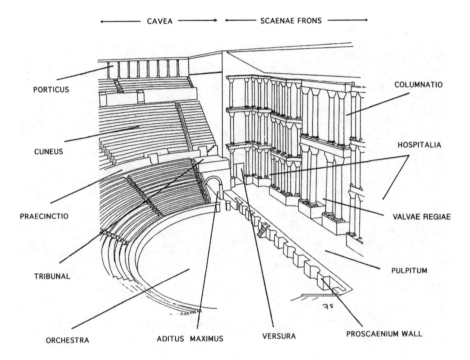

Fig. 1. Arrangement of the parts of a Roman theatre and their terminology.

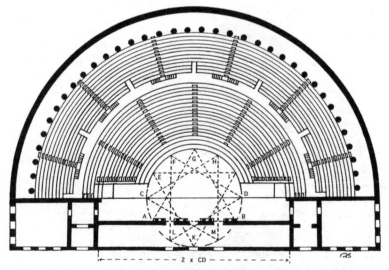

Fig. 2. Plan of a Roman theatre according to Vitruvius.

Fig. 3. View of a Roman theatre: the late Augustan theatre in Arausio (Orange, France).

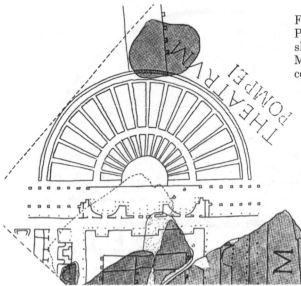

Fig. 4. The Theatre of Pompey in Rome as shown on the Severan Marble Plan (early third century CE).

Fig. 5. Plan of the Theatre of Pompey in Rome.

→ N

Fig. 6. Red-figure bell-krater, showing a scene from South Italian comedy; attributed to the McDaniel Painter, made in Puglia, 380-370 BCE (height: 37.4 cm; diameter: 39.4 cm): British Museum London (reg. no. GR 1849.6-20.13; Vase F 151).

Appendix 1
Roman dramatic poets and their plays

Question marks after some titles indicate uncertainty over the form of the
title or its ascription to a particular poet.

Lucius Livius Andronicus (*c.* 280/60-200 BCE)
Fabulae crepidatae: *Achilles, Aegisthus, Aiax mastigophorus, Andromeda,
Danae, Equos Troianus, Hermiona, Ino* (?), *Tereus, Teucer* (?)
Fabulae palliatae: *Gladiolus, Ludius, Virgo* (?)

Gnaeus Naevius (*c.* 280/60-200 BCE)
Fabulae crepidatae: *Danae, Equos Troianus, Hector proficiscens, Hesiona,
Iphigenia, Lycurgus*
Fabulae praetextae: *Clastidium, Romulus/Lupus*
Fabulae palliatae: *Acontizomenos, Agitatoria, Agrypnuntes, Appella,
Ariolus, Astiologa* (?), *Carbonaria, Clamidaria, Colax, Commotria,
Corollaria, Dementes, Demetrius, Dolus, Figulus, Glaucoma,
Guminasticus, Lampadio, Leon, Nagido, Nautae* (?), *Nervolaria, Paelex,
Personata, Proiectus, Quadrigemini, Stalagmus, Stigmatias, Tarentilla,
Technicus, Testicularia, Tribacelus* (?), *Triphallus, Tunicularia*

Quintus Ennius (239-169 BCE)
Fabulae crepidatae: *Achilles (Aristarchi), Aiax, Alcmeo, Alexander,
Andromacha (aechmalotis), Andromeda, Athamas, Cresphontes,
Erechtheus, Eumenides, Hectoris lytra, Hecuba, Iphigenia, Medea
(exul), Melanippa, Nemea, Phoenix, Telamo, Telephus, Thyestes*
Fabulae praetextae: *Ambracia, Sabinae*
Fabulae palliatae: *Caupuncula, Pancratiastes*

Marcus Pacuvius (*c.* 220-130 BCE)
Fabulae crepidatae: *Antiopa, Armorum iudicium, Atalanta, Chryses,
Dulorestes, Hermiona, Iliona, Medus, Niptra, Orestes, Pentheus* (vel
Bacchae), *Periboea, Teucer*
Fabula praetexta: *Paulus*

Lucius Accius (170-*c.* 80 BCE)
Fabulae crepidatae: *Achilles, Aegisthus, Agamemnonidae, Alcestis,
Alcmeo, Alphesiboea, Amphitruo, Andromeda, Antenoridae, Antigona,*

Appendix 1

Armorum iudicium, Astyanax, Athamas, Atreus, Bacchae, Chrysippus, Clytaemestra, Deiphobus, Diomedes, Epigoni, Epinausimache, Erigona, Eriphyla, Eurysaces, Hecuba, Hellenes, Io, Medea, Melanippus, Meleager, Minos sive Minotaurus (?), *Myrmidones, Neoptolemus, Nyctegresia, Oenomaus, Pelopidae, Persidae, Philocteta, Phinidae, Phoenissae, Prometheus, Stasiastae vel Tropaeum Liberi, Telephus, Tereus, Thebais, Troades*
Fabulae praetextae: *Aeneadae vel/aut Decius, Brutus*

Titus Maccius Plautus (*c.* 250-184 BCE)
Fabulae palliatae: *Amphitruo, Asinaria, Aulularia, Bacchides, Captivi, Casina, Cistellaria, Curculio, Epidicus, Menaechmi, Mercator, Miles gloriosus, Mostellaria, Persa, Poenulus, Pseudolus, Rudens, Stichus, Trinummus, Truculentus, Vidularia*
Fragmentary fabulae palliatae (some presumably spurious): *Acharistio, Addictus, Agroecus, Artemo, Astraba, Bacaria, Boeotia, Caecus vel Praedones, Calceolus, Carbonaria, Cesistio* (?), *Colax, Commorientes, Condalium, Cornicula, Dyscolus, Faeneratrix, Fretum, Frivolaria, Fugitivi, Hortulus, Lenones gemini, Lipargus, Nervolaria, P<h>ago, Parasitus medicus, Parasitus piger, Plocinus, Saturio, Schematicus, Sitellitergus, Trigemini*

Caecilius Statius (*c.* 230/20-168/7 BCE)
Fabulae palliatae: *Aethrio, Andrea, Androgynos, Asotus, Chalcia, Chrysion, Dardanus, Davos, Demandati, Ephesio, Epicleros, Epistathmos, Epistula, Exhautuhestos, Exul, Fallacia, Gamos, Harpazomene, Hymnis, Hypobolimaeus sive Subditivos, Hypobolimaeus Chaerestratus, Hypobolimaeus Rastraria, Hypobolimaeus Aeschinus, Imbrii, Karine, Meretrix, Nauclerus, Nothus Nicasio, Obolostates sive Faenerator, Pausimachus, Philumena, Plocium, Polumeni, Portitor, Progamos, Pugil, Symbolum, Synaristosae, Synephebi, Syracusii, Titthe, Triumphus, Venator*

Publius Terentius Afer (*c.* 195/4-159 BCE)
Fabulae palliatae: *Andria, Heautontimorumenos, Eunuchus, Phormio, Hecyra, Adelphoe*

Sextus Turpilius (d. 104/3 BCE)
Fabulae palliatae: *Boethuntes, Canephoros, Demetrius, Demiurgus, Epiclerus, Hetaera, Lemniae, Leucadia, Lindia, Paedium, Paraterusa, Philopator, Thrasyleon*

Titinius (*fl. c.* 200 BCE)
Fabulae togatae: *Barbatus, Caecus, Fullones* (vel *Fullonia*), *Gemina,*

Hortensius, Insubra (?), *Iurisperita, Prilia, Privigna, Psaltria sive Ferentinatis, Quintus, Setina, Tibicina, Varus, Veliterna*

Lucius Afranius (*fl. c.* 160-120 BCE)
Fabulae togatae: *Abducta, Aequales, Auctio, Augur, Brundisinae, Cinerarius, Compitalia, Consobrini, Crimen, Deditio, Depositum, Divortium, Emancipatus, Epistula, Exceptus, Fratriae, Ida* (?), *Incendium, Inimici, Libertus, Mariti, Materterae, Megalensia, Omen, Panteleus, Pompa, Privignus, Prodigus, Proditus, Promus, Prosa* (?), *Purgamentum, Repudiatus, Sella, Simulans, Sorores, Suspecta, Talio, Temerarius, Thais, Titulus, Virgo, Vopiscus*

Titus Quinctius Atta (d. 77 BCE)
Fabulae togatae: *Aedilicia, Aquae Caldae, Conciliatrix, Gratulatio, Lucubratio, Materterae, Megalensia, Nurus, Satura, Socrus, Supplicatio, Tiro proficiscens*

Lucius Pomponius (*fl.* 89 BCE)
Fabulae Atellanae: *Adelphi, Aeditumus, Agamemno suppositus, Aleones, Anulus posterior, Ariadne* (?), *Armorum iudicium, Aruspex vel Pexor rusticus, Asina, Atalante* (?), *Auctoratus, Augur, Bucco adoptatus, Bucco auctoratus, Campani, Capella, Citharista, Collegium, Concha, Condiciones, Cretula vel Petitor, Decuma, Decuma fullonis, Dives* (?), *Dotalis* (?), *Dotata, Ergastilus* (?), *Fullones, Galli Transalpini, Heres petitor, Hirnea Pappi, Kalendae Martiae, Lar familiaris, Leno, Maccus, Macci gemini, Maccus miles, Maccus sequester, Maccus virgo, Maialis, Marsya* (?), *Medicus, Mevia, Munda, Nuptiae, Pannuceati, Pappus agricola, Pappus praeteritus, Parci, Patruus, Philosophia, Pictores* (?), *Piscatores, Pistor, Placenta, Porcetra* (?), *Praeco posterior, Praefectus morum, Prostibulum, Pytho Gorgonius, Quinquatrus, Rusticus, Sarcularia, Satura, Sisyphus* (?), *Sponsa Pappi, Synephebi, Syri, Vacca vel Marsuppium, Verniones, Verres aegrotus, Verres salvos*

Novius (*fl. c.* 85 BCE)
Fabulae Atellanae: *Agricola, Andromacha, Asinus* (?), *Bucculus, Bubulcus cerdo, Dapatici* (?), *Decuma, Dotata, Duo Dossenni, Eculeus, Exodium, Ficitor, Fullones, Fullones feriati, Fullonicum, Funus, Gallinaria, Gemini, Hercules coactor, Hetaera, Lignaria, Maccus, Maccus copo, Maccus exul, Malivoli, Mania medica, Milites Pometinenses, Mortis et vitae iudicium, Optio, Pacilius* (?), *Paedium, Pappus praeteritus, Parcus, Phoenissae, Picus, Quaestio, Sanniones, Surdus, Tabellaria, Togularia, Tripertita, Vindemiatores, Virgo praegnans, Zona*

Decimus Laberius (*c.* 106-43 BCE)
Mimi: *Alexandrea, Anna Peranna, Aquae caldae, Aries, Augur, Aulularia* (?), *Belonistria, Cacomnemon, Caeculi, Cancer, Carcer, Catularius, Centonarius, Colax, Colorator, Compitalia, Cophinus, Cretensis, Ephebus, Fullo* (?), *Galli, Gemelli, Hetaera* (?), *Imago, Lacus Avernus, Late loquens, Natalis, Necyomantia, Nuptiae, Parilicii, Paupertas, Piscator, Restio, Salinator, Saturnalia, Scylax, Sedigitus, Sorores, Staminariae, Stricturae* (?), *Taurus, Tusca, Virgo*

Publilius Syrus (*fl.* 46-43 BCE)
Mimi: *Murmurco, Putatores*
Sententiae

Lucius Annaeus Seneca (*c.* 1 BCE-65 CE)
Fabulae crepidatae: *Hercules furens, Troades, Phoenissae, Phaedra, Medea, Thyestes, Agamemnon, Oedipus*; *Hercules Oetaeus*
Fabula praetextata (spurious): *Octavia*

Appendix 2
Chronological table

The following synoptic table lists key events in Rome's dramatic history and shows how the life times and active periods of the dramatists, the presence of the various dramatic genres as well as the existence of venues and opportunities for dramatic performances in Rome overlapped and succeeded each other.

Unless otherwise indicated all dates are BCE; by necessity a number of them are approximate.

FESTIVALS AND BUILDINGS	DRAMATIC GENRES AND ACTIVE POETS	DATES OF DRAMATIC POETS
509/7 first regular *Ludi Romani*		
	364 **first scenic performance** at a public festival (Etruscan dancers in Rome)	
		c. 280/70 **Livius Andronicus** born
		c. 280/60 **Naevius** born
		c. 250 **Plautus** born
	240 first literary drama (*tragoedia* and/or *comoedia* in Greek style) produced in Rome by Livius Andronicus	
	c. 240-205 Livius Andronicus active	
		239 **Ennius** born
	c. 235-204 Naevius active	
		c. 230/20 **Caecilius Statius** born
		c. 220 **Pacuvius** born

FESTIVALS AND BUILDINGS	DRAMATIC GENRES AND ACTIVE POETS	DATES OF DRAMATIC POETS
	c. 220 first *praetexta* produced by Naevius	
c. 220 first regular *Ludi plebeii*		
c. 220/19 first regular *Ludi Ceriales*		
	c. 215-184 Plautus active	
208 first regular *Ludi Apollinares*		
	c. 204-169 Ennius active	
		c. 200 Livius Andronicus died
		c. 200 Naevius died
	c. 200-160 Titinius active	
	c. 200-180 first *togata* produced	
	c. 195-168/7 Caecilius active	
	c. 195-135 Pacuvius active	
		c. 195/4 **Terentius** born
194 first step to **stratified seating** (special seats for senators)		
191 first regular *Ludi Megalenses*		
		184 Plautus died
179 first attempt at **theatre building** (unsuccessful)		
174 another attempt at erecting a stage (unsuccessful)		
173 first regular *Ludi Florales*	since 173 **non-literary *mimi*** at *Ludi Florales*	

FESTIVALS AND BUILDINGS	DRAMATIC GENRES AND ACTIVE POETS	DATES OF DRAMATIC POETS
		170 **Accius** born
		169 Ennius died
		168/7 Caecilius Statius died
	166-160 Terentius active	
	c. 160-120 Afranius active	
		c. 159 Terentius died
154 another attempt at theatre building (demolished in its early stages)		
	c. 140-100 Turpilius active	
	c. 140-80 Accius active	
		130 Pacuvius died
		120 Afranius died
	c. 120 first **literary *Atellana*** produced	
107 possibly another attempt at theatre building		
		c. 106 **Decimus Laberius** born
		104/3 Turpilius died
	c. 100-77 Atta active	
	c. 89 Pomponius active	
	c. 85 Novius active	
81 first regular *Ludi Victoriae (Sullanae)*		
		c. 80 Accius died
		77 Atta died

FESTIVALS AND BUILDINGS	DRAMATIC GENRES AND ACTIVE POETS	DATES OF DRAMATIC POETS
67 special seats assigned to equestrians		
	c. 60 first **literary *mimus*** produced	
	c. 60-43 Decimus Laberius active	
	c. 50-40 Publilius Syrus active	
58 **luxurious temporary theatre of Aemilius Scaurus**		
55 first **permanent theatre** in Rome (Theatre of Pompeius)		
45 first regular *Ludi Victoriae Caesaris*		
		43 Decimus Laberius died
	probably *c.* 45-40 first *pantomimus* produced	
	29 **last** 'Republican' **drama performed on stage** (*Thyestes* after battle at Actium)	
13 permanent Theatre of Balbus		
13/11 permanent Theatre of Marcellus		
		c. 1 **Seneca** born
	c. 40-60 CE Seneca active	
		65 CE Seneca died

Testimonia on Roman Drama

T 1. On the introduction of drama to Rome

(Livy, *Ab urbe condita* 7.2; Valerius Maximus, *Facta et dicta memorabilia* 2.4.4)

Although details are disputed among scholars, the description of the early stages of Roman drama as given in the Augustan historian Livy and, with slight variations, in Valerius Maximus, an early imperial writer of a collection of exempla, is among the most important pieces of evidence for the evolution and initial development of dramatic performances at Rome (both versions probably going back to the same source). Livy inserts this excursus presumably in order to make a comment on his own time and to show how

(a) Livy, *Ab urbe condita* 7.2

[1] et hoc et insequenti anno C. Sulpicio Petico C. Licinio Stolone consulibus pestilentia fuit. eo nihil dignum memoria actum, [2] nisi quod pacis deum exposcendae causa tertio tum post conditam urbem lectisternium fuit; [3] et cum vis morbi nec humanis consiliis nec ope divina levaretur, victis superstitione animis ludi quoque scenici – nova res bellicoso populo, nam circi modo spectaculum fuerat – inter alia caelestis irae placamina instituti dicuntur; [4] ceterum parva quoque, ut ferme principia omnia, et ea ipsa peregrina res fuit. sine carmine ullo, sine imitandorum carminum actu ludiones ex Etruria acciti, ad tibicinis modos saltantes, haud indecoros motus more Tusco dabant. [5] imitari deinde eos iuventus, simul inconditis inter se iocularia fundentes versibus, coepere; nec absoni a voce motus erant. [6] accepta itaque res saepiusque usurpando excitata. vernaculis artificibus, quia ister Tusco verbo ludio vocabatur, nomen histrionibus inditum; [7] qui non, sicut ante, Fescennino versu similem incompositum temere ac rudem alternis iaciebant sed impletas modis saturas descripto iam ad tibicinem cantu motuque congruenti peragebant.
[8] Livius post aliquot annis, qui ab saturis ausus est primus argumento fabulam serere, idem scilicet – id quod omnes tum erant – suorum carminum actor, [9] dicitur, cum saepius revocatus vocem obtudisset, venia petita puerum ad canendum ante tibicinem cum statuisset, canticum egisse aliquanto magis vigente motu quia nihil vocis usus impediebat. [10] inde † ad manum cantari histrionibus † coeptum diverbiaque tantum ipsorum voci relicta. [11] postquam lege hac fabularum ab risu ac soluto ioco res avocabatur et ludus in artem paulatim

Testimonia on Roman Drama

T 1. On the introduction of drama to Rome

(Livy, *Ab urbe condita* 7.2; Valerius Maximus, *Facta et dicta memorabilia* 2.4.4)

the institution developed from small, acceptable beginnings to something unhealthy and intolerable; yet the facts mentioned are still likely to contain a nucleus of truth. Out of the five phases into which the evolutionary model can be divided, the most important ones are the introduction of scenic performances to Rome in 364 BCE, as a supplement to the already existing circus games, and the move to dramas with a plot made by Livius Andronicus in 240 BCE.

(a) Livy, *Ab urbe condita* 7.2

[1] Both in this year and in the following one, when C. Sulpicius Peticus and C. Licinius Stolo were consuls [in 364 BCE], there was a pestilence. Therefore nothing worth remembering happened, [2] apart from the fact that, in order to gain peace from the gods, there was a *lectisternium*[1], then held for the third time since the foundation of the city[2]. [3] And since the power of the illness could not be eased, neither by human counsel nor by divine help, the minds of the people were conquered by superstition; and, among other attempts to placate the wrath of heaven, scenic games[3] are said to have also been established – a novel feature for the warlike nation, for there had only been spectacle in the circus. [4] Moreover, this was also a small matter, as all beginnings commonly are, and a foreign one on top of this. Without any song, without acting in imitation of the songs, stage-performers, fetched from Etruria and dancing according to the music of a piper, performed not inelegant movements in Tuscan[4] style. [5] Then youths began to imitate them, at the same time exchanging jest in uncouth verses among themselves; and their movements were not out of tune with the words. [6] Hence this matter was accepted and established by rather frequent use. To the native artists the term *histriones* ('actors') was applied, since the stage-performer was called *ister* with a Tuscan word. [7] These men did not, as before, utter something disordered and rude, improvised and in turns, in the style of Fescennine verses[5], but performed *saturae* ('medleys'), filled with musical measures, while song was now arranged according to the music of the piper and the movements corresponded with it.

43

verterat, iuventus histrionibus fabellarum actu relicto ipsa inter se more antiquo ridicula intexta versibus iactitare coepit; unde exorta quae exodia postea appellata consertaque fabellis potissimum Atellanis sunt; [12] quod genus ludorum ab Oscis acceptum tenuit iuventus nec ab histrionibus pollui passa est; eo institutum manet, ut actores Atellanarum nec tribu moveantur et stipendia, tamquam expertes artis ludicrae, faciant.

[13] inter aliarum parva principia rerum ludorum quoque prima origo ponenda visa est, ut appareret quam ab sano initio res in hanc vix opulentis regnis tolerabilem insaniam venerit.

---

1 a 'banquet for the gods'. 2 i.e. since the foundation of Rome, traditionally dated to 753 BCE. 3 i.e. dramatic performances. 4 i.e. Etruscan. 5 traditional Italic improvised verses. 6 this is presumably the meaning of the difficult Latin text. 7 a people in southern Italy. 8 i.e. they are treated like ordinary citizens and not like actors.

(b) Valerius Maximus, *Facta et dicta memorabilia* 2.4.4

nunc causam instituendorum ludorum ab origine sua repetam. C. Sulpicio Petico C. Licinio Stolone consulibus intoleranda vis ortae pestilentiae civitatem nostram a bellicis operibus revocatam domestici atque intestini mali cura adflixerat, iamque plus in exquisito et novo cultu religionis quam in ullo humano consilio positum opis videbatur. itaque placandi caelestis numinis gratia compositis carminibus vacuas aures praebuit, ad id tempus circensi spectaculo contenta, quod primus Romulus raptis virginibus Sabinis Consualium nomine celebravit.

verum, ut est mos hominum parvola initia pertinaci studio prosequendi, venerabilibus erga deos verbis iuventus rudi atque incomposito motu corporum iocabunda gestus adiecit, eaque res ludium ex Etruria arcessendi causam dedit. cuius decora pernicitas vetusto ex more Curetum Lydorumque, a quibus Tusci originem traxerunt, novitate grata Romanorum oculos permulsit, et quia ludius apud eos ister appellabatur, scaenico nomen histrionis inditum est.

paulatim deinde ludicra ars ad saturarum modos perrepsit, a quibus

[8] After a number of years [in 240 BCE] Livius [i.e. Livius Andronicus], who was the first to venture to compose a play with a plot, moving forward from medleys, was himself also an actor in his own plays – as everyone was at the time. [9] The story goes that when he had lost his voice, after having been called upon for repeated encores, and, having been granted permission, had placed a boy to do the singing in front of the piper, he acted the song with significantly more vigorous movement, since the use of the voice restrained him in no way. [10] From that time onwards singing to the gestures of actors began[6], and the spoken parts only were left for their own voices. [11] After the matter had been removed from laughter and loose joking by these rules for the plays and the game had gradually turned into art, the youths themselves, as the acting of plays had been left to professional actors, began to proclaim jocular utterances in verse among themselves, following an ancient custom; hence perform-ances arose that were later called after-pieces and joined in particular with Atellana plays. [12] This kind of performances had been adopted from the Oscans[7] and was retained by the youths, and they did not allow it to be polluted by professional actors; therefore the institution remains that actors of Atellanae are not removed from their tribes and do military service, as if they had no connection with the theatrical art[8].

[13] It seems that among small beginnings of other things the first origin of the games too should be placed, so that it becomes clear how the matter has turned from a healthy start to this madness, hardly bearable even for wealthy kingdoms.

(b) Valerius Maximus, *Facta et dicta memorabilia* 2.4.4

Now I will trace the reason for the institution of games back from its beginning. When C. Sulpicius Peticus and C. Licinius Stolo were consuls [in 364 BCE], an unbearably strong pestilence had broken out and had crushed our community with concern for a domestic and internal problem, calling it away from military activities. And soon it seemed advisable to place more support in a specially selected and new religious practice than in any human counsel. Therefore, in order to placate the heavenly divinities, the community lent open ears to well-composed poems, having been content up to this point in time with spectacle in the circus, which Romulus was the first to celebrate under the name of Consualia[1], when the Sabine maidens had been abducted.

But, as it is the custom of human beings to pursue small beginnings with zealous eagerness, the young men, in jocular mood, added to the respectful words addressed to the gods gestures with rude and clumsy movement of the bodies, and this situation provided the incentive to summon a stage-performer from Eturia[2]. His graceful agility, according

primus omnium poeta Livius ad fabularum argumenta spectantium animos transtulit, isque sui operis actor, cum saepius a populo revocatus vocem obtudisset, adhibito pueri ac tibicinis concentu gesticulationem tacitus peregit.

Atellani autem ab Oscis acciti sunt; quod genus delectationis Italica severitate temperatum ideoque vacuum nota est: nam neque tribu movetur <actor> nec a militaribus stipendiis repellitur.

---

1 an annual festival held on 21 August and 15 December, determined by the agricultural cycle and featuring games in the circus. 2 i.e. as a consequence of the events in 364 BCE. 3 ancient inhabitants of Crete, known as dancers. 4 Etruscans ('Tuscans') were thought to stem from the people of Lydia, at the west coast of Asia Minor. 5 a people in southern Italy.

T 2. On the introduction of Greek literature to Rome

(Horace, *Epistula* 2.1.145-67)

In one of his epistles on literary history and literary criticism (cf. also T 5; 11b), the Augustan poet Horace gives his version of the development of early drama at Rome, against the background of the aesthetic standards of his time. His description starts with an indigenous form of verse composition, the so-called Fescennine verses, simple alternate verses, which turned from innocent jest to biting comments and therefore had to be limited by law. In another step, according to Horace, the arts were taken over from Greece,

[145] Fescennina per hunc invecta licentia morem
versibus alternis opprobria rustica fudit.
libertasque recurrentis accepta per annos
lusit amabiliter, donec iam saevus apertam
in rabiem coepit verti iocus et per honestas
[150] ire domos impune minax. doluere cruento
dente lacessiti; fuit intactis quoque cura
condicione super communi. quin etiam lex
poenaque lata, malo quae nollet carmine quemquam
describi. vertere modum, formidine fustis
[155] ad bene dicendum delectandumque redacti.
    Graecia capta ferum victorem cepit et artis
intulit agresti Latio. sic horridus ille
defluxit numerus Saturnius et grave virus

to the old custom of the Curetes[3] and Lydians, from whom the Tuscans drew their origin[4], pleased the eyes of the Romans with welcome novelty, and because the stage-performer was called *ister* among them, the person on stage was given the name *histrio* ('actor').

Then the theatrical art gradually moved towards the rhythms of *saturae* ('medleys'); from there the poet Livius [i.e. Livius Andronicus] was the first of all to turn the minds of spectators to plots of plays [in 240 BCE]; and being himself the actor of his own work, when he had been called by the people for repeated encores and had lost his voice, he arranged for a boy and a piper to sing and play together and then carried out the gesticulation without speaking himself.

Atellana actors on the other hand were summoned from the Oscans[5]; this kind of entertainment is regulated by Italian severity and therefore free from the censorial mark: for the actor [i.e. of Atellana plays] is neither removed from his tribe nor excluded from military service.

T 2. On the introduction of Greek literature to Rome

(Horace, *Epistula* 2.1.145-67)

conquered by Roman military force, but culturally more advanced, and thus literature in Rome became more refined. Horace dates the adoption of tragedy, to which the Romans were well suited, to a late period, to the quiet time after the Punic Wars. If he refers to the conclusion of the Second Punic War, he probably has Ennius in mind, whose writings were regarded as more sophisticated than those of the actual pioneers and whom he calls the 'father' of Roman literature elsewhere.

[145] Owing to this custom[1] the Fescennine licence[2] was introduced, and it poured forth rustic reproaches in alternate verses. And the outspokenness, condoned each returning year, sported nicely until the jest, already fierce, began to turn into open rabies and [150] to move threateningly through honest houses without punishment. Those who had been provoked by a biting tooth felt pain; even for those untouched there was some concern for the common cause. Eventually a law and a punishment were introduced, which did not permit anyone to be portrayed in a damaging song. They changed the tune, and in fear of the cudgel [155] were brought back to speaking well and entertaining.

Captured Greece captured the savage victor and brought the arts to rustic Latium. Thus that rough Saturnian metre[3] ran dry, and good taste put the foul odour to flight; still for a long time [160] there remained and remain to the present day traces of rustic features. For late did he [i.e.

munditiae pepulere; sed in longum tamen aevum
[160] manserunt hodieque manent vestigia ruris.
serus enim Graecis admovit acumina chartis
et post Punica bella quietus quaerere coepit
quid Sophocles et Thespis et Aeschylus utile ferrent.
temptavit quoque rem, si digne vertere posset,
[165] et placuit sibi, natura sublimis et acer;
nam spirat tragicum satis et feliciter audet,
sed turpem putat inscite metuitque lituram.

T 3. On the dates of the early dramatists

(Cicero, *Brutus* 71-6; Gellius, *Noctes Atticae* 17.21.42-9)

By the first century BCE early scholars had started to look at Rome's first poets as part of their heritage and to discuss issues such as the genuineness of their works or their chronology. Cicero reports the chronology established by his friend Atticus and the alternative version by the late Republican tragic poet Accius, who also wrote treatises on literary questions. Cicero supports Atticus' chronology, which was the dominant view in antiquity

(a) Cicero, *Brutus* 71-6

[Cicero:] "... [71] et nescio an reliquis in rebus omnibus idem eveniat: nihil est enim simul et inventum et perfectum; nec dubitari debet quin fuerint ante Homerum poetae, quod ex eis carminibus intellegi potest, quae apud illum et in Phaeacum et in procorum epulis canuntur. quid, nostri veteres versus ubi sunt? 'quos olim Fauni vatesque canebant, cum neque Musarum scopulos * * * nec dicti studiosus quisquam erat ante hunc' ait ipse de se [Ennius, *Ann.* 214-16 V.^{2} = 232-4 W. = 207-9 Skutsch] nec mentitur in gloriando: sic enim sese res habet. nam et Odyssia Latina est sic tamquam opus aliquod Daedali et Livianae fabulae non satis dignae quae iterum legantur. [72] atqui hic Livius primus fabulam C. Claudio Caeci filio et M. Tuditano consulibus docuit anno ipso ante quam natus est Ennius, post Romam conditam autem quartodecimo et quingentensimo, ut hic ait, quem nos sequimur. est enim inter scriptores de numero annorum controversia. Accius autem a Q. Maximo quintum consule captum Tarento scripsit Livium annis XXX post quam eum fabulam docuisse et Atticus scribit et nos in antiquis commentariis invenimus, [73] docuisse autem

the Roman] turn his wit to Greek writings, and only in the tranquillity after the Punic Wars did he begin to ask what useful stuff Sophocles, Thespis and Aeschylus might bring. He also made an attempt at this matter, whether he could transfer it acceptably, [165] and he was pleased with himself, by nature lofty and passionate; for he breathes forth tragic spirit sufficiently and ventures happily, but, for lack of understanding, he considers polishing as disgraceful and fears it[4].

---

1 i.e. harvest festivals. 2 traditional Italic improvised verses. 3 a metre of early Roman epics and inscriptions. 4 refers to (earlier) poets who did not polish their writings as much as poetic conventions in Horace's time would require.

T 3. On the dates of the early dramatists

(Cicero, *Brutus* 71-6; Gellius, *Noctes Atticae* 17.21.42-9)

and has become accepted in modern scholarship: in this model Livius Andronicus is Rome's first poet and is followed by Naevius, Plautus and Ennius, which triggers a corresponding assessment of the early writers.

The archaist Gellius in the second century CE gives a historical overview of the early poets and tries to place them in the context of their time, building on the evidence of various earlier sources.

(a) Cicero, *Brutus* 71-6

[Cicero:] "... [71] And something similar may happen in all other arts: for nothing is at the same time invented and accomplished; and one should not doubt that there were poets before Homer, which can be inferred from those songs that are sung at the dinners of the Phaeacians and of the suit-ors in Homer[1]. Well, where are our old verses? 'which the Fauni and seers once sang, when neither the cliffs of the Muses[2] (had been surmounted by anyone) ... nor was there a student of the word before this man', he [i.e. Ennius] says about himself[3], and he does not lie in his self-praise: for this is how the matter is. For the Latin *Odyssey*[4] is just like some work of Daedalus[5], and the plays of Livius [i.e. Livius Andronicus] are not so valuable that they should be read a second time. [72] And yet this Livius was the first to produce a play, when C. Claudius, son of Caecus, and M. Tuditanus were consuls [in 240 BCE], in the very year before Ennius was born [in 239 BCE] and in the 514th year after the foundation of Rome [in 753 BCE according to Roman tradition], as he [i.e. Atticus] says, whom we follow. For there is a controversy about the number of years among writers. Ac-

fabulam annis post XI C. Cornelio Q. Minucio consulibus ludis Iuventatis, quos Salinator Senensi proelio voverat. in quo tantus error Acci fuit, ut his consulibus XL annos natus Ennius fuerit: quoi si aequalis fuerit Livius, minor fuit aliquanto is, qui primus fabulam dedit, quam ei, qui multas docuerant ante hos consules, et Plautus et Naevius. [74] haec si minus apta videntur huic sermoni, Brute, Attico adsigna, qui me inflammavit studio inlustrium hominum aetates et tempora persequendi."

"ego vero", inquit Brutus, "et delector ista quasi notatione temporum et ad id quod instituisti, oratorum genera distinguere aetatibus, istam diligentiam esse accommodatum puto."

[75] "recte", inquam, "Brute, intellegis. atque utinam exstarent illa carmina, quae multis saeculis ante suam aetatem in epulis esse cantitata a singulis convivis de clarorum virorum laudibus in Originibus scriptum reliquit Cato [Cato, fr. 118 Peter]! tamen illius, quem in vatibus et Faunis adnumerat Ennius, bellum Punicum quasi Myronis opus delectat. [76] sit Ennius sane, ut est certe, perfectior; qui si illum, ut simulat, contemneret, non omnia bella persequens primum illud Punicum acerrimum bellum reliquisset. sed ipse dicit cur id faciat. 'scripsere', inquit, 'alii rem vorsibus' [Ennius, *Ann.* 213-14 V.² = 231-2 W. = 206-7 Skutsch] – et luculente quidem scripserunt, etiam si minus quam tu polite. nec vero tibi aliter videri debet, qui a Naevio vel sumpsisti multa, si fateris, vel, si negas, surripuisti. [77] ..."

---

1 cf. Hom. *Od.* 8.43b-95; 1.153-361; 17.261b-3a; 22.330-53. 2 referring to Parnassus or Helicon. 3 Cicero incorporates some of the wording of Ennius' verses into his argument, which explains the somewhat disjointed syntax; at any rate Cicero alludes to Ennius' comments in his *Annales* on his status as the first true poet in Rome. 4 Livius Andronicus' epic *Odusia*. 5 a legendary Greek artist of archaic times. 6 a town in southern Italy. 7 'Games of Youth', an old Roman cult. 8 when Hasdrubal was defeated on the river Metaurus, near the town of Sena in Umbria, in 207 BCE. 9 Cato's historiographical work on the development of Rome up to his own time. 10 Naevius' historical epic on the First Punic War. 11 in the context of the lines just referred to by Cicero. 12 a Greek sculptor in the fifth century BCE. 13 in Ennius' epic *Annales*, covering all of Roman history up to his own time.

(b) Gellius, *Noctes Atticae* 17.21.42-9

[42] annis deinde postea paulo pluribus quam viginti pace cum Poenis facta consulibus <C.> Claudio Centhone, Appii Caeci filio, et M. Sempronio Tuditano primus omnium L. Livius poeta fabulas docere Romae coepit post Sophoclis et Euripidis mortem annis plus fere centum et sexaginta, post Menandri annis circiter quinquaginta duobus. [43] Claudium et Tuditanum consules secuntur Q. Valerius et C. Mamilius, quibus natum esse

cius, on the contrary, wrote that Livius was taken captive by Q. Maximus, when he was consul for the fifth time [in 209 BCE], in Tarentum[6], thirty years after he had produced a play according to both what Atticus writes and what we find in ancient commentaries; [73] Accius went on to say that he [i.e. Livius Andronicus] had produced a play eleven years later, when C. Cornelius and Q. Minucius were consuls [in 197 BCE], at the Ludi Iuventatis[7], which Salinator [i.e. M. Livius Salinator] had vowed at the battle of Sena[8]. In this Accius' error was so great that, when these men were consuls, Ennius had already lived for forty years: if Livius would have been a contemporary of his, he who was the first to produce a play was significantly younger than those who had produced many plays before the consulship of these men, both Plautus and Naevius. [74] If this seems not sufficiently appropriate to this conversation, Brutus, attribute it to Atticus, who has inspired me with an eagerness to go through the lifetimes and dates of illustrious men."

"But I", said Brutus, "am both delighted by this marking of dates as it were and believe that this exactness is suitable to what you set out to do, to distinguish types of orators by their lifetimes."

[75] "Rightly", I said, "Brutus, do you see this. And if only those songs were extant, which were sung about the praiseworthy deeds of outstanding men by individual guests at dinner parties many centuries before his time, as Cato has left written testimony in his *Origines*[9]! Nevertheless, the *Bellum Poenicum*[10] by him, whom Ennius counts among the seers and Fauns[11], pleases like a work by Myron[12]. [76] May Ennius indeed be more perfect, as he certainly is; if he looked down upon him [i.e. Naevius] as he pretends, he had not left out this very fierce First Punic War, when he was going through all wars[13]. But he himself says why he does so. 'Others', he says, 'have written about this matter in verse' – and splendidly at any rate did they write, even though in a less polished style than you. And it cannot seem otherwise to you, who have taken much from Naevius, if you confess it, or, if you deny it, have stolen it. [77] ..."

(b) Gellius, *Noctes Atticae* 17.21.42-9

[42] Then, a little more than twenty years later, when peace with the Carthaginians had been made[1], when C. Claudius Centho, son of Appius Caecus, and M. Sempronius Tuditanus were consuls [in 240 BCE], the poet L. Livius [i.e. Livius Andronicus] was the first of all to begin to produce plays at Rome, more than about one hundred and sixty years after the deaths of Sophocles and Euripides, around fifty-two years after that of

Q. Ennium poetam M. Varro in primo de poetis libro scripsit [Varro, fr. 61 Funaioli] eumque, cum septimum et sexagesimum annum ageret, duodecimum annalem scripssise idque ipsum Ennium in eodem libro dicere [Enn. *Ann.* XII.V V.² = p. 134 W. = inc. sed. lxx Skutsch]. [44] anno deinde post Romam conditam quingentesimo undevicesimo Sp. Carvilius Ruga primus Romae de amicorum sententia divortium cum uxore fecit, quod sterila esset iurassetque apud censores uxorem se liberum quaerundorum causa habere, [45] eodemque anno Cn. Naevius poeta fabulas apud populum dedit, quem M. Varro in libro de poetis primo stipendia fecisse ait bello Poenico primo [Varro, fr. 56 Funaioli] idque ipsum Naevium dicere in eo carmine, quod de eodem bello scripsit [Naev. *Bell. Pun.* fr. 2 *FPL*³ = p. 47 W.].

Porcius autem Licinus serius poeticam Romae coepisse dicit in his versibus: 'Poenico bello secundo Musa pinnato gradu / intulit se bellicosam in Romuli gentem feram' [Porcius Licinus, fr. 1 *FPL*³ = fr. 1 Funaioli]. [46] ac deinde annis fere post quindecim bellum adversum Poenos sumptum est, [47] atque non nimium longe <post> M. Cato orator in civitate et Plautus poeta in scaena floruerunt; [48] isdemque temporibus Diogenes Stoicus et Carneades Academicus et Critolaus Peripateticus ab Atheniensibus ad senatum populi Romani negotii publici gratia legati sunt. [49] neque magno intervallo postea Q. Ennius et iuxta Caecilius et Terentius et subinde et Pacuvius et Pacuvio iam sene Accius clariorque tunc in poematis eorum obtrectandis Lucilius fuit.

---

1 after the First Punic War (264-241 BCE). 2 Ennius' epic on the history of Rome. 3 Naevius' epic *Bellum Poenicum*. 4 a Roman scholar in the second half of the second century BCE (cf. T 15a). 5 the Second Punic War (218-201 BCE). 6 three Greek philosophers, representing the major philosophical schools. 7 the satires of the second-century poet Lucilius included comments on contemporary poets and their poetry.

T 4. On the assessment of comic poets

(Volcacius Sedigitus, fr. 1 *FPL*³ = fr. 1 Funaioli, ap. Gellius, *Noctes Atticae* 15.24)

Volcacius Sedigitus was one of the early Roman scholars who discussed literary questions around 100 BCE. Like the works of some of the poets he talks about, his own writings only survive in fragments. The most interesting extant piece is the so-called 'canon' of ten palliatae writers, transmitted in a chapter by the archaist Gellius (writing in the second century CE). Here Volcacius Sedigitus gives his own definitive answer to the question of who

Menander. [43] Claudius and Tuditanus [i.e. the consuls in 240 BCE] were followed by Q. Valerius and C. Mamilius [in 239 BCE], under whom the poet Q. Ennius was born, as M. Varro has recorded in the first book of his work on poets, and he has also transmitted that he [i.e. Ennius], when he was in his sixty-seventh year, had written the twelfth book of the *Annales*[2] and that Ennius himself said so in this very book. [44] In the 519th year after the foundation of Rome [in 235 BCE] Sp. Carvilius Ruga was the first at Rome to divorce his wife, on the advice of his friends, because she was barren and he had sworn before the censors that he had a wife for the purpose of having children. [45] And in the same year the poet Cn. Naevius presented plays to the people; of him M. Varro says in the first book of his work on poets that he did military service in the First Punic War and that Naevius himself said so in that poem that he has written about this very war[3].

But Porcius Licinus[4] says that poetry started in Rome rather late, in the following verses: 'In the Second Punic War the Muse introduced herself with winged step to the savage warrior nation of Romulus'. [46] And then about fifteen years later war against the Carthaginians was taken up[5]. [47] And not too long afterwards M. Cato flourished as an orator in the community and Plautus as a poet on the stage. [48] And at the same time the Stoic Diogenes, the Academic Carneades and the Peripatetic Critolaus[6] were sent as envoys by the Athenians to the senate of the Roman people for the purpose of public business [in 155 BCE]. [49] And not a long time later came Q. Ennius, and next Caecilius and Terence, and soon also Pacuvius and, when Pacuvius was already an old man, Accius and Lucilius, rather famous at the time for criticizing their poetry[7].

T 4. On the assessment of comic poets

(Volcacius Sedigitus, fr. 1 *FPL*[3] = fr. 1 Funaioli, ap. Gellius, *Noctes Atticae* 15.24)

the best comic poets were, which was apparently discussed in his time. He places Caecilius Statius first, followed by Plautus and Naevius, and then goes on to list seven further comic poets. Unfortunately, he does not always give criteria for his ranking, and his table might have been idiosyncratic. Still, it provides an overview of recognized palliata poets and a glimpse into the sort of issues addressed in his time.

Quid Volcacius Sedigitus in libro, quem de poetis scripsit, de comicis Latinis iudicarit.

Sedigitus in libro, quem scripsit de poetis, quid de his sentiat, qui co-moedias fecerunt, et quem praestare ex omnibus ceteris putet ac deinceps, quo quemque in loco et honore ponat, his versibus suis demonstrat:
'multos incertos certare hanc rem vidimus,
palmam poetae comico cui deferant.
eum meo iudicio errorem dissolvam tibi,
ut, contra si quis sentiat, nihil sentiat.
[5] Caecilio palmam Statio do comico.
Plautus secundus facile exuperat ceteros.
dein Naevius, qui fervet, pretio in tertiost.
si erit, quod quarto detur, dabitur Licinio.
post insequi Licinium facio Atilium.
[10] in sexto consequetur hos Terentius,
Turpilius septimum, Trabea octavum optinet,
nono loco esse facile facio Luscium.
decimum addo causa antiquitatis Ennium.'

T 5. On the assessment of early Roman dramatists

(Horace, *Epistula* 2.1.50-62)

In his discussions of literary questions (cf. also T 2; 11b), the Augustan poet Horace complains about the admiration for earlier writers just because they are 'old'; in this context he gives a list of Republican poets whose works were still read, performed and discussed in his time. Although one need not agree with the assessments by Horace or his contemporaries, his comments

[50] Ennius, et sapiens et fortis et alter Homerus,
ut critici dicunt, leviter curare videtur
quo promissa cadant et somnia Pythagorea.
Naevius in manibus non est et mentibus haeret
paene recens? adeo sanctum est vetus omne poema.
[55] ambigitur quotiens, uter utro sit prior, aufert
Pacuvius docti famam senis, Accius alti,
dicitur Afrani toga convenisse Menandro,
Plautus ad exemplar Siculi properare Epicharmi,
vincere Caecilius gravitate, Terentius arte.
[60] hos ediscit et hos arto stipata theatro
spectat Roma potens; habet hos numeratque poetas
ad nostrum tempus Livi scriptoris ab aevo.

What judgements Volcacius Sedigitus made about the Latin comic play-wrights in the book that he wrote about poets.

In the book that he wrote about poets, Sedigitus demonstrates in the following verses of his what he thinks of those who wrote comedies and whom he believes to surpass all others, and finally to which position of honour he assigns each individual:

'We see that many debate this matter, being uncertain to which comic playwright they should assign the victory palm. By my judgement I will resolve this uncertainty for you, so that, if anyone has a contrary opinion, they will have no opinion at all. [5] I give the victory palm to the comic poet Caecilius Statius. Plautus is second and easily surpasses the others. Then Naevius, who is passionate, is in the third rank. If there is something that can be given to the person in fourth place, it will be given to Licinius. I have Atilius follow Licinius. [10] In sixth place Terence will follow them, Turpilius holds seventh, Trabea eighth place. I easily place Luscius [i.e. Luscius Lanuvinus] in ninth place. As the tenth poet I add Ennius for the sake of his antiquity.'

T 5. On the assessment of early Roman dramatists

(Horace, *Epistula* 2.1.50-62)

on early playwrights are an interesting piece of evidence for their early re-ception, as they provide an indication of who was counted among the major representatives from Livius Andronicus onwards and what characteristics were assigned to each of them.

[50] Ennius, wise, heroic and a second Homer, as the critics say, seems to care only little where the expectations he raises and the Pythagorean dreams end up[1]. Is not Naevius in our hands and clinging to our minds as if recent? So holy is every old poem. [55] Whenever there is a dispute on which is the better of the two, Pacuvius carries the fame of the learned old man, Accius that of the lofty one. The toga of Afranius is said to have fitted Menander, Plautus to hurry along according to the example of Sicilian Epicharmus[2]; Caecilius is said to win by dignity, Terence by art. [60] Mighty Rome learns these poets by heart and watches them, crowded together in a narrow theatre; she regards these as her poets and counts them from the age of the writer Livius [i.e. Livius Andronicus] to our own time.

1 refers to Ennius mentioning at the beginning of his epic *Annales* that Homer's soul had migrated into his own body. 2 a Sicilian writer of Greek comedies in the sixth/fifth centuries BCE.

T 6. On the assessment of Roman dramatists

(Quintilian, *Institutio oratoria* 10.1.97-100)

The rhetorician Quintilian's textbook for aspiring orators, written in the late first century CE, includes a famous overview of the various literary genres and their Greek and Roman representatives. In this context Quintilian outlines his views on Roman tragic poets from the late Republic to his own time and on Republican poets of Greek-style and Roman-style

[97] tragoediae scriptores veterum Accius atque Pacuvius clarissimi gravitate sententiarum, verborum pondere, auctoritate personarum. ceterum nitor et summa in excolendis operibus manus magis videri potest temporibus quam ipsis defuisse: virium tamen Accio plus tribuitur, Pacuvium videri doctiorem qui esse docti adfectant volunt. [98] iam Vari Thyestes cuilibet Graecarum comparari potest. Ovidi Medea videtur mihi ostendere quantum ille vir praestare potuerit si ingenio suo imperare quam indulgere maluisset. eorum quos viderim longe princeps Pomponius Secundus, quem senes parum tragicum putabant, eruditione ac nitore praestare confitebantur.

[99] in comoedia maxime claudicamus. licet Varro Musas, Aeli Stilonis sententia, Plautino dicat sermone locuturas fuisse si Latine loqui vellent [Aelius Stilo, fr. 50 Funaioli = Varro, fr. 321 Funaioli], licet Caecilium veteres laudibus ferant, licet Terenti scripta ad Scipionem Africanum referantur (quae tamen sunt in hoc genere elegantissima, et plus adhuc habitura gratiae si intra versus trimetros stetissent): [100] vix levem consequimur umbram, adeo ut mihi sermo ipse Romanus non recipere videatur illam solis concessam Atticis venerem, cum eam ne Graeci quidem in alio genere linguae optinuerint. togatis excellit Afranius: utinam non inquinasset argumenta puerorum foedis amoribus, mores suos fassus.

---

1 a tragedy written by the poet L. Varius Rufus for celebrations after Octavian's victory at Actium in 31 BCE. 2 a tragedy by Ovid, of which only two lines survive. 3 i.e. tragic poets. 4 a writer of tragedies and praetextae under Claudius and Nero. 5 a Roman literary critic and grammarian of the late second century BCE. 6 P. Cornelius Scipio Aemilianus Africanus; for accusations that Terence relied on the help of friends for writing his plays cf. Ter. *Haut.* 22-4; *Ad.* 15-21. 7 alludes to the difference between the more regulated spoken metre in Greek comedy (trimeter) and the less strict form in Roman comedy (senarius). 8 alludes to the fact that Greek drama used the Attic dialect. 9 an allegation that is not confirmed by other evidence.

T 6. On the assessment of Roman dramatists

(Quintilian, *Institutio oratoria* 10.1.97-100)

comedy. Again, one need not agree with his assessments, but his list is indicative of a later period of reception, since it gives an idea of which poets were remembered and discussed in the late first century CE and what qualities were attributed to each of them.

[97] As regards writers of tragedy, Accius and Pacuvius are the most distinguished among the old ones, by the gravity of their thoughts, the weightiness of their expressions and the dignity of their characters. Further, elegance and the last hand in polishing one's works may seem to have been absent from their times rather than from themselves: nevertheless more force is attributed to Accius; those who aspire to be learned wish Pacuvius to be seen as the more learned. [98] Varius' *Thyestes*[1] can already be compared with any of the Greek tragedies. Ovid's *Medea*[2] seems to me to indicate how much this man could have excelled if he had preferred to govern his genius rather than to indulge in it. Out of those[3] who I could see myself, Pomponius Secundus[4] is by far the best; older men regarded him as not tragic enough, but they admitted that he stood out in learning and elegance.

[99] In comedy we are furthest behind. Even if Varro says, on the authority of Aelius Stilo[5], that the Muses would speak in Plautine idiom if they wished to speak Latin, even if older people extol Caecilius, even if the writings of Terence are attributed to Scipio Africanus[6] (which are nevertheless the most elegant in this genre, and they would have even more charm if they had remained within trimeters[7]), [100] we scarcely achieve a light shadow, so much so that, in my opinion, the Latin language itself does not take up that grace that was given only to the Attics, since not even the Greeks achieved it in another dialect of their language[8]. In togatae Afranius excels: if only he had not stained his plots with indecent love affairs with boys, admitting his own way of life[9].

T 7. On theatre buildings

(Vitruvius, *De architectura* 5.6; Tertullian, *De spectaculis* 10.1-9)

The architect Vitruvius has left the most extensive textual evidence for the structure of Roman theatres, outlining detailed instructions on how to build a perfect theatre (as part of his treatise on architecture). His description dates to the late Republican/early Augustan period, when permanent stone theatres started to be built in Rome, and it may also reflect his view of an ideal structure; therefore his discussion has to be applied with caution to archaeological remains, and it does not cover early, temporary stages. However, although it is very technical, it illustrates the constituent features of a fully developed Roman theatre in contrast to a Greek one, and it is thus a useful

(a) Vitruvius, *De architectura* 5.6

[1] ipsius autem theatri conformatio sic est facienda uti, quam magna futura est perimetros imi, centro medio conlocato circumagatur linea rotundationis, in eaque quattuor scribantur trigona paribus lateribus <quae paribus> intervallis extremam lineam circinationis tangant, [quibus etiam in duodecim signorum caelestium astrologi ex musica convenientia astrorum ratiocinantur]. ex his trigonis cuius latus fuerit proximum scaenae, ea regione qua praecidit curvaturam circinationis, ibi finiatur scaenae frons, et ab eo loco per centrum parallelos linea ducatur, quae disiungat proscaenii pulpitum et orchestrae regionem. [2] ita latius factum fuerit pulpitum quam Graecorum, quod omnes artifices in scaena dant operam, in orchestra autem senatorum sunt sedibus loca designata. et eius pulpiti altitudo sit ne plus pedum quinque, uti qui in orchestra sederint, spectare possint omnium agentium gestus.

cunei spectaculorum in theatro ita dividantur, uti anguli trigonorum, qui currunt circum curvaturam circinationis, dirigant ascensus scalasque inter cuneos ad primam praecinctionem, supra autem alternis itineribus superiores cunei medii dirigantur. [3] i autem qui sunt in imo et dirigunt scalaria, erunt numero VII, reliqui quinque scaenae designabunt compositionem: et unus medius contra se valvas regias habere debet, et qui erunt dextra ac sinistra hospitaliorum designabunt compositionem, extremi duo spectabunt itinera versurarum. gradus spectaculorum ubi subsellia componantur ne minus alti sint palmopede, <ne plus pedem> et digitos sex, latitudinis eorum ne plus pedes semis, ne minus pedes duo constituantur.

[4] tectum porticus, quod futurum est in summa gradatione, cum scaenae altitudine libratum prospiciatur, ideo quod vox crescens

T 7. On theatre buildings

(Vitruvius, *De architectura* 5.6; Tertullian, *De spectaculis* 10.1-9)

complement to preserved theatre structures from the Roman Empire (cf. Fig. 2).
   Like other late-antique Christian writers, Tertullian talked about the theatre as a pagan institution that was condemned and opposed by the Christians. Apart from this particular perspective, his treatise De spectaculis *('On spectacles') includes interesting information about the Roman 'theatre temple' as realized, for instance, in Pompey's theatre in Rome (55 BCE), i.e. a combination of theatre and temple, where a temple towers above the auditorium and the central wedge of the rows of seats functions as monumental access to this temple.*

(a) Vitruvius, *De architectura* 5.6

[1] And the structure of the theatre itself has to be arranged as follows: in the middle of an area that is as large as the perimeter of the lowest (row of the auditorium) will be, a pair of compasses is to be placed and a line of circumference to be drawn around, and therein four triangles are to be inscribed with sides of equal length and which touch with their edges the line of the circumference at equally spaced intervals. Out of these triangles that one whose side is nearest to the stage shall determine the front of the stage by this spot where it cuts the curvature of the circle, and from this spot a parallel line shall be drawn through the centre, which is to separate the platform of the stage and the area of the orchestra. [2] Thus the stage should be made deeper than that of the Greeks, since all artists are active on the stage, while spaces for seats of senators are assigned in the orchestra. And the height of this platform shall not be more than five feet, so that those who sit in the orchestra can see the gestures of all those acting.
   The wedges for seats in the theatre shall be divided so that the angles of the triangles that run around the circumference of the circle give the direction for the ascending flights of steps between the wedges up to the first curved cross-aisle; and above, the higher wedges shall be laid out with alternating aisles in the middle. [3] These then that are at the bottom and direct the flights of steps will be seven in number; the remaining five will determine the form of the stage: and the single one in the middle ought to have the royal door[1] opposite itself, and those that will be to the right and to the left will determine the arrangement of the quarters for guests[2], the two outermost ones will look to the passages in the wings. The stairs for seats, where benches are placed, shall not be less high than

aequaliter ad summas gradationes et tectum perveniet. namque si non erit aequale, quo minus fuerit altum, vox praeripietur ad eam altitudinem ad quam perveniet primo. [5] orchestra inter gradus imos quod diametron habuerit, eius sexta pars sumatur, et in cornibus utrimque ad eius mensurae perpendiculum inferiores sedes praecidiantur, et qua praecisio fuerit, ibi constituantur itinerum supercilia. ita enim satis altitudinis habebunt eorum confornicationes. [6] scaenae longitudo ad orchestrae diametron duplex fieri debet. podii altitudo ab libramento pulpiti cum corona et lysi duodecuma orchestrae diametri. supra podium columnae cum capitulis et spiris altae quarta parte eiusdem diametri, epistylia et ornamenta earum columnarum altitudinis quinta parte. pluteum insuper cum unda et corona inferioris plutei dimidia parte. supra id pluteum columnae quarta parte minore altitudine sint quam inferiores, epistylia et ornamenta earum columnarum quinta parte. item si tertia episcenos futura erit, mediani plutei summum sit dimidia parte, columnae summae medianarum minus altae sint quarta parte, epistylia cum coronis earum columnarum item habeant altitudinis quintam partem.

[7] nec tamen in omnibus theatris symmetriae ad omnes rationes et effectus possunt respondere, sed oportet architectum animadvertere quibus proportionibus necesse sit sequi symmetriam et quibus ad loci naturam aut magnitudinem operis temperari. sunt enim res quas et in pusillo et in magno theatro necesse est eadem magnitudine fieri propter usum, uti gradus, diazomata, pluteos, itinera, ascensus, pulpita, tribunalia et si qua alia intercurrunt, ex quibus necessitas cogit discedere ab symmetria, ne inpediatur usus. non minus si qua exiguitas copiarum, id est marmoris, materiae reliquarumque rerum quae parantur, in opere fuerit, paulum demere aut adicere, dum id ne nimium inprobe fiat sed cum sensu, non erit alienum. hoc autem erit si architectus erit usu peritus, praeterea ingenio mobili sollertiaque non fuerit viduatus.

[8] ipsae autem scaenae suas habent rationes explicatas ita, uti mediae valvae ornatus habeant aulae regiae, dextra ac sinistra hospitalia, secundum autem spatia ad ornatus comparata, quae loca Graeci περιάκτους dicunt ab eo quod machinae sunt in his locis versatiles trigonoe habentes singulae tres species ornationis, quae, cum aut fabularum mutationes sunt futurae seu deorum adventus cum tonitribus repentinis versentur mutentque speciem ornationis in fronte. secundum ea loca versurae sunt procurrentes, quae efficiunt una a foro, altera a peregre aditus in scaenam. [9] genera autem sunt scaenarum tria, unum quod dicitur tragicum, alterum comicum, tertium satyricum. horum autem ornatus sunt inter se dissimili disparique ratione, quod tragicae deformantur columnis et fastigiis et signis reliquisque regalibus rebus, comicae autem aedificiorum privatorum et maenianorum habent speciem prospectusque fenestris

a foot and a palm and not more than a foot and six fingers; their breadth shall be fixed at not more than two and a half feet, not less than two feet.

[4] The roof of the portico, which will be at the top of the ascending rows, shall be seen in line with the height of the stage house, so that the rising voice will reach the top of the auditorium and the roof evenly. For if this will not be equal, in proportion as it is lower, the voice will be cut off at the height that it will reach first. [5] What the diameter of the orchestra will be at the lowest rows, the sixth part of this shall be taken, and at the end of the half-circle on both sides the lower seats shall be cut off in a straight line of this size; and where the cutting away will occur, there shall be lintels over the passages. For thus their vaulting will have sufficient height. [6] The length of the stage must be twice the diameter of the orchestra. The height of the podium from the horizontal plane of the platform with crown and talon shall be the twelfth part of the diameter of the orchestra. Above the podium there shall be columns, with capitals and bases, of the fourth part of the same diameter in height; architraves and ornaments of these columns shall be of the fifth part of their height. A parapet above with talon and crown shall be of half the size of the lower parapet. Above this parapet there shall be columns one fourth less in height than the lower ones; architraves and ornaments of these columns shall be of the fifth part of their height. Equally if there will be three storeys above the stage, the highest one shall be of half the size of the middle parapet; the highest columns shall be one fourth less high than the middle ones; the architraves with the crowns of these columns shall also have the fifth part of the height.

[7] Nevertheless not in all theatres can the symmetries correspond to all these calculations and realizations, but the architect must consider for which proportions it is necessary to follow the symmetry and for which proportions it must be adjusted to the nature of the site or the size of the work. For there are items that must be of the same size both in a tiny and in a big theatre because of their use, such as steps, walkways between seats, parapets, paths, flights of steps, platforms, spaces for seats of magistrates and if there is anything else as a result of which one is forced to depart from symmetry, lest use be hindered. Equally, if by some lack of resources, i.e. of marble, timber and the other things that are provided, there is a shortage in the construction, it will not be unsuitable to take away or add a little, as long as this does not happen in too inappropriate a way, but rather with sense. But this will be the case if the architect is experienced and besides is not bereft of a flexible mind and dexterity.

[8] And the stage walls themselves have their own clear rationale so that the middle door has the decoration of a royal palace, the right and the left doors are for guests, and next to them there are spaces for decoration, places that the Greeks call *periaktoi* (Gr. 'revolving machines')

dispositos imitatione, communium aedificiorum rationibus, satyricae vero ornantur arboribus, speluncis, montibus reliquisque agrestibus rebus in topiodis speciem deformati.

---

1 the central door of the three stage-doors. 2 refers to the two doors on either side of the central door.

(b) Tertullian, *De spectaculis* 10.1-9

[1] transeamus ad scaenicas, quarum et originem communem et titulos pares secundum ipsam ab initio ludorum appellationem et administrationem coniunctam cum re equestri iam ostendimus. [2] apparatus etiam ex ea parte consortes, qua ad scaenam a templis et aris et illa infelicitate turis et sanguinis inter tibias et tubas itur duobus inquinatissimis arbitris funerum et sacrorum, dissignatore et haruspice. [3] ita cum de originibus ludorum ad circenses transiimus, inde nunc ad scaenicos ludos dirigemus. a loci vitio theatrum proprie sacrarium Veneris est. hoc denique modo id genus operis in saeculo evasit. [4] nam saepe censores nascentia cum maxime theatra destruebant, moribus consulentes, quorum scilicet periculum ingens de lascivia providebant, ut iam hic ethnicis in testimonium cedat sententia ipsorum nobiscum faciens et nobis in exaggerationem disciplinae etiam humanae praerogativa.

[5] itaque Pompeius Magnus, solo theatro suo minor, cum illam arcem omnium turpitudinum exstruxisset, veritus quandoque memoriae suae censoriam animadversionem Veneris aedem superposuit et ad dedicationem edicto populum vocans non theatrum, sed Veneris templum nuncupavit, 'cui subiecimus', inquit, 'gradus spectaculorum'. [6] ita damnatum et damnandum opus templi titulo praetexit et disciplinam superstitione delusit.

sed Veneri et Libero convenit. duo ista daemonia conspirata et coniurata inter se sunt ebrietatis et libidinis. [7] itaque theatrum Veneris Liberi quoque domus est. nam et alios ludos scaenicos Liberalia proprie vocabant, praeterquam Libero devotos, quae sunt Dionysia penes Graecos, etiam a Libero institutos. [8] et est plane in artibus quoque scaenicis Liberi et Veneris patrocinium. quae privata et propria sunt scaenae de gestu et corporis flexu mollitiam Veneri et Libero immolant, illi per sexum,

62

for the reason that in these areas there are revolving three-sided machines with three types of individual decoration, which, when there will be changes in the plays or the arrival of gods with sudden thunders, they can revolve and change the style of decoration in front. Next to these spots are the protruding wings, which provide entrances to the stage, one from the Forum and the other one from abroad. [9] And there are three types of scenery: one that is called tragic, another one that is comic, and the third one is in the style of satyr-play. And the decorations of these are of different and unequal types, since tragic scenes are created by columns, pediments, statues and the other royal things; comic scenes on the other hand have the appearance of private buildings and balconies and projections in imitation of windows, in the style of ordinary buildings; and satyr-play scenes are embellished by trees, caves, mountains and other rural things, in the shape of recreated landscape.

(b) Tertullian, *De spectaculis* 10.1-9

[1] Let us move on to stage business; we have already shown both that its origin is the same and that the names are identical, owing to the very term 'games' used from the outset and to the organization shared with the equestrian business[1]. [2] The set-up is also similar in the respect that there is a procession to the stage from the temples and altars and that infelicitous use of incense and blood, among pipes and trumpets, under the two most polluted masters of funerals and sacrifices, the undertaker and the soothsayer. [3] So, as we moved from the origins of the games to the circus games, from there we will now turn to the scenic games. Because of the vices of the site, the theatre actually is a shrine of Venus. This, in short, is how this kind of structure emerged into the world. [4] For the censors frequently destroyed theatres, particularly when they were just appearing, looking after public morals, as they obviously foresaw immense danger to them on account of the theatrical licentiousness, so that here already the opinion of the pagans themselves coincides with ours as evidence, providing reinforcement for us by the precedent of basic human morality.

[5] Therefore, when Pompeius Magnus [i.e. Pompey the Great], second only to his own theatre, had erected that citadel of all foulness, he feared censorial censure of his memory at some point and therefore built a temple of Venus on top of it; summoning the people to the dedication by edict, he called it not a theatre, but a temple of Venus, 'under which', he said, 'we have set up steps for the shows'[2]. [6] Thus he covered a condemned and condemnable structure by the name of 'temple' and deceived morality with superstition.

But there is unanimity between Venus and Liber[3]. These two demons

illi per fluxum dissolutis. [9] quae vero voce et modis et organis et litteris transiguntur, Apollines et Musas et Minervas et Mercurios mancipes habent. oderis, Christiane, quorum auctores non potes non odisse.

---

1 both performances in the circus and those in the theatre were called 'games' and organized by the same officials. **2** Pompey's theatre, inaugurated in 55 BCE, consisted of a theatre and a temple to Venus on top of the auditorium. **3** i.e. Bacchus, here understood as the god of theatre in analogy to the Greek Dionysus. **4** an ancient festival in Rome on 17 March, but without dramatic performances in Republican times. **5** the main festival in Athens.

T 8. On the development of theatre buildings

(Valerius Maximus, *Facta et dicta memorabilia* 2.4.1-3, 6)

In his chapter on Roman theatre and dramatic performances (cf. T 1b) Valerius Maximus, the early imperial writer of a collection of exempla, not only discusses the history of the institution, but also the development of its physical setting. Although his description is not an entirely logical exposition throughout, he refers to the following significant facts in the history of the Roman theatre: difficulties with erecting a permanent theatre building in the mid-Republic due to opposition from within the nobility, allegedly

[1] proximus <a> militaribus institutis ad urbana castra, id est theatra, gradus faciendus est, quoniam haec quoque saepe numero animosas acies instruxerunt, excogitataque cultus deorum et hominum delectationis causa non sine aliquo pacis rubore voluptatem et religionem civili sanguine scaenicorum portentorum gratia macularunt. [2] quae incohata quidem sunt a Messalla et Cassio censoribus. ceterum auctore P. Scipione Nasica omnem apparatum operis eorum subiectum hastae venire placuit, atque etiam senatus consulto cautum est ne quis in urbe propiusve passus mille subsellia posuisse sedensve ludos spectare vellet, ut scilicet † remissioni animorum standi virilitas propria Romanae gentis iuncta esset †.
    [3] per quingentos autem et quinquaginta et octo annos senatus populo mixtus spectaculo ludorum interfuit. sed hunc morem <A.> Atilius Serranus et L. Scribonius aediles ludos Matri deum facientes, posterioris Africani sententiam secuti, discretis senatus et populi locis solverunt, eaque res avertit volgi animum et favorem Scipionis magnopere quassavit. [4] ...
    [6] religionem ludorum crescentibus opibus secuta lautitia est. eius instinctu Q. Catulus, Campanam imitatus luxuriam, primus spectantium

64

of drunkenness and lust have conspired and both joined in a plot. [7] Therefore the theatre of Venus is also the house of Liber. For, appropriately, they called other scenic games Liberalia[4]; besides being dedicated to Liber, these games, which are Dionysia among the Greeks[5], have even been introduced by Liber. [8] And obviously in the arts of the stage, too, there is patronage of Liber and Venus. What is specific and distinctive of the stage, the effeminacy of gesture and body movement, they offer it to Venus and Liber, both licentious, one by her sex and the other by his extravagance. [9] But what is accomplished by voice, songs, instruments and texts, for this they have Apollos, Muses, Minervas and Mercuries as responsible. Hate, you Christian, those whose patrons you cannot but hate.

T 8. On the development of theatre buildings

(Valerius Maximus, *Facta et dicta memorabilia* 2.4.1-3, 6)

partly caused by the aim of maintaining the virility of the Roman people; the introduction of stratified seating with special seats reserved for senators; the increasing sophistication and lavishness of temporary stages. These facts illustrate how dramatic performances and their setting became an important part of Roman public and social life during the latter part of the Republican period.

[1] From military institutions the next step is to be made to camps in the city, i.e. theatres, since they too have often drawn up vigorous battle lines and, invented for the benefit of the worship of gods and the entertainment of men, have stained pleasure and religion with citizen blood for the sake of monstrosities on stage, not without some blushing of peace[1]. [2] They [i.e. theatre buildings] were begun by the censors Messalla and Cassius[2]. But at the instance of P. Scipio Nasica[3] it was decided to auction off all equipment belonging to their building, and precautions were also taken by a senate decree that no one in the city of Rome or at a distance of less than a mile should wish to put up benches and watch the shows seated, obviously so that the virility of remaining standing, distinctive of the Roman nation, should be joined with the relaxation of minds[4].
[3] For 558 years[5] the senate attended the spectacle of the games mingled with the people. But this custom was discontinued by the aediles A. Atilius Serranus and L. Scribonius [in 194 BCE], when they were organizing the games for the Mother of the Gods[6]; following the view of the younger Africanus[7], they had the areas for the senate and the people

65

consessum velorum umbraculis texit. Cn. Pompeius ante omnes aquae per semitas decursu aestivum minuit fervorem. Claudius Pulcher scaenam varietate colorum adumbravit, vacuis ante pictura tabulis extentam. quam totam argento C. Antonius, auro Petreius, ebore Q. Catulus praetexuit. versatilem fecerunt Luculli, argentatis choragiis P. Lentulus Spinther adornavit. translatum, antea poenicis indutum tunicis, M. Scaurus exquisito genere vestis cultum induxit.

---

1 apparently refers to riots in the theatre, though those mentioned in Cicero and the Ciceronian tradition are not so bloody. 2 M. Valerius Messalla and C. Cassius Longinus in 154 BCE. 3 P. Cornelius Scipio Nasica Corculum, initiating a senate decree slightly later. 4 this seems to be the sense of the Latin, as the precise wording here is in doubt. 5 since 753 BCE, the legendary date of Rome's foundation. 6 Magna Mater, honoured by *Ludi Megalenses*. 7 P. Cornelius Scipio Africanus, consul in this year, actually the elder Africanus.

T 9. On revival performances of 'old' plays

(Plautus, *Casina* 5-20)

The extant prologue to Plautus' Casina *does not go back to Plautus himself, but was supplied for a revival performance of the play about a generation after its first production. Hence this text provides valuable evidence for the practice of revival performances in the middle of the second century* BCE *and the assessment of dramatic poets in this period. According to this*

[5] qui utuntur vino vetere sapientis puto
et qui lubenter veteres spectant fabulas;
anticua opera et verba quom vobis placent,
aequom est placere ante <alias> veteres fabulas:
nam nunc novae quae prodeunt comoediae
[10] multo sunt nequiores quam nummi novi.
nos postquam populi rumore intelleximus
studiose expetere vos Plautinas fabulas,
anticuam eiius edimus comoediam,
quam vos probastis qui estis in senioribus;
[15] nam iuniorum qui sunt non norunt, scio;
verum ut cognoscant dabimus operam sedulo.
haec quom primum acta est, vicit omnis fabulas.
ea tempestate flos poetarum fuit,
qui nunc abierunt hinc in communem locum.
[20] sed tamen apsentes prosunt <pro> praesentibus.

separated; and this step alienated the attitude of the populace and severely shattered Scipio's popularity. [4] ... [for 2.4.4 cf. T 1b] ...

[6] The sacredness of the games was followed by elegance as wealth increased. At its prompting Q. Catulus, imitating Campanian luxury, was the first to cover the seats of the spectators with the shade of awnings [in 69 BCE]. Cn. Pompeius, before all others, reduced the summer heat with water flowing down in channels [in 55 BCE]. Claudius Pulcher covered the stage with a variety of colours; previously it had been made up of boards without painting [in 99 BCE]. The whole of it was covered over with silver by C. Antonius [in 66 BCE], with gold by Petreius [before 64 BCE], with ivory by Q. Catulus [prob. in 81 BCE]. The Luculli made it revolving [in 79 BCE], P. Lentulus Spinther decorated it with silver stage equipment [in 63 BCE]. M. Scaurus brought on the procession dressed in an exquisite kind of costume, while it had previously been clothed in purple tunics [in 58 BCE].

T 9. On revival performances of 'old' plays

(Plautus, *Casina* 5-20)

prologue, a play by Plautus was put on again since 'new' plays written at this time were worthless, while 'old' plays were appreciated and called for by audiences. The 'flower of poets' active in an earlier period was dead, but their work could be kept alive and enjoyed by means of revivals (to the advantage also of theatre companies).

[5] Those who use old wine I regard as wise men, as well as those who watch old plays with pleasure; since old works and words please you, it is right that old plays please you more than others: for new comedies that appear nowadays [10] are far more worthless than new coins. After we have learned by popular rumour that you eagerly desire plays by Plautus, we produce an old comedy of his; it has been approved by those of you who are among the older men. [15] For those who belong to the younger men do not know it, I am sure; but we will make every effort so that they will get to know it. When this play was first performed, it surpassed all other plays. In that age there was a flower of poets, who have now gone away from here to the place where all men go. [20] Yet, though absent, they profit us as if present.

T 10. On revival performances in the late Republic

(Cicero, *Ad Atticum* 2.19.3; *Pro Sestio* 106-26)

While only few new tragedies and comedies were written for the stage in the late Republic, revival performances of 'classic' plays continued (cf. also T 9). According to Cicero, who provides almost all the evidence, a distinctive feature of revivals in this period was their political application and exploitation, which is not attested for dramatic performances in earlier centuries. This politicization could concern the event as a whole, when audiences reacted to appearances or absences of well-known public figures, for instance by greeting them with the appropriate noises, or to the choice of plays. And it could affect the presentation of the plays, when individual lines were interpreted out of context and understood as referring to the

(a) Cicero, *Ad Atticum* 2.19.3

populi sensus maxime theatro et spectaculis perspectus est; nam gladia-toribus qua dominus qua advocati sibilis conscissi; ludis Apollinaribus Diphilus tragoedus in nostrum Pompeium petulanter invectus est: 'nostra miseria tu es magnus' [*Trag. inc. inc.* 115 R.³ = 125 W.], miliens coactus est dicere; 'eandem virtutem istam veniet tempus cum graviter gemes' [*Trag. inc. inc.* 116 R.³ = 126 W.], totius theatri clamore dixit itemque cetera. nam et eius modi sunt ii versus, ut in tempus ab inimico Pompei scripti esse videantur: 'si neque leges neque mores cogunt' [*Trag. inc. inc.* 117 R.³ = 127 W.], et cetera magno cum fremitu et clamore sunt dicta.

Caesar cum venisset mortuo plausu, Curio filius est insecutus. huic ita plausum est ut salva re publica Pompeio plaudi solebat. tulit Caesar graviter. litterae Capuam ad Pompeium volare dicebantur. inimici erant equitibus qui Curioni stantes plauserant, hostes omnibus; Rosciae legi, etiam frumentariae minitabantur. sane res erat perturbata. equidem malueram quod erat susceptum ab illis silentio transiri, sed vereor ne non liceat. non ferunt homines quod videtur esse tamen ferendum; sed est iam una vox omnium magis odio firmata quam praesidio.

---

1 probably A. Gabinius, a candidate for the consulship. 2 Games for Apollo, celebrated in mid-July. 3 a quotation from an unidentified tragedy. 4 another quotation from an unidentified tragedy. 5 a further quotation from an unidentified tragedy. 6 C. Scribonius Curio, tr. pl. 50 BCE, hostile to the political allies Caesar, Pompey and Crassus. 7 a town in southern Italy. 8 apparently Caesar and Pompey. 9 a law carried by the tribune L. Roscius Otho, assigning the first fourteen rows in the theatre to the knights. 10 one of the Roman laws regulating the price and distribution of corn.

T 10. On revival performances in the late Republic

(Cicero, *Ad Atticum* 2.19.3; *Pro Sestio* 106-26)

contemporary situation by actors and/or audiences; actors might even include relevant lines from other plays or of their own invention into the play currently performed.

Even though Cicero did not approve of dramatic performances turning into spectacles (cf. T 11a), he enjoyed their political exploitation when it supported his own views and standing in society. This is shown by the extensive description of games in his speech On behalf of Sestius, *where they are seen as a venue for political expression in connection with Cicero's recall from exile in 57 BCE.*

(a) Cicero, *Ad Atticum* 2.19.3 [59 BCE]

The feelings of the people can be seen most clearly at the theatre and the spectacles. For at the gladiatorial shows both the organizer[1] and his associates[2] were torn to pieces with hisses. At the *Ludi Apollinares*[2] the tragic actor Diphilus insolently attacked our Pompeius [i.e. Pompey the Great]: 'By our misery you are great!'[3] He was forced to say it a thousand times. 'There will come a time when you will bitterly lament the same courage'[4], he said amid shouting from the whole theatre, and similarly the rest. For these verses are indeed of such a kind that they seem to be written by an enemy of Pompeius for this time. 'If neither laws nor morals exert force'[5], and the rest was delivered amid great noise and shouting.

When Caesar had come with applause non-existent, he was followed by Curio the son[6]. He got such an applause as Pompeius used to get when the Republic was intact. Caesar took it badly. A letter is said to be flying to Pompeius in Capua[7]. They[8] are opposed to the equestrians, who gave Curio a standing ovation, and hostile to everybody; they threaten the Roscian Law[9], even the corn law[10]. Public matters are truly in disarray. I myself would have preferred that what had been organized by them could be passed over in silence, but I fear that it might not be possible. People do not bear what, all the same, apparently has to be borne; but already there is one voice of all men, strengthened more by hatred than by powerful defence.

(b) Cicero, *Pro Sestio* 106-26

[106] nunc, nisi me fallit, in eo statu civitas est ut, si operas conductorum removeris, omnes idem de re publica sensuri esse videantur. etenim tribus locis significari maxime de <re publica> populi Romani iudicium ac voluntas potest: contione, comitiis, ludorum gladiatorumque consessu. ...
    [115] veniamus ad ludos; ... [116] ...
    semel, inquam, se ludis homo popularis commisit omnino, cum in templo Virtutis honos habitus esset virtuti, Gaique Mari, conservatoris huius imperi, monumentum municipi eius et rei publicae defensori sedem ad salutem praebuisset. [117] quo quidem tempore quid populus Romanus sentire se ostenderet utroque in genere declaratum est: primum cum audito senatus consulto rei ipsi atque absenti senatui plausus est ab universis datus, deinde cum senatoribus singulis spectatum e senatu redeuntibus: cum vero ipse qui ludos faciebat consul adsedit, stantes ei manibus passis gratias agentes et lacrimantes gaudio suam erga me benivolentiam ac misericordiam declararunt. at cum ille furibundus incitata illa sua vaecordi mente venisset, vix se populus Romanus tenuit, vix homines odium suum a corpore eius impuro atque infando represserunt; voces quidem et palmarum intentus et maledictorum clamorem omnes profuderunt.
    [118] sed quid ego populi Romani animum virtutemque commemoro, libertatem iam ex diuturna servitute dispicientis, in eo homine cui tum petenti iam aedilitatem ne histriones quidem coram sedenti pepercerunt? nam cum ageretur togata Simulans, ut opinor, caterva tota clarissima concentione in ore impuri hominis imminens contionata est: 'haec, Tite, tua post principia atque exitus vitiosae vitae!' [Afranius, *Tog.* 304/5 R.[3]] sedebat exanimatus, et is qui antea cantorum convicio contiones celebrare suas solebat cantorum ipsorum vocibus eiciebatur. et quoniam facta mentio est ludorum, ne illud quidem praetermittam, in magna varietate sententiarum numquam ullum fuisse locum, in quo aliquid a poeta dictum cadere in tempus nostrum videretur, quod aut populum universum fugeret aut non exprimeret ipse actor. [119] ...
    [120] quid fuit illud quod, recenti nuntio de illo senatus consulto quod factum est in templo Virtutis ad ludos scaenamque perlato, consessu maximo summus artifex et me hercule semper partium in re publica tam quam in scaena optimarum, flens et recenti laetitia et mixto dolore ac desiderio mei, egit apud populum Romanum multo gravioribus verbis meam causam quam egomet de me agere potuissem? summi enim poetae ingenium non solum arte sua, sed etiam dolore exprimebat. qua enim <vi>: 'qui rem publicam animo certo adiuverit, statuerit, steterit cum Achivis' [Accius, *Trag.* 357-8 R.[3] = 351-2 W.], vobiscum me stetisse dicebat, vestros ordines demonstrabat! revocabatur ab universis 're dubia haut

(b) Cicero, *Pro Sestio* 106-26 [56 BCE]

[106] Now, unless I am mistaken, our community is in such a state that all would be seen to have the same feelings about the Republic if one eliminated the activities of hired henchmen. For truly the Roman people's judgement and desires concerning the Republic can be observed most clearly in three places: at popular assemblies, at voting assemblies, at gatherings for games and gladiator shows. ...
    [115] Let's move on to the games. ... [116] ...
    Only once, I stress, did this 'man of the people'[1] entrust himself to the games at all[2], when in the Temple of Virtus honour had been paid to virtue, and the monument of Gaius Marius[3], the preserver of the power of this state, had provided a townsman of his and defender of the Republic[4] with a spot for salvation. [117] On this occasion it was made clear in two ways what feelings the Roman people showed: first, when they had heard the senate decree[5], applause was granted by all to the matter itself and to the absent senate, second, when individual senators returned from the senate to watch the games; and when the consul himself, who was organizing the games[6], took his seat, they rose and showed their gratitude to him with upturned hands, and weeping for joy they demonstrated their goodwill and pity for me. But when this madman[7] had arrived, urged on by his own insane mind, the Roman people could scarcely hold back, the men scarcely restrained their hatred from his polluted and abominable body; at any rate all poured fourth cries, gestures of their hands and shouts of abuse.
    [118] But why should I recall the Roman people's spirit and courage, when they were just discerning liberty after long servitude, in the case of this man[8], whom not even the actors have spared, when he was already a candidate for the aedileship and sitting before them? For when a togata, entitled *Simulans* ('*The Pretender*'), I believe, was being performed, the whole group of actors publicly harangued him in splendid harmony, bending towards the face of the polluted man: 'This, Titus, is the sequel for you and the outcome of your vicious life!'[9] He sat there entirely put out of his senses, and he who previously used to fill his popular assemblies[10] with abuse of hired singers was now driven off by the voices of actual singers. And since mention has been made of the games, I will not omit this detail, namely that amid the great variety of utterances there has never been a passage in which something said by the poet seemed to apply to our time that either escaped the whole populace or was not expressed by the actor himself. [119] ...
    [120] What about this: when the recent news about the senate decree that had been passed in the temple of Virtus had been brought to the games and the stage[11], amid a great gathering, this supreme artist[12],

71

dubitarit vitam offerre nec capiti pepercerit' [Accius, *Trag.* 359-60 R.³ = 353-4 W.]. haec quantis ab illo clamoribus agebantur! [121] cum iam omisso gestu verbis poetae et studio actoris et exspectationi nostrae plauderetur: 'summum amicum summo in bello', nam illud ipse actor adiungebat amico animo et fortasse homines propter aliquod desiderium adprobabant: 'summo ingenio praeditum'.

iam illa quanto cum gemitu populi Romani ab eodem paulo post in eadem fabula sunt acta! 'o pater' [Ennius, *Trag.* 81 R.³ = 101 W. = Accius, *Trag.* 355 W.], me, me ille absentem ut patrem deplorandum putabat, quem Q. Catulus, quem multi alii saepe in senatu patrem patriae nominarant. quanto cum fletu de illis nostris incendiis ac ruinis, cum patrem pulsum, patriam adflictam deploraret, domum incensam eversamque, sic egit ut, demonstrata pristina fortuna, cum se convertisset: 'haec omnia vidi inflammari' [Ennius, *Trag.* 86 R.³ = 106 W. = Accius, *Trag.* 356 W.] fletum etiam inimicis atque invidis excitaret! [122] pro di immortales! quid? illa quem ad modum dixit idem! quae mihi quidem ita et acta et scripta videntur esse ut vel a Q. Catulo, si revixisset, praeclare posse dici viderentur; is enim libere reprehendere et accusare populi non numquam temeritatem solebat aut errorem senatus: 'o ingratifici Argivi, immunes Grai, inmemores benefici!' [Accius, *Trag.* 364 R.³ = 358 W.] non erat illud quidem verum; non enim ingrati, sed miseri, quibus reddere salutem a quo acceperant non liceret, nec unus in quemquam umquam gratior quam in me universi; sed tamen illud scripsit disertissimus poeta pro me, egit fortissimus actor, non solum optimus, de me, cum omnis ordines demonstraret, senatum, equites Romanos, universum populum Romanum accusaret: 'exsulare sinitis, sistis pelli, pulsum patimini!' [Accius, *Trag.* 365 R.³ = 359 W.] quae tum significatio fuerit omnium, quae declaratio voluntatis ab universo populo Romano in causa hominis non popularis, equidem audiebam: existimare facilius possunt qui adfuerunt.

[123] et quoniam huc me provexit oratio, histrio casum meum totiens conlacrimavit, cum ita dolenter ageret causam meam ut vox eius illa praeclara lacrimis impediretur; neque poetae, quorum ego semper ingenia dilexi, tempori meo defuerunt; eaque populus Romanus non solum plausu sed etiam gemitu suo comprobavit. utrum igitur haec Aesopum potius pro me aut Accium dicere oportuit, si populus Romanus liber esset, an principes civitatis? nominatim sum appellatus in Bruto: 'Tullius, qui libertatem civibus stabiliverat' [Accius, *Praet.* 40 R.³ = 40 W.]. miliens revocatum est. parumne videbatur populus Romanus iudicare id a me et a senatu esse constitutum quod perditi cives sublatum per nos criminabantur? [124] ...

[126] at vero ille praetor, qui de me non patris, avi, proavi, maiorum denique suorum omnium, sed Graeculorum instituto contionem interrogare solebat, 'velletne me redire', et, cum erat reclamatum

by Hercules, always playing the best roles in the Republic as well as on stage, weeping for fresh joy, mixed with grief and longing for me, pled my case before the Roman people with far weightier words than I could have done it for myself. For he expressed the genius of the best poet[13] not only through his art, but also through his grief. For with what force did he say: 'he who has supported the public cause with determined mind, has established it and has stood beside the Achivi [i.e. the Greeks]'[14] – he said that I had stood beside you, he pointed to your ranks! He was asked back again by everyone: 'in uncertain circumstances he did not hesitate to offer his life, nor did he spare his person'[15]. Amid what shouting was this performed by him! [121] When, already in neglect of gesture, applause was given to the words of the poet, the zeal of the actor and the expectation of us[16]: 'the greatest friend in the greatest war', for the actor himself added this out of feelings of friendship, and perhaps the people approved due to some yearning: 'endowed with greatest talent'.

Moreover, amid what amount of sighing of the Roman people was the following acted by the same actor slightly later in the same play! 'Oh father'[17]: me, me it was that he believed had to be mourned like a father, me, whom Q. Catulus[18] and many others had often called 'father of the fatherland'[19] in the senate. With what amount of tears did he act concerning this our conflagration and ruin, when he mourned the father expelled, the fatherland ruined, the house set afire and burnt down, so that, after he had demonstrated the previous good fortune[20] and then turned round: 'I have seen all this go up in flames'[21], he provoked tears even among those hostile and ill-wishing! [122] By the immortal gods! Now, how the same actor delivered this! This seems to me to be both acted and written in such a way that it seems that it could even be spoken splendidly by Q. Catulus, if he had come back to life; for he was accustomed to criticize freely and to frequently find fault with the rashness of the people or errors of the senate: 'oh ungrateful Argives, disobliging Greeks, forgetful of favours!'[22] This was not true; for these people were not ungrateful, but rather pitiable, as it was not possible for them to return well-being to a man from whom they had received it, and never was one individual more thankful to anyone than all were to me; but still the most eloquent poet has written this for me, and the bravest actor, not only the best, delivered it about me, while he pointed to all ranks and accused the senate, the Roman knights and the whole Roman people: 'You allow him to be in exile, you have allowed him to be driven out; you put up with him driven out!'[23] What expression of assent from everyone then occurred, what declaration of their will from the entire Roman people in the case of a man who is not 'a man of the people', I for my part have heard[24]; those who were present can judge more easily.

semivivis mercennariorum vocibus, populum Romanum negare dicebat, is, cum cotidie gladiatores spectaret, numquam est conspectus cum veniret. emergebat subito, cum sub tabulas subrepserat, ut 'mater, te appello' [Pacuvius, *Trag.* 197 R.[3] = 205 W.] dicturus videretur; itaque illa via latebrosior, qua spectatum ille veniebat, Appia iam vocabatur; qui tamen quoquo tempore conspectus erat, non modo gladiatores sed equi ipsi gladiatorum repentinis sibilis extimescebant.

---

1 P. Clodius Pulcher. 2 at games in 57 BCE, after the first senate decree in support of Cicero's recall from exile. 3 who had erected this Temple of Honos and Virtus. 4 Cicero, a native of Arpinum like Marius. 5 i.e. the first senate decree in support of Cicero's recall from exile. 6 P. Cornelius Lentulus Spinther, in 57 BCE. 7 P. Clodius Pulcher. 8 P. Clodius Pulcher. 9 a line from this togata, applied to Clodius' situation. 10 i.e. those he held as a tribune of the people. 11 as described above. 12 i.e. the famous actor Clodius Aesopus, named below. 13 presumably Accius. 14 to be understood as a quotation from Accius' tragedy *Eurysaces*, as suggested by comments of the scholiast on the passage. 15 another quotation from Accius' tragedy. 16 i.e. of Cicero's return. 17 a quotation from Ennius' *Andromacha* (cf. D 1), apparently inserted in a play of Accius by the actor. 18 Q. Lutatius Catulus, consul in 78 and censor in 65 BCE. 19 a honorary title applied to Cicero after the suppression of the Catilinarian conspiracy in 63 BCE. 20 the actor perhaps pointing in the direction of Cicero's house. 21 another quotation from Ennius' *Andromacha* (cf. D 1). 22 again a quotation from Accius' tragedy. 23 another quotation from Accius' tragedy. 24 since Cicero was still in exile at the time. 25 a quotation from Accius' praetexta *Brutus* (cf. D 6), originally referring to the Roman king Servius Tullius. 26 i.e. liberty. 27 Clodius' brother, Appius Clodius Pulcher, praetor in 57 BCE. 28 Cicero has now turned to audience reactions at gladiatorial shows. 29 a quotation from Pacuvius' *Iliona*, where the shade of the dead son, emerging from the underworld, appears to his mother. 30 alludes to the name of a road from Rome to the south, begun by Appius' ancestor Appius Claudius Caecus in 312 BCE.

T 11. On sensational spectacle on stage

(Cicero, *Ad familiares* 7.1; Horace, *Epistula* 2.1.177-207)

Over the course of the Republican period dramatic performances became more and more spectacular as dramas gradually included more sophisticated stage props, exciting stage action or stunning effects of various kinds and as new dramatic genres with a large proportion of song and dance developed. These tendencies also affected revival performances, which were adapted to the taste of the period (cf. also T 10).

Intellectuals, who preferred meaningful dialogues and serious messages,

[123] And since the course of my speech has brought me to this point, the actor wept over my misfortune again and again, while he pleaded my cause with so much grief that this magnificent voice of his was hindered by tears. Nor were poets, whose talents I have always appreciated, lacking in my situation; and the Roman people showed their approval to this not only by applause, but also by groaning. Should Aesopus then or Accius rather have said this for me, if the Roman people were free, or the foremost men in the community? In *Brutus* I was mentioned by name: 'Tullius, who established liberty for the citizens'[25]. Encores of this line were requested countless times. Did the Roman people seem to be not firm enough of the view that I and the senate had established what ruined citizens accused us of having removed[26]? [124] ...

[126] But that praetor[27], who was accustomed to ask the popular assembly about me not in the established way of his father, grandfather, great-grandfather, all his ancestors in short, but of little Greeks, 'whether they wish that I return', and, when it was rejected by the lifeless voices of his recruits, said that the Roman people denied it, he, although he watched the gladiators every day, was never seen when he came[28]. He emerged suddenly, when he had crept along under the planks, so that he seemed to be about to say 'Mother, I call on you!'[29]. Therefore this rather shadowy path, by which he used to come to see the games, was already called the 'Appian way'[30]; still, whenever he was seen, not only the gladiators, but even the horses of the gladiators were struck by fear at the sudden hissing.

T 11. On sensational spectacle on stage

(Cicero, *Ad familiares* 7.1; Horace, *Epistula* 2.1.177-207)

were disgusted. Some criticism was already voiced by the satirist Lucilius in the second century BCE, *but the most famous instances come from the first century* BCE, *when these features might have increased: Cicero describes the spectacle at the opening of Pompey's theatre in 55* BCE *(cf. also T 7b) with utter contempt, and Horace is enraged at people, even of higher social classes, who are interested in actors' costumes and other paraphernalia, but do not pay attention to the words spoken (cf. also T 2; 5).*

(a) Cicero, *Ad familiares* 7.1

M. Cicero s. d. M. Mario.

[1] si te dolor aliqui corporis aut infirmitas valetudinis tuae tenuit quo minus ad ludos venires, fortunae magis tribuo quam sapientiae tuae; sin haec quae ceteri mirantur contemnenda duxisti et, cum per valetudinem posses, venire tamen noluisti, utrumque laetor, et sine dolore corporis te fuisse et animo valuisse, cum ea quae sine causa mirantur alii neglexeris, modo ut tibi constiterit fructus oti tui; quo quidem tibi perfrui mirifice licuit cum esses in ista amoenitate paene solus relictus. neque tamen dubito quin tu in illo cubiculo tuo, ex quo tibi Stabianum perforasti et patefecisti sinum, per eos dies matutina tempora lectiunculis consumpseris, cum illi interea qui te istic reliquerunt spectarent communis mimos semisomni. reliquas vero partis diei tu consumebas iis delectationibus quas tibi ipse ad arbitrium tuum compararas; nobis autem erant ea perpetienda quae Sp. Maecius probavisset.

[2] omnino, si quaeris, ludi apparatissimi, sed non tui stomachi; coniecturam enim facio de meo. nam primum honoris causa in scaenam redierant ii quos ego honoris causa de scaena decessisse arbitrabar. deliciae vero tuae, noster Aesopus, eius modi fuit ut ei desinere per omnis homines liceret; is iurare cum coepisset, vox eum defecit in illo loco: 'si sciens fallo' [*Trag. inc. poet.* 9 R.³]. quid tibi ego alia narrem? nosti enim reliquos ludos; qui ne id quidem leporis habuerunt quod solent mediocres ludi. apparatus enim spectatio tollebat omnem hilaritatem; quo quidem apparatu non dubito quin animo aequissimo carueris. quid enim delectationis habent sescenti muli in Clytaemestra aut in Equo Troiano creterrarum tria milia aut armatura varia peditatus et equitatus in aliqua pugna? quae popularem admirationem habuerunt, delectationem tibi nullam attulissent.

[3] quod si tu per eos dies operam dedisti Protogeni tuo, dum modo is tibi quidvis potius quam orationes meas legerit, ne tu haud paulo plus quam quisquam nostrum delectationis habuisti. non enim te puto Graecos aut Oscos ludos desiderasse, praesertim cum Oscos vel in senatu vestro spectare possis, Graecos ita non ames ut ne ad villam quidem tuam via Graeca ire soleas. nam quid ego te athletas putem desiderare, qui gladiatores contempseris? in quibus ipse Pompeius confitetur se et operam et oleum perdidisse. reliquae sunt venationes binae per dies quinque, magnificae, nemo negat; sed quae potest homini esse polito delectatio cum aut homo imbecillus a valentissima bestia laniatur aut praeclara bestia venabulo transverberatur? quae tamen, si videnda sunt, saepe vidisti, neque nos qui haec spectavimus quicquam novi vidimus. extremus elephantorum dies fuit. in quo admiratio magna vulgi atque turbae, delectatio nulla exstitit; quin etiam misericordia quaedam consecuta est

76

(a) Cicero, *Ad familiares* 7.1 [55 BCE]

Marcus Cicero sends greetings to Marcus Marius[1].

[1] If some bodily pain or the weakness of your health has prevented you from coming to the games[2], I assign this to fortune rather than to your wisdom; if however you regard what others admire as despicable and, although you were able to on account of your health, did not wish to come all the same, I am delighted at both: that you were without bodily pain and that you were healthy in your mind, since you disregarded what others admire without reason, if only you have reaped the fruit of your leisure. To enjoy it you have indeed had a wonderful opportunity, when you had been left almost on your own in that pleasant spot[3]. And after all, I do not doubt that in that private chamber of yours, in which you broke a window and opened it to the bay of Stabiae[4], you spent the morning period throughout these days with light readings, while in the meantime those who left you there were watching common mimes, half-asleep. But you spent the rest of the day in those diversions that you had prepared for yourself according to your own fancy; we, however, had to endure what Sp. Maecius[5] had approved.

[2] To be sure, if you ask, the games were most sumptuous, but not to your taste; for I make a guess on the basis of my own taste. For in the first place those actors had returned to the stage out of respect[6] who I believed had left the stage out of respect[7]. Indeed your favourite, our Aesopus[8], was in such a state that he would have been allowed to stop by everyone's permission. When he had begun to swear an oath, his voice failed him at this point: 'if I knowingly deceive'[9]. What else shall I tell you? For you know the remaining spectacles; these did not even have this attractiveness that mediocre games usually have. For watching the elaborate equipment removed all cheerfulness; and I do not doubt that you could do without this elaborate equipment with your mind completely at ease. For what enjoyment do six hundred mules in a *Clytaemestra*[10] or three thousand craters in an *Equus Troianus* ('*Trojan Horse*')[11] or various kinds of armour of soldiers on foot and on horseback in some battle provide? What won the admiration of the people would not have brought any enjoyment to you.

[3] If you paid attention to your Protogenes[12] throughout these days, as long as he read anything else to you rather than my speeches, you have indeed had not a little more enjoyment than any of us. For I do not believe that you missed the Greek or the Oscan games, particularly since you can see Oscans[13] even in the senate of your town[14], and you do not appreciate the Greeks to such an extent that you are accustomed not to walk along Greek street even to get to your house. For why should I believe that you have a desire for athletes, you who have scorned gladiators? As for those,

atque opinio eius modi, esse quandam illi beluae cum genere humano societatem.

[4] his ego tamen diebus, ludis scaenicis, ne forte videar tibi non modo beatus sed liber omnino fuisse, dirupi me paene in iudicio Galli Canini, familiaris tui. quod si tam facilem populum haberem quam Aesopus habuit, libenter mehercule artem desinerem tecumque et cum similibus nostri viverem. nam me cum antea taedebat, cum et aetas et ambitio me hortabatur et licebat denique quem nolebam non defendere, tum vero hoc tempore vita nulla est; neque enim fructum ullum laboris exspecto et cogor non numquam homines non optime de me meritos rogatu eorum qui bene meriti sunt defendere. [5] itaque quaero causas omnis aliquando vivendi arbitratu meo teque et istam rationem oti tui et laudo vehementer et probo, quodque nos minus intervisis, hoc fero animo aequiore, quod, si Romae esses, tamen neque nos lepore tuo neque te, si qui est in me, meo frui liceret propter molestissimas occupationes meas. quibus si me relaxaro (nam ut plane exsolvam non postulo), te ipsum, qui multos annos nihil aliud commentaris, docebo profecto quid sit humaniter vivere. tu modo istam imbecillitatem valetudinis tuae sustenta et tuere, ut facis, ut nostras villas obire et mecum simul lecticula concursare possis.

[6] haec ad te pluribus verbis scripsi quam soleo non oti abundantia sed amoris erga te, quod me quadam epistula subinvitaras, si memoria tenes, ut ad te aliquid eius modi scriberem quo minus te praetermisisse ludos paeniteret. quod si adsecutus sum, gaudeo; sin minus, hoc me tamen consolor, quod posthac ad ludos venies nosque vises neque in epistulis relinques meis spem aliquam delectationis tuae.

---

1 known only from Cicero's letters to him. 2 those given at the opening of Pompey's theatre. 3 in his villa near Pompeii. 4 a small town on the coast of Campania near Pompeii. 5 the person in charge of selecting the performances for these games. 6 for Pompey, the organizer of the games. 7 for themselves. 8 Clodius Aesopus, a famous actor in Cicero's time. 9 a quotation from an unidentified tragedy. 10 perhaps Accius' tragedy of this title. 11 perhaps Livius Andronicus' or Naevius' tragedy of this title. 12 the addressee's attendant, reading aloud to him. 13 a people of southern Italy. 14 presumably Pompeii in Campania. 15 L. Caninius Gallus, tribunus plebis in 56 BCE. 16 presumably Cicero's villas on the Bay of Naples.

---

even Pompeius admits that he has wasted both effort and oil. What is left are the hunts, two a day for five days, magnificent, nobody denies it; but what enjoyment can this be for a cultivated man when either a weak human is torn to pieces by a very strong animal or a splendid animal is pierced through by a hunting spear? If indeed these things are worth watching, you have often seen them; neither did we who watched these see anything new. The last day was for the elephants. Their admiration by the people and the mob was great, but there was no enjoyment. Even some sort of compassion arose and a view along the lines that there is some fellowship of this animal with the human race.

[4] All the same, during these days, during the scenic games, so that I do not by any chance appear to you to have been not only happy, but entirely free, I have almost ruptured myself in the trial of Gallus Caninius, your friend[15]. And if I had as good-natured an audience as Aesopus had, I would gladly, by Hercules, give up this art and live with you and those similar to us. For while I was already weary of it even earlier, when both age and ambition spurred me on and it was actually possible not to defend whom I did not wish, now indeed, in this time, it is no life at all. For I do not expect any fruit of my labours, and I am sometimes forced to defend people who have not done the best service to me, upon the request of those who have done good service. [5] Therefore I seek out all excuses for eventually living according to my fancy and strongly praise and approve this organization of your leisure, and as regards your visiting us less, I bear that with my mind more at ease, since, if you were in Rome, it would still be possible neither for me to enjoy your charm nor for you to enjoy mine, whatever is in me, because of my most troublesome occupations. If I have loosened my grip on those (for I do not demand that I discharge myself completely), I will indeed teach you, who have thought about nothing else for many years, what it is to live like a human being. You, however, keep this weakness of your health in check and care for yourself, as you do, so that you are able to visit our villas[16] and move around together with me in a litter.

[6] I have written to you about this with more words than I am used to, not due to abundance of leisure, but out of love towards you, since you had somehow invited me in some letter, if you remember this, that I should write to you something of this kind, so that you would regret less that you had missed the games. If I have achieved this, I rejoice; if not, I still comfort myself by this: that you will come to games in the future, will visit us and will not leave some hope of enjoying yourself to my letters.

(b) Horace, *Epistula* 2.1.177-207

quem tulit ad scaenam ventoso Gloria curru,
exanimat lentus spectator, sedulus inflat;
sic leve, sic parvum est, animum quod laudis avarum
[180] subruit aut reficit (valeat res ludicra si me
palma negata macrum, donata reducit opimum).
saepe etiam audacem fugat hoc terretque poetam,
quod numero plures, virtute et honore minores,
indocti stolidique et depugnare parati
[185] si discordet eques, media inter carmina poscunt
aut ursum aut pugiles; his nam plebecula gaudet.
   verum equitis quoque iam migravit ab aure voluptas
omnis ad incertos oculos et gaudia vana.
quattuor aut pluris aulaea premuntur in horas,
[190] dum fugiunt equitum turmae peditumque catervae;
mox trahitur manibus regum fortuna retortis,
esseda festinant, pilenta, petorrita, naves,
captivum portatur ebur, captiva Corinthus.
   si foret in terris, rideret Democritus, seu
[195] diversum confusa genus panthera camelo
sive elephans albus vulgi converteret ora;
spectaret populum ludis attentius ipsis,
ut sibi praebentem nimio spectacula plura;
scriptores autem narrare putaret asello
[200] fabellam surdo. nam quae pervincere voces
evaluere sonum referunt quem nostra theatra?
Garganum mugire putes nemus aut mare Tuscum,
tanto cum strepitu ludi spectantur et artes
divitiaeque peregrinae, quibus oblitus actor
[205] cum stetit in scaena, concurrit dextera laevae.
'dixit adhuc aliquid?' 'nil sane.' 'quid placet ergo?'
'lana Tarentino violas imitata veneno.'

(b) Horace, *Epistula* 2.1.177-207

Him whom Fame has carried to the stage in a windy chariot does the
sluggish spectator deprive of his spirit, the zealous one puff up; it is
so trivial, so little what [180] undermines or restores the mind eager
for praise (farewell shall be said to the theatrical art if the victory
palm, when denied, brings me back home poor, when given, rich).
Often even the bold poet is put to flight and terrified when those,
stronger in number, but weaker in qualities and rank, unlearned and
stupid and ready to fight to the end, [185] – if the knights disagree –
demand either a bear or boxers in the middle of a play; for at these
things the mob rejoices.

But even the desires of the knights have now gone from the ear to
wandering eyes and vain delights. The curtains are kept down for four
or more hours[1], [190] while troops of soldiers on horseback and groups
of foot soldiers pass quickly; then kings, fallen from fortune, are
dragged past, with their hands bound behind their backs, chariots,
coaches, carriages, ships hurry past, captured ivory is carried along,
as is captured Corinth[2].

If he were on earth, Democritus[3] would laugh, whether [195] a
panther crossed with a camel, a hybrid form, or a white elephant
attracted the gazes of the masses; he would watch the people more
attentively than the games themselves, since they offered him more
than enough spectacle; and he would believe that the poets tell their
story to [200] a deaf ass. For what voices have been strong enough to
overcome the noise with which our theatres resound? One might think
that the Garganian forest[4] or the Tuscan sea[5] was roaring: amid so
much noise are the games watched and the works of art and foreign
riches; when the actor, laden with these, [205] has taken his position
on the stage, right and left hands join for a round of applause. 'Has he
said anything yet?' 'Nothing at all.' 'What then causes delight?' 'The
wool[6] that imitates violets with its Tarentine dye[7].'

---

1 i.e. plays last for this length of time, since the curtain was lowered at the
beginning and raised at the end of a performance. 2 presumably images of the
city, which were typically carried in triumphal processions; alludes to the conquest
of Corinth by the Romans in 146 BCE. 3 'the laughing philosopher', a Greek
philosopher of the fifth/fourth centuries BCE. 4 on a stormy promontory in
Apulia. 5 between the west coast of Italy, Sardinia and Sicily. 6 of the actor's
costume. 7 from Tarentum in southern Italy.

T 12. On dramatic genres

(Diomedes, *Ars grammatica* 3, *Gramm. Lat.* 1, pp. 482-91; Euanthius, *De fabula* 4.1-3; Donatus, *De comoedia* 6.1-2, 5)

Early Roman dramatists, who were active in a variety of dramatic and other literary genres, seem to have observed some generic distinctions from the start. However, most of the time, this is implicit; just a few playwrights make comments about their own dramatic genre and occasionally about others in their dramas, triggered by specific contexts (cf. T 13-14). The late Republican tragic poet Accius is the only playwright who also wrote treatises that may have dealt with such questions.

When Roman scholars started to approach drama as a literary genre worth studying in the late Republic, they established definitions and characteristics of the individual dramatic genres, the polymath Varro in particular. These works have not been preserved; what survives are outlines

(a) Diomedes, *Ars grammatica* 3, *Gramm. Lat.* 1, pp. 482-91

(i) poematos dramatici vel activi genera sunt quattuor, apud Graecos tragica comica satyrica mimica, apud Romanos praetextata tabernaria Atellana planipes (p. 482.27-9).

(ii) tragoedia est heroicae fortunae in adversis conprehensio. a Theophrasto ita definita est, τραγῳδία ἐστὶν ἡρωικῆς τύχης περίστασις [T 708 Fortenbaugh]. tragoedia, ut quidam, a τράγῳ et ᾠδῇ dicta est, quoniam olim actoribus tragicis τράγος, id est hircus, praemium cantus proponebatur; qui Liberalibus die festo Libero patri ob hoc ipsum immolabatur, quia, ut Varro ait, depascunt vitem; et Horatius in arte poetica [Hor. *Ars P.* 220-1] 'carmine qui tragico vilem certavit ob hircum, / mox etiam agrestis Satyros nudavit', et Vergilius in georgicon secundo [Verg. *Georg.* 2.380-1], cum et sacri genus monstrat et causam talis hostiae reddit his versibus, 'non aliam ob culpam Baccho caper omnibus aris / caeditur'. alii autem putant a faece, quam Graecorum quidam τρύγα appellant, tragoediam nominatam, per mutationem litterarum υ in α versa, quoniam olim nondum personis a Thespide repertis, tales fabulas peruncti ora faecibus agitabant, ut rursum est Horatius testis sic [Hor. *Ars P.* 275-7], 'ignotum tragicae genus invenisse Camenae / dicitur et plaustris vexisse poemata Thespis, / quae canerent agerentque infecti faecibus ora'. alii a vino arbitrantur, propterea quod olim τρύξ dictitabatur, a quo τρύγητος hodieque vindemia est, quia Liberalibus apud Atticos, die festo Liberi patris, vinum cantoribus pro corollario dabatur, cuius rei testis est Lucilius in duodecimo [Lucilius, fr. 437 Marx = p. 146 W.] (pp. 487.1-488.2).

(iii) comoedia est privatae civilisque fortunae sine periculo vitae

T 12. On dramatic genres

(Diomedes, *Ars grammatica* 3, *Gramm. Lat.* 1, pp. 482-91; Euanthius, *De fabula* 4.1-3; Donatus, *De comoedia* 6.1-2, 5)

in late-antique grammarians, commentators and scholiasts that ultimately derive from earlier sources. These later scholars, such as the grammarian Diomedes and the Terentian commentators Euanthius and Donatus, present descriptions and explanations of all Greek and Roman dramatic genres, organized in fully-fledged systems with slight variations, including tragedy (tragoedia or crepidata), praetexta (or praetextata), comedy (comoedia or palliata), togata (or tabernaria), Atellana and mimus. These overviews provide useful starting points for defining and distinguishing the various serious and light dramatic forms present in (Republican) Rome (cf. I 2).

(a) Diomedes, *Ars grammatica* 3, *Gramm. Lat.* 1, pp. 482-91

(i) There are four types of dramatic poetry or poetry with action: among the Greeks 'tragic', 'comic', 'satyric' and 'mimic', among the Romans 'praetextata', 'tabernaria', 'Atellana' and 'planipes'.

(ii) Tragoedia is the presentation of the fate of heroes in adversity. It is defined by Theophrastus[1] as follows: 'Tragoedia is a crisis of heroic fortune.' The term 'tragoedia', according to some, is derived from *tragos* (Gr. 'he-goat') and *ode* (Gr. 'song'), since once upon a time a *tragos*, i.e. a he-goat, was offered to tragic actors as a prize for their singing; at the festival of the Liberalia[2] that [i.e. the he-goat] was sacrificed to Father Liber[3], for the very reason that, as Varro says, they eat up the vine; and Horace, in his *Art of poetry*, says 'who competed in tragic song because of a humble he-goat, soon also had the rustic satyrs appear naked', and Vergil, in the second book of the *Georgics*, when he explains the type of sacrifice and describes the reason for this sacrificial victim in the following verses, says: 'for no other crime is a he-goat killed for Bacchus at all altars'. Others, however, believe, that tragoedia is named after the dregs, which some of the Greeks call *tryx* (Gr. 'dregs'), after *y* had turned into *a* by a change of letters; for once upon a time, when masks had not yet been invented by Thespis[4], they acted such stories, their faces covered with the dregs. For this again Horace is a witness, by the following: 'Thespis is said to have discovered the genre of the tragic Muse as yet unknown and to have carried his poems in wagons, which they would sing and act, their faces smeared with the dregs'. Others think that it is named after wine, since it was once called *tryx*, from which derives *trygetos* (Gr. 'vintage')

conprehensio, apud Graecos ita definita, κωμῳδία ἐστὶν ἰδιωτικῶν πραγμάτων ἀκίνδυνος περιοχή. comoedia dicta ἀπὸ τῶν κωμῶν. κῶμαι enim appellantur pagi, id est conventicula rusticorum. itaque iuventus Attica, ut ait Varro, circum vicos ire solita fuerat et quaestus sui causa hoc genus carminis pronuntiabat. aut certe a ludis vicinalibus. nam postea quam ex agris Athenas conmigratum est hi ludi instituti sunt, sicut Romae conpitalicii, ad canendum prodibant, et ab urbana κώμῃ καὶ ᾠδῇ comoedia dicta est: vel quod in ea viculorum, id est humilium domuum, fortunae conprehendantur, non ut in tragoedia publicarum regiarumque: vel ἀπὸ τοῦ κώμου, id est comessatione, quia olim in eius modi fabulis amantium iuvenum κῶμοι canebantur (p. 488.3-14).

(iv) comoedia a tragoedia differt, quod in tragoedia introducuntur heroes duces reges, in comoedia humiles atque privatae personae; in illa luctus exilia caedes, in hac amores, virginum raptus; deinde quod in illa frequenter et paene semper laetis rebus exitus tristes et liberorum fortunarumque priorum in peius adgnitio *. quare varia definitione discretae sunt. altera enim ἀκίνδυνος περιοχή, altera τύχης περίστασις dicta est. tristitia namque tragoediae proprium; ideoque Euripides petente Archelao rege ut de se tragoediam scriberet abnuit ac precatus est ne accideret Archelao aliquid tragoediae proprium, ostendens nihil aliud esse tragoediam quam miseriarum conprehensionem (p. 488.14-23).

(v) poetae primi comici fuerunt Susarion Mullus et Magnes. hi veteris disciplinae iocularia quaedam minus scite ac venuste pronuntiabant, in quibus hi versus fuerunt, Σουσαρίων ταῦτα λέγει· / κακὸν γυναῖκες· ἀλλ᾽ ὅμως, ὦ δημόται, / οὐκ ἔστιν εὑρεῖν οἰκίαν ἄνευ κακοῦ [Susario, fr. 1 Kassel-Austin]. secunda aetate fuerunt Aristophanes Eupolis et Cratinus, qui et principum vitia sectati acerbissimas comoedias conposuerunt. tertia aetas fuit Menandri Diphili et Philemonis, qui omnem acerbitatem comoediae mitigaverunt atque argumenta multiplicia Graecis erroribus secuti sunt. ab his Romani fabulas transtulerunt, et constat apud illos primum Latino sermone comoediam Livium Andronicum scripsisse (pp. 488.23-489.8).

(vi) initio togatae comoediae dicebantur, quod omnia in publico honore confusa cernebantur. quae togatae postea in praetextatas et tabernarias dividebantur. togatae fabulae dicuntur quae scriptae sunt secundum ritus et habitum hominum togatorum, id est Romanorum (toga namque Romana est), sicut Graecas fabulas ab habitu aeque palliatas Varro ait nominari [Varro, fr. 306 Funaioli]. togatas autem, cum sit generale nomen, specialiter tamen pro tabernariis non modo communis error usurpat, qui Afrani togatas appellat, sed et poetae, ut Horatius, qui ait 'vel qui praetextas vel qui docuere togatas' [Hor. *Ars P.* 288]. togatarum fabularum species tot fere sunt quot et palliatarum. nam prima species est togatarum quae praetextatae dicuntur, in quibus imperatorum negotia

and which is called vintage today, since among the Attics on the Liberalia, on a festival for Father Liber, wine was given to the singers instead of a garland; a witness for this is Lucilius[5] in his twelfth book.

(iii) Comoedia is a presentation of private and civil fortune without danger to life; among the Greeks it is defined as follows: 'Comoedia is a piece of literature about private affairs without danger.' It is called comoedia after the *komai* (Gr. 'small villages'). For country districts, i.e. the resorts of farmers, are called *komai*. Hence, the Attic youths, as Varro says, were accustomed to go round the villages and performed this kind of song for the sake of earning money. Or surely it has been named after the 'local games'. For after people had moved to Athens from the fields and these games had been introduced, just as the Compitalicii at Rome[6], they came forth for singing, and after the urban *kome and ode* (Gr. 'village and song') it was called comoedia. Or because in such a play the fortunes of small villages, i.e. of humble dwellings, are dealt with, not, like in tragoedia, of public and royal ones. Or after the *komos* (Gr. 'revelry'), i.e. revelry, since once upon a time *komoi* (Gr. 'revelries') of young men in love were sung about in plays of this kind.

(iv) Comoedia differs from tragoedia, since in tragoedia heroes, leaders and kings are presented, in comoedia humble and private persons; in the former there is grief, exile and death, in the latter love and abduction of maidens. Secondly, since in the former there are frequently and almost always sad endings following on happy circumstances and recognition of children and former good fortune turning to worse *[7]. Accordingly, they are distinguished by different definitions. For one of the pair is called 'a piece of literature without danger', the other one 'a crisis of fortune'. For sadness is a characteristic of tragoedia; and therefore Euripides refused, when king Archelaus[8] asked him to write a tragoedia about him, and wished that nothing might happen to Archelaus characteristic of tragoedia, thereby showing that tragoedia is nothing other than a presentation of miseries.

(v) The first comic poets were Susarion, Mullus and Magnes[9]. They voiced some pleasantries of the old style, in a less refined and elegant way. Among them were the following verses: 'Susarion says this: women are an evil; but still, citizens, one cannot find a house without evil.' In a second age there were Aristophanes, Eupolis and Cratinus, who, even attacking the faults of foremost men, wrote extremely sharp comoediae[10]. The third age was that of Menander, Diphilus and Philemon, who softened all the harshness of comoedia and constructed complex plots full of aberrations as they are common among Greeks[11]. From them the Romans took over the dramas[12], and it is well known that among them Livius Andronicus was the first to write a comoedia in the Latin language.

(vi) In the beginning togatae were just called comoediae, since

agebantur et publica et reges Romani vel duces inducuntur, personarum dignitate et sublimitate tragoediis similes. praetextatae autem dicuntur, quia fere regum vel magistratuum qui praetexta utuntur in eius modi fabulas acta conprehenduntur. secunda species est togatarum quae tabernariae dicuntur et humilitate personarum et argumentorum similitudine comoediis pares, in quibus non magistratus regesve sed humiles homines et privatae domus inducuntur, quae quidem olim quod tabulis tegerentur, communiter tabernae vocabantur. tertia species est fabularum Latinarum quae a civitate Oscorum Atella, in qua primum coeptae, appellatae sunt Atellanae, argumentis dictisque iocularibus similes satyricis fabulis Graecis. quarta species est planipedis, qui Graece dicitur mimus. ideo autem Latine planipes dictus, quod actores pedibus planis, id est nudis, proscenium introirent, non ut tragici actores cum cothurnis neque ut comici cum soccis; sive quod olim non in suggestu scenae sed in plano orchestrae positis instrumentis mimicis actitabant. cuius planipedis Atta togatarum scriptor ita in Aedilicia fabula meminit, 'daturin estis aurum? exultat planipes' [Atta, *Tog.* 1 R.³]. siquas tamen ex soccis fabulas fecerant, palliati pronuntiabant (pp. 489.14-490.10).

(vii) togata praetextata a tragoedia differt, quod in tragoedia heroes inducuntur, ut Pacuvius tragoedias nominibus heroicis scripsit, Orestem Chrysen et his similia, item Attius; in praetextata autem quae inscribitur Brutus vel Decius, item Marcellus (p. 490.10-14).

(viii) togata tabernaria a comoedia differt, quod in comoedia Graeci ritus inducuntur personaeque Graecae, Laches Sostrata; in illa vero Latinae. togatas tabernarias in scenam dataverunt praecipue duo, L. Afranius et G. Quintius. nam Terentius et Caecilius comoedias scripserunt (p. 490.14-18).

(ix) Latina Atellana a Graeca satyrica differt, quod in satyrica fere Satyrorum personae inducuntur, aut siquae sunt ridiculae similes Satyris, Autolycus Busiris; in Atellana Oscae personae, ut Maccus (p. 490.18-20).

(x) mimus est sermonis cuiuslibet imitatio et motus sine reverentia, vel factorum et dictorum turpium cum lascivia imitatio; a Graecis ita definitus, μῖμός ἐστιν μίμησις βίου τά τε συγκεχωρημένα καὶ ἀσυγχώρητα περιέχων. mimus dictus παρὰ τὸ μιμεῖσθαι, quasi solus imitetur, cum et alia poemata idem faciant; sed solus quasi privilegio quodam quod fuit commune possedit: similiter atque is qui versum facit dictus ποιητής, cum et artifices, cum aeque quid faciant, non dicantur poetae (p. 491.13-19).

everything that was publicly respected was perceived without distinctions. These togatae were later divided into praetextatae and tabernariae. Togatae is the name for those dramas that are written according to the customs and dress of men in the *toga*, i.e. the Romans (for the *toga* is Roman), just as, according to Varro, Greek dramas are named after the dress in the same way and called palliatae. This term 'togata', even though it is a general expression, is nevertheless used in a special sense instead of tabernariae, not only by common error, which calls Afranius' plays togatae, but also by that of a poet, such as Horace, who says 'both those who produced praetextae and those who produced togatae'. There are basically as many forms of togata plays as there are also of palliata plays. For the first form of togatae are those plays that are called praetextatae, in which business of generals and public affairs are carried out and Roman kings or leaders are shown, similar to tragoediae in the dignity and elevation of the characters. And these are called praetextatae, since generally the deeds of kings and magistrates, who use the *toga praetexta* ('purple-bordered gown'), are presented in dramas of this type. The second form of togatae are those plays that are called tabernariae and are corresponding to comoediae in the humility of characters and the similarity of plot; in these dramas, instead of magistrates or kings, humble men and private dwellings are presented, which once upon a time were generally called *tabernae* ('huts') as they were covered with *tabulae* ('wooden tiles'). The third species of Latin plays are those that are called Atellanae after the Oscan community of Atella[13], in which they first began, in plot and jocular expressions similar to Greek satyr-plays. The fourth form is that of planipes, which is called mimus in Greek. But it is called planipes in Latin for the reason that the actors come on stage with bare feet, i.e. naked, not like the tragic actors with high buskins nor like the comic ones with slippers; or because once upon a time they played not on the elevated platform of the stage, but in the plain of the orchestra, after they had arranged their mimic equipment. This planipes is mentioned by Atta, a writer of togatae, in a play entitled *Aedilicia* ('*Matters concerning aediles*') in the following way: 'Will you be giving gold? The planipes[14] exults.' If, however, they had made any plays with slippers, they used to deliver them as palliata actors.

(vii) Togata praetextata differs from tragoedia in that in tragoedia heroes appear, just as Pacuvius has written tragoediae with heroic names, Orestes, Chryses and others similar to these[15], likewise Attius[16]; in a praetextata, however, which is entitled Brutus or Decius, likewise Marcellus[17], (Roman citizens appear on stage)[18].

(viii) Togata tabernaria differs from comoedia in that in comoedia Greek customs are presented and Greek characters, like Laches or Sostrata[19], but in the former Latin ones. Togatae tabernariae for the stage

1 a Peripatetic philosopher in the late fourth century BCE, a pupil of Aristotle. 2 an ancient festival in Rome on 17 March, but without dramatic performances in Republican times. 3 i.e. Bacchus/Dionysus. 4 an early Greek actor and writer of tragedies. 5 an early Roman writer of satires. 6 'festival of the cross-roads', ancient Roman rural festival. 7 the Latin text here is uncertain and probably lacunose. 8 a king of Macedon. 9 very early, somewhat shadowy Greek comic poets, here regarded as representing the initial stage of Greek comedy. 10 refers to Greek Old Comedy. 11 refers to Greek New Comedy. 12 i.e. the Romans adopted Greek New Comedy. 13 a town in Campania. 14 i.e. the mime actor. 15 Pacuvius' *Dulorestes* and *Chryses*. 16 i.e. Accius. 17 Accius' *Brutus* and *Aeneadae vel Decius* as well as Naevius' *Clastidium*. 18 the Latin text seems to be incomplete here. 19 characters in Greek comedy. 20 i.e. T. Quinctius Atta. 21 characters in satyr-plays by Euripides. 22 one of the stock characters of Atellanae. 23 i.e. imitation.

(b) Euanthius, *De fabula* 4.1-3

[1] illud vero tenendum est, post νέαν κωμῳδίαν Latinos multa fabularum genera protulisse, ut togatas ab scaenicis atque argumentis Latinis, praetextatas a dignitate personarum tragicarum ex Latina historia, Atellanas a civitate Campaniae, ubi actitatae sunt primae, Rinthonicas ab auctoris nomine, tabernarias ab humilitate argumenti ac stili, mimos ab diuturna imitatione vilium rerum ac levium personarum. [2] inter tragoediam autem et comoediam cum multa tum inprimis hoc distat, quod in comoedia mediocres fortunae hominum, parvi impetus periculorum laetique sunt exitus actionum, at in tragoedia omnia contra, ingentes personae, magni timores, exitus funesti habentur; et illic prima turbulenta, tranquilla ultima, in tragoedia contrario ordine res aguntur; tum quod in tragoedia fugienda vita, in comoedia capessenda exprimitur; postremo quod omnis comoedia de fictis est argumentis, tragoedia saepe de historica fide petitur. [3] Latinae fabulae primo a Livio Andronico scriptae sunt, adeo cuncta re etiam tum recenti, ut idem poeta et actor suarum fabularum fuisset.

(c) Donatus, *De comoedia* 6.1-2, 5

[1] fabula generale nomen est: eius duae primae partes tragoedia et comoedia. <tragoedia>, si Latina argumentatio sit, praetexta dicitur. comoedia autem multas species habet: aut enim palliata est aut togata

88

were primarily produced by two poets, L. Afranius and C. Quintius[20]. For Terence and Caecilius wrote *comoediae*.

(ix) The Latin Atellana differs from the Greek satyr-play in that in satyr-play generally the characters of satyrs appear or if any other figures are similarly ridiculous, like Autolycus and Busiris[21]; in Atellana there are Oscan characters, like Maccus[22].

(x) Mimus is an imitation of any kind of speech and movement without reverence, or an imitation of base deeds and words with licentiousness. It is defined by the Greeks as follows: 'Mimus is an imitation of life, covering things permitted and things forbidden.' Mimus is named after *mimeisthai* (Gr. 'to imitate'), as if this was the only genre to imitate, even though other poems, too, do the same. But it is the only one to own by some kind of privilege what was common[23]. And in the same way he who makes verses is called *poietes* (Gr. 'maker'), even though artisans, though equally making something, are not called poets.

(b) Euanthius, *De fabula* 4.1-3

[1] But what has to be borne in mind is that, after New Comedy, the Latins have produced many kinds of dramas, such as togatae based on Latin actors and plots, praetextatae based on characters of tragic dignity and stories from Latin history, Atellanae named after a township in Campania, where they were first acted [i.e. Atella], Rhinthonicae called after the author's name [i.e. Rhinthon], tabernariae with humble plot and style, mimi named after the constant imitation of cheap things and unimportant characters. [2] And between tragoedia and comoedia there are many differences, but primarily the following one: in comoedia there are mediocre fates of men, small onsets of dangers and happy endings of the action; but in tragoedia everything is the opposite, there are towering characters, great fears, fatal endings. And in the former the beginning is turbulent and the ending is quiet, but in tragoedia things are done in reverse order. Further, in tragoedia life is to be eschewed, in comoedia it is presented as to be seized eagerly. Finally, that every comoedia is built on fictional plots, but tragoedia is often based on historical tradition. [3] Latin dramas were first written by Livius Andronicus, when the whole matter was still so recent that the same man was the author and the actor of his own plays.

(c) Donatus, *De comoedia* 6.1-2, 5

[1] 'Play' (*fabula*) is a general term: its two foremost types are tragoedia and comoedia. Tragoedia, if the plot is Latin, is called praetexta. Comoedia, however, has many forms: for it is either palliata or togata or

aut tabernaria aut Atellana aut mimus aut Rinthonica aut planipedia. [2] planipedia autem dicta ob humilitatem argumenti eius ac vilitatem actorum, qui non coturno aut socco nituntur in scaena aut pulpito sed plano pede, vel ideo quod non ea negotia continet, quae personarum in turribus aut in cenaculis habitantium sunt, sed in plano atque in humili loco. [3] ...

[5] comoediarum formae sunt tres: palliatae Graecum habitum referentes, togatae iuxta formam personarum habitum togarum desiderantes, quas nonnulli tabernarias vocant, Atellanae salibus et iocis compositae, quae in se non habent nisi vetustatum elegantias.

T 13. On comedy

(Plautus, *Amphitruo* 50-63; *Captivi* 55-62; 1029-36; Terence, *Heautontimorumenos* 35-42; *Eunuchus* 35-41)

Since prologues and epilogues to dramas are detached from the plot proper, it is here that explicit comments on dramatic genres and forms are most likely to be found if dramas contain any. The two palliata poets by whom entire plays are extant, Plautus and Terence, use some of these sections to discuss their dramatic genre, particularly if there is anything that deviates from the standard in the respective plays; this demonstrates interest in and awareness of generic features among both playwrights and audiences. Dramatists may comment on stock elements of the standard comic plot and

(a) Plautus, *Amphitruo* 50-63

[50] nunc quam rem oratum huc veni primum proloquar;
post argumentum huius eloquar tragoediae.
quid? contraxistis frontem quia tragoediam
dixi futuram hanc? deu' sum, commutavero.
eandem hanc, si voltis, faciam <iam> ex tragoedia
[55] comoedia ut sit omnibus isdem vorsibus.
utrum sit an non voltis? sed ego stultior,
quasi nesciam vos velle, qui divos siem.
teneo quid animi vostri super hac re siet:
faciam ut commixta sit; <sit> tragico[co]moedia;
[60] nam me perpetuo facere ut sit comoedia,
reges quo veniant et di, non par arbitror.
quid igitur? quoniam hic servos quoque partis habet,
faciam sit, proinde ut dixi, tragico[co]moedia.

tabernaria or Atellana or mimus or Rhinthonica or planipedia. [2] And planipedia is named after the humbleness of its plot and the baseness of the actors, who do not rest themselves on the high buskin or the slipper on the stage or the podium, but rather on their bare feet, or for the reason that it does not contain those affairs that belong to persons living in towers and big houses, but in a plain and humble place. [3] ...

[5] Of comedy there are three types: palliatae, reproducing Greek attire, togatae, requiring in addition to the type of characters the wearing of togas, which some call tabernariae, Atellanae, consisting of puns and jokes, which have nothing in them if not the elegance of age.

T 13. On comedy

(Plautus, *Amphitruo* 50-63; *Captivi* 55-62; 1029-36; Terence, *Heautonti-morumenos* 35-42; *Eunuchus* 35-41)

their essential sameness, outline how the present play stands out or define it against other dramatic genres.

The prologue to Plautus' Amphitruo is particularly noteworthy since here the poet does not describe the play as a slightly irregular comedy, but apparently feels that it includes elements of other dramatic genres to such an extent that it can no longer be defined as 'comedy'. The piece is therefore presented as a specific dramatic form, for which the term 'tragi-comedy' is coined (cf. D 7).

(a) Plautus, *Amphitruo* 50-63

[50] Now I will first explain what matter to ask of you I have come here; then I will tell you the plot of this tragedy. What? You have wrinkled your brows because I said that this would be a tragedy? I am a god; I will have it changed. The very same play, if you wish, I am about to turn from a tragedy [55] into a comedy, with all verses exactly the same. Shall it be one or not: what do you wish? But I am too stupid, as if I did not know that you want it, being a god as I am. I know what your view is on this matter. I will see to it that it is mixed; it shall be a tragi-comedy; [60] for I do not think that it is right for me to turn the play into a comedy entirely, in which kings and gods take part. What then? Since a slave has a part here as well, I will turn it, as I have said, into a tragi-comedy.

(b) Plautus, *Captivi* 55-62

[55] non pertractate facta est neque item ut ceterae:
neque spurcidici insunt vorsus inmemorabiles;
hic neque peiiurus leno est nec meretrix mala
neque miles gloriosus; ne vereamini
quia bellum Aetolis esse dixi cum Aleis:
[60] foris illi extra scaenam fient proelia.
nam hoc paene iniquomst, comico choragio
conari desubito agere nos tragoediam.

(c) Plautus, *Captivi* 1029-36

spectatores, ad pudicos mores facta haec fabula est,
[1030] neque in hac subigitationes sunt neque ulla amatio
nec pueri suppositio nec argenti circumductio,
neque ubi amans adulescens scortum liberet clam suom patrem.
huius modi paucas poetae reperiunt comoedias,
ubi boni meliores fiant. nunc vos, si vobis placet
[1035] et si placuimus neque odio fuimus, signum hoc mittite:
qui pudicitiae esse voltis praemium, plausum date.

(d) Terence, *Heautontimorumenos* 35-42

[35] adeste aequo animo, date potestatem mihi
statariam agere ut liceat per silentium,
ne semper servo' currens, iratus senex,
edax parasitu', sycophanta autem inpudens,
avaru' leno adsidue agendi sint seni
[40] clamore summo, cum labore maxumo.
mea causa causam hanc iustam esse animum inducite,
ut aliqua pars labori' minuatur mihi.

(e) Terence, *Eunuchus* 35-41

[35] quod si personis isdem huic uti non licet:
qui mage licet currentem servom scribere,
bonas matronas facere, meretrices malas,
parasitum edacem, gloriosum militem,
puerum supponi, falli per servom senem,
[40] amare odisse suspicari? denique
nullumst iam dictum quod non dictum sit prius.

(b) Plautus, *Captivi* 55-62

[55] It [i.e. this play] is not composed in the hackneyed fashion, nor is it just like others; nor are there filthy verses in it that one must not repeat; here there is neither a perjured pimp nor a bad courtesan nor a braggart soldier; do not be alarmed because I said that the Aetolians have a war with the Eleans[1]: [60] battles will happen off the stage over there[2]. For this would be almost inappropriate: to try to act a tragedy with comic equipment.

---

1 such a war is not attested in the historical record. 2 the speaker pointing to one of the exits from the stage.

(c) Plautus, *Captivi* 1029-36

Spectators, this play has been composed in accordance with decent manners; [1030] in it there are neither illicit intercourses nor any love affair nor the substitution of a young child nor cheating out of money, nor a story where the young lover sets free a prostitute in secret from his father. Poets hit upon few comedies of this type, whereby good men may become better. Now if it pleases you [1035] and if we have pleased you and have not caused boredom, give us this sign: those of you who want there to be a prize for virtue, give us applause.

(d) Terence, *Heautontimorumenos* 35-42

[35] Pay attention with fair minds, give me a chance so that I am allowed to put on a quiet play without noisy interruption, so that the running slave, the angry old man, the gluttonous parasite, the shameless trickster and the greedy pimp do not have to be continuously acted by an old man for ever, [40] at the top of his voice, with the greatest effort. For my sake, be convinced that this cause is just, so that some part of my effort can be reduced.

(e) Terence, *Eunuchus* 35-41

[35] If this poet is not allowed to use the same characters[1]: how is it more admissible to write about a running slave, to create good matrons, bad courtesans, a gluttonous parasite, a braggart soldier, a young child being substituted, an old man deceived by his slave, [40] loving, hating, suspecting? In short, nothing is now said that has not been said before.

---

1 that had appeared in previous, similar plays.

T 14. On the experiences of a dramatist upon staging a play

(Terence, *Hecyra* 1-57)

According to what Terence has his producer Ambivius Turpio say in the prologues to Hecyra *('The mother-in-law'), this comedy suffered from particularly bad fortune: it took three attempts to get a full staging, since the first two performances were soon interrupted and had to be abandoned (the extant prologues belonging to the second and the third productions). From Terence's report it seems that rumours were spread that other, more exciting spectacles were about to be given in the same venue; hence another group of people broke in, which forced the dramatic performance to stop. The speaker obliquely suggests that this was not due to coincidence, but that this rumour rather originated with Terence's opponents, who wished*

Hecyra est huic nomen fabulae. haec quom datast
nova, ei novom intervenit vitium et calamitas
ut neque spectari neque cognosci potuerit:
ita populu' studio stupidus in funambulo
[5] animum occuparat. nunc haec planest pro nova,
et is qui scripsit hanc ob eam rem noluit
iterum referre ut iterum possit vendere.
alias cognostis eiu': quaeso hanc noscite.

orator ad vos venio ornatu prologi:
[10] sinite exorator sim eodem ut iure uti senem
liceat quo iure sum usus adulescentior,
novas qui exactas feci ut inveterascerent,
ne cum poeta scriptura evanesceret.
in is quas primum Caecili didici novas
[15] partim sum earum exactu', partim vix steti.
quia scibam dubiam fortunam esse scaenicam,
spe incerta certum mihi laborem sustuli:
easdem agere coepi ut ab eodem alias discerem
novas, studiose ne illum ab studio abducerem.
[20] perfeci ut spectarentur: ubi sunt cognitae,
placitae sunt. ita poetam restitui in locum
prope iam remotum iniuria advorsarium
ab studio atque ab labore atque arte musica.
quod si scripturam sprevissem in praesentia
[25] et in deterrendo voluissem operam sumere,
ut in otio esset potiu' quam in negotio,
deterruissem facile ne alias scriberet.
    nunc quid petam mea causa aequo animo attendite.

T 14. On the experiences of a dramatist upon staging a play

(Terence, *Hecyra* 1-57)

to drive the poet from the stage. There is also a reference to the precedent of Terence's predecessor Caecilius Statius, whom opponents equally prevented from having his plays performed in full straightaway. However, their impresario Ambivius Turpio persevered: he brought these and other plays on stage again, when they were appreciated and ultimately successful. Therefore the prologues appeal to the audience to give Hecyra *a fair hearing. Even though details of this story are questioned by some modern scholars, it provides an interesting glimpse into conditions at the theatre in Republican Rome and the possible rivalry among playwrights and impresarios.*

[prologue to the second performance]
   Hecyra ('*The mother-in-law*') is the title of this play. When it was given as a new play, a novel disaster and misfortune happened to it, so that it could neither be watched nor be understood properly. With so much eagerness had the foolish people fixed their minds [5] on a tightrope walker. Now this play absolutely has the status of a new one, and he who wrote it did not wish to bring it on again just for the reason that he could sell it again. You got to know other plays of his: I pray, get to know this one.

[prologue to the third performance]
   I come to you as an orator in the guise of a prologue [i.e. of a prologue speaker]: [10] allow me to be a successful pleader so that I am granted to enjoy the same right as an old man that I enjoyed when I was younger, when I saw to it that new plays that had been driven off the stage became established and that the script did not vanish along with the poet. As for those that I first produced as new plays for Caecilius, [15] in some of them I was driven off the stage, in some of them I hardly stood my ground. Since I knew that fortune on the stage was dubious, I took on myself certain toil with uncertain hope: I started to put on the same ones, so that I would produce others, new ones, from the same playwright, so that I would not actively discourage him from his vocation. [20] I managed to have them watched: as soon as they were understood, they pleased. Thus I reinstated the poet in his position, when he had almost been removed from his vocation, his work and the dramatic art by insults of his opponents. But if I had scorned his writing at the time [25] and had wished to make an effort to discourage him, so that he was in a state of idleness rather than activity, I would have easily discouraged him from writing further ones.
   Now pay attention to my request with fair minds for my sake. I

Hecyram ad vos refero, quam mihi per silentium
[30] numquam agere licitumst; ita eam oppressit calamitas.
eam calamitatem vostra intellegentia
sedabit, si erit adiutrix nostrae industriae.
quom primum eam agere coepi, pugilum gloria
(funambuli eodem accessit exspectatio),
[35] comitum conventu', strepitu', clamor mulierum
fecere ut ante tempus exirem foras.
vetere in nova coepi uti consuetudine
in experiundo ut essem; refero denuo.
primo actu placeo; quom interea rumor venit
[40] datum iri gladiatores, populu' convolat,
tumultuantur clamant, pugnant de loco:
ego interea meum non potui tutari locum.
  nunc turba nulla est: otium et silentiumst:
agendi tempu' mihi datumst; vobis datur
[45] potestas condecorandi ludos scaenicos.
nolite sinere per vos artem musicam
recidere ad paucos: facite ut vostra auctoritas
meae auctoritati fautrix adiutrixque sit.
si numquam avare pretium statui arti meae
[50] et eum esse quaestum in animum induxi maxumum
quam maxume servire vostris commodis,
sinite impetrare me, qui in tutelam meam
studium suom et se in vostram commisit fidem,
ne eum circumventum inique iniqui inrideant.
[55] mea causa causam accipite et date silentium,
ut lubeat scribere aliis mihique ut discere
novas expediat posthac pretio emptas meo.

T 15. On 'translating' Greek literature into Latin

(Cicero, *De finibus* 1.4-7; *Academica* 1.10; *De optimo genere oratorum* 18)

Since literary Roman drama, the genres of Greek-style tragedy (crepidata) and Greek-style comedy (palliata) in particular, were adopted from the Greeks, a major question, which was already addressed by ancient scholars and is still relevant in modern scholarship, is the relationship between Greek and Roman plays with the same title or dramatizing the same story: are the Roman versions word-for-word translations and therefore not actually worth reading in their own right, or did Roman poets transpose the sense of Greek models and otherwise adapt them to their own culture so as to create new and different pieces of literature; did the dramas become better or worse in this process?

bring *Hecyra* to you again, which I have [30] never been allowed to put on without noisy interruption; so much has misfortune overwhelmed it. This misfortune will be assuaged by your discernment if it supports our efforts. When I first began to perform it, enthusiastic talk of boxers (to this the expectation of a tightrope walker was added), [35] the gathering of supporters, general noise and the cries of women brought it about that I left the stage early. I began to use the old custom for the new play, so as to carry out an experiment; I bring it on again. I please in the first act; when a rumour intervenes [40] that a gladiatorial show was going to be given, people flock together, there is an uproar, they shout, they fight for a place: I meanwhile could not keep my place.

Now there is no disturbance: there is peace and silence: a chance to put on the play has been given to me; the opportunity [45] to adorn the scenic games is given to you. Do not allow the dramatic art to fall into the hands of a few on account of you: see to it that your influence is a patron and supporter of my influence. If I have never greedily fixed a price for my art [50] and regarded this reward as the greatest, namely to serve your interests as well as possible, allow me to obtain that he [i.e. the poet] who has entrusted his vocation to my guardianship and himself to your protection, is not deceived and mocked unfairly by adversaries. [55] For my sake approve of this cause and grant me silence, so that others may wish to write and that it is expedient for me to produce new plays, bought at my price, in the future.

T 15. On 'translating' Greek literature into Latin

(Cicero, *De finibus* 1.4-7; *Academica* 1.10; *De optimo genere oratorum* 18)

Among others (cf. also D 9), this issue was discussed by Cicero, who was interested in the problem in relation to his own renderings of Greek philosophical treatises into Latin. Some of Cicero's remarks are contradictory at first glance, but they are probably triggered by the respective argument: he wishes to stress that Latin philosophical works are well worth reading, because they are not word-for-word translations and offer additional comment; in one instance he adduces translations of plays as precedents and in the other he contrasts translations in the two literary genres. At any rate he seems to be convinced that Latin plays are literary creations that merit study.

97

(a) Cicero, *De finibus* 1.4-7

[4] iis igitur est difficilius satisfacere qui se Latina scripta dicunt contemnere. in quibus hoc primum est in quo admirer, cur in gravissimis rebus non delectet eos sermo patrius, cum idem fabellas Latinas ad verbum e Graecis expressas non inviti legant. quis enim tam inimicus paene nomini Romano est qui Enni Medeam aut Antiopam Pacuvi spernat aut reiciat, quod se isdem Euripidis fabulis delectari dicat, Latinas litteras oderit? Synephebos ego, inquit, potius Caecili aut Andriam Terenti quam utramque Menandri legam? [5] a quibus tantum dissentio ut, cum Sophocles vel optime scripserit Electram, tamen male conversam Atili mihi legendam putem, de quo Licinus 'ferreum scriptorem; verum, opinor, scriptorem tamen, ut legendus sit' [Porcius Licinus, fr. 5 *FPL*³ = fr. 3 Funaioli]. rudem enim esse omnino in nostris poetis aut inertissimae segnitae est aut fastidi delicatissimi. mihi quidem nulli satis eruditi videntur quibus nostra ignota sunt. an 'utinam ne in nemore ...' [Ennius, *Trag.* 205 R.³ = 253 W.] nihilo minus legimus quam hoc idem Graecum, quae autem de bene beateque vivendo a Platone disputata sunt, haec explicari non placebit Latine?

[6] quid? si nos non interpretum fungimur munere, sed tuemur ea quae dicta sunt ab iis quos probamus eisque nostrum iudicium et nostrum scribendi ordinem adiungimus, quid habent cur Graeca anteponant iis quae et splendide dicta sint neque sint conversa de Graecis? nam si dicent ab illis has res esse tractatas, ne ipsos quidem Graecos est cur tam multos legant quam legendi sunt. quid enim est a Chrysippo praetermissum in Stoicis? legimus tamen Diogenem, Antipatrum, Mnesarchum, Panaetium, multos alios, in primisque familiarem nostrum Posidonium. quid? Theophrastus mediocriterne delectat cum tractat locos ab Aristotele ante tractatos? quid? Epicurei num desistunt de isdem de quibus et ab Epicuro scriptum est et ab antiquis ad arbitrium suum scribere? quod si Graeci leguntur a Graecis, isdem de rebus alia ratione compositis, quid est cur nostri a nostris non legantur?

[7] quamquam si plane sic verterem Platonem aut Aristotelem ut verterunt nostri poetae fabulas, male, credo, mererer de meis civibus si ad eorum cognitionem divina illa ingenia transferrem. sed id neque feci adhuc nec mihi tamen ne faciam interdictum puto. locos quidem quosdam, si videbitur, transferam, et maxime ab iis quos modo nominavi, cum inciderit ut id apte fieri possit, ut ab Homero Ennius, Afranius a Menandro solet.

(a) Cicero, *De finibus* 1.4-7

[4] Therefore it is more difficult to satisfy those who say that they scorn Latin writings. As regards those people, the first thing I am amazed at is this: why does their native language not provide them with pleasure in most serious matters, while the same people read Latin plays, translated word for word from Greek ones, not unwillingly? For who is so inimical almost to the very name of 'Roman' that he despises and rejects Ennius' *Medea*[1] or Pacuvius' *Antiopa*, since he says that he finds pleasure in the corresponding plays of Euripides, but hates Latin literature? Shall I, he says, read Caecilius' *Synephebi* ('*The young comrades*') or Terence's *Andria* ('*The woman from Andros*') rather than either of these comedies by Menander? [5] With these people I disagree to such an extent that, although, assuredly, Sophocles has written *Electra* in the very best way, I still believe that I should read the bad translation by Atilius[2], about whom Licinus[3] says: 'an iron writer; but, I believe, a writer all the same, so that he should be read'. For being completely unversed in our poets is a sign either of the most sluggish indolence or of the most choosy arrogance. To me at any rate no one to whom our writings are unknown seems sufficiently educated. Or indeed do we read 'if only in the grove ...'[4] no less than the very same passage in the Greek, but what has been argued about living well and happily by Plato will not please when it is outlined in Latin?

[6] Now, if we do not fulfil the job of mere translators, but keep what has been said by those of whom we approve and add to this our own judgement and our own arrangement of the writing, what reason do they have why they give preference to the Greek over what is splendidly said and also not just translated from the Greek? For if they will say that these matters have been treated by those, there is no reason why they should read so many of the Greeks themselves as should be read. For what has been passed over by Chrysippus[5] among the Stoics? Still we read Diogenes, Antipater, Mnesarchus, Panaetius[6], many others, and in particular our friend Posidonius[7]. Again, does Theophrastus[8] please us only moderately when he treats topics previously treated by Aristotle? Again, do the Epicureans stop writing at will about the same things about which has been written both by Epicurus and by the ancients[9]? If Greeks are read by Greeks, on the same subjects arranged in a different way, what reason is there why our writers are not read by our people?

[7] However, if I translated Plato or Aristotle exactly as our poets have translated plays, I would do a bad service, I believe, to my countrymen if I transferred these divine intellects for them to get to know them. But

---

1 cf. D 2. **2** a Roman dramatic poet, probably active in the first half of the second century BCE. **3** Porcius Licinus, a Roman scholar in the second half of the second century BCE (cf. T 3a). **4** the famous beginning of Ennius' *Medea* (cf. D 2). **5** the head of the Stoa in the third century BCE; his works outlining the Stoic system came to be identified with Stoic orthodoxy. **6** later Stoic philosophers. **7** a Stoic philosopher and historian, who wrote about Roman history and was in touch with Cicero and other Romans. **8** a Peripatetic philosopher in the late fourth century BCE, a pupil of Aristotle. **9** Epicurean philosophers soon after Epicurus. **10** for Ennius' Roman epic *Annales* and for Afranius' Roman comedies.

(b) Cicero, *Academica* 1.10

"... causam autem probabilem tu quidem affers: aut enim Graeca legere malent qui erunt eruditi, aut ne haec quidem qui illa nescient. sed eam mihi non sane probas; immo vero et haec qui illa non poterunt, et qui Graeca poterunt non contemnent sua. quid enim causae est cur poetas Latinos Graecis litteris eruditi legant, philosophos non legant? an quia delectat Ennius Pacuvius Accius multi alii, qui non verba sed vim Graecorum expresserunt poetarum – quanto magis philosophi delectabunt, si ut illi Aeschylum Sophoclem Euripidem sic hi Platonem imitentur Aristotelem Theophrastum. oratores quidem laudari video si qui e nostris Hyperidem sint aut Demosthenem imitati. ..."

(c) Cicero, *De optimo genere oratorum* 18

huic labori nostro duo genera reprehensionum opponuntur. unum hoc: 'verum melius Graeci.' a quo quaeratur ecquid possint ipsi melius Latine. alterum: 'quid istas potius legam quam Graecas?' idem Andriam et Synephebos nec minus Andromacham aut Antiopam aut Epigonos Latinos recipiunt. quod igitur est eorum in orationibus e Graeco conversis fastidium, nullum cum sit in versibus?

---

1 comedies by Terence and Caecilius as well as tragedies by Ennius (cf. D 1), Pacuvius and Accius respectively; cf. T 15a.

---

neither have I done this so far nor indeed do I believe that I am forbidden to do so. I will translate certain passages, if this seems fit, and particularly from those writers whom I have just mentioned, when the occasion arises that this can be done appropriately, just as Ennius is accustomed to borrow from Homer and Afranius from Menander[10].

(b) Cicero, *Academica* 1.10

"... But you put forward a case that has some probability: for on the one hand those who are educated will prefer to read Greek writings, and on the other hand those who do not know those [i.e. Greek writings] will not even read these [i.e. Latin writings]. Yet you do not sufficiently prove this case in my view; on the contrary: both those who will not be able to read those [i.e. Greek writings] and those who will be able to read Greek texts will not spurn writings in their own language. For what reason is there why people educated in Greek literature should read Latin poets, but not read philosophers? Is it because Ennius, Pacuvius, Accius, many others, who have expressed not the words, but the sense of Greek poets, provide pleasure – how much more pleasure will philosophers provide, if they imitate Plato, Aristotle, Theophrastus as those imitated Aeschylus, Sophocles, Euripides. I see that orators at any rate are praised if anyone of our men has imitated Hyperides or Demosthenes. ..."

(c) Cicero, *De optimo genere oratorum* 18

Against this project of ours two types of objections are brought forward. One of them is this: 'But the Greeks do it better.' Such a person should be asked whether they themselves can produce anything better in Latin. The other one is: 'Why should I read those texts rather than the Greek ones?' The same people accept *Andria* ('*The woman from Andros*') and *Synephebi* ('*The young comrades*') and equally *Andromacha, Antiopa* or *Epigoni* ('*The after-born*') in Latin[1]. Why then do they have an aversion as regards orations translated from the Greek, when there is none with respect to poetry?

Dramatic Texts

D 1. Ennius, *Andromacha aechmalotis* (some fragments)

*Ennius (239-169 BCE) was regarded as the actual founder of their
literature by some Roman authorities. And even though his entire output
is preserved in fragments only, his are the earliest tragedies of which any
substantial pieces remain. The majority of Ennius' tragedies were adapted
from Euripides; and Cicero and Varro seem to have believed that this was
the case for his* Andromacha *too. Yet although there is a general similarity
to Euripides'* Andromache *(as well as to his* Troades *and* Hekabe*), as all
these tragedies are set against the background of events towards the end
of the Trojan War, no particular and decisive connections have yet been
established. Some sources give Ennian fragments under the title of* Andromacha aechmalotis *('Andromacha captive'); these apparently belong to the*

[Andromacha]
vidi, videre quod me passa aegerrume,
Hectorem curru quadriiugo raptarier ... (*Trag.* 91-2 R.³ = 91-2 W.)

ex opibus summis opis egens, Hector, tuae (*Trag.* 89 R.³ = 94 W.)

quid petam praesidi aut exequar? quove nunc
auxilio exili aut fugae freta sim?
arce et urbe orba sum. quo accedam? quo applicem?
cui nec arae patriae domi stant, fractae et disiectae iacent,
fana flamma deflagrata, tosti alti stant parietes
deformati atque abiete crispa ... (*Trag.* 75-80 R.³ = 95-100 W.)

o pater, o patria, o Priami domus,
saeptum altisono cardine templum!
vidi ego te adstante ope barbarica
tectis caelatis lacuatis,
auro ebore instructam regifice (*Trag.* 81-5 R.³ = 101-5 W.)

haec omnia videi inflammarei,
Priamo vi vitam evitarei,
Iovis aram sanguine turparei (*Trag.* 86-8 R.³ = 106-8 W.)

Dramatic Texts

D 1. Ennius, *Andromacha aechmalotis* (some fragments)

same play that is elsewhere referred to as Andromacha, *and the title may have been intended to distinguish this drama from others about* Andromacha.

Ennius' tragedy is about Andromacha, the wife of Priam's son Hector, who had been killed by Achilles; the play is set at a point in time after the fall of Troy. The tragedy seems to have included the killing of Andromacha's little son Astyanax and of Priam's daughter Polyxena by the Greeks. It shows Andromacha in a correspondingly despondent mood. Her desperate lament in this tragedy, various parts of which have been preserved, became famous and was frequently quoted and alluded to by Cicero (cf. esp. Tusc. 3.44-6).

[Andromacha]

I saw what I could bear to see only with the greatest sorrow: Hector dragged along by a four-horse chariot ...

From the greatest resources, now needing your might, Hector.

What protection shall I seek or pursue? What help in exile or flight can I now rely on? I am bereft of citadel and city. Where shall I turn? Where can I find support? Me, for whom no paternal altars stand at home; they lie broken and torn apart; the sanctuaries are burnt down by fire; high walls stand scorched, out of shape and with firwood beams crisped ...

O father, o fatherland, o house of Priam, temple guarded by high-sounding hinges. I saw you [i.e. the buildings] furnished in kingly fashion with carved and fretted ceilings, with gold and ivory, while barbarian might stood.

I saw all this go up in flames, Priam's life snatched away by force, the altar of Jupiter defiled by blood.

D 2. Ennius, *Medea exul* (all fragments)

Ancient sources refer to Ennius' dramatization of the Medea story, a popular myth among Roman playwrights (cf. D 3; 5; 14), under the titles of Medea *and* Medea exul; *in this case these are likely to denote two different plays (cf. D 1). The majority of extant fragments come from the tragedy that is also referred to as* Medea exul; *and it is clear from these fragments and other evidence (cf. T 15a) that it was modelled upon Euripides'* Medea.

The play is set in Corinth and shows Medea enraged at the infidelity of her husband Jason (after she has helped him to gain the Golden Fleece,

[**Nutrix Medeae**]
utinam ne in nemore Pelio securibus
caesa accidisset abiegna ad terram trabes,
neve inde navis incohandi exordium
coepisset, quae nunc nominatur nomine
Argo, quia Argivi in ea delecti viri
vecti petebant pellem inauratam arietis
Colchis, imperio regis Peliae, per dolum.
nam numquam era errans mea domo ecferret pedem
Medea, animo aegra, amore saevo saucia (*Trag.* 205-13 R.[3] = 253-61 W.)

[**Paedagogus**]
antiqua erilis fida custos corporis,
quid sic te extra aedis exanimata eliminas? (*Trag.* 214-15 R.[3] = 262-3 W.)

[**Nutrix**]
cupido cepit miseram nunc me proloqui
caelo atque terras Medeai miserias (*Trag.* 216-17 R.[3] = 264-5 W.)

[**Chorus**?]
fructus verborum aures aucupant (*Trag.* 218 R.[3] = 288 W.)

[**Medea**]
quae Corinthum arcem altam habetis, matronae opulentae, optumates ...
multi suam rem bene gessere et publicam patria procul,
multi qui domi aetatem agerent propterea sunt inprobati
(*Trag.* 219-21 R.[3] = 266-8 W.)

[**Medea**]
  nam ter sub armis malim vitam cernere,
quam semel modo parere (*Trag.* 222-3 R.[3] = 269-70 W.)

D 2. Ennius, *Medea exul* (all fragments)

even forsaking her father and her native country Colchis); it includes her plans to take revenge on him, on his new bride Creusa and on his prospective father-in-law, Creon, king of the country, before she is sent into exile. The structure of the plot and the speakers of individual lines are inferred from the testimony of later authors who transmit the fragments and by comparison with Euripides' Medea. All fragments preserved for this drama or plausibly attributed to it are here given in a probable order that is based on a reconstructed plot.

[Medea's Nurse]
If only the firwood timber had not fallen to the ground in the Pelian grove[1], hewn by axes, and if only the ship had not taken the first steps to the beginning from there – the ship that is now known by the name of Argo, since selected Argive[2] men travelling in her sought the Golden Fleece of the ram from the Colchians, at the behest of king Pelias, by trickery[3]. For never would my mistress, Medea, going astray, set her foot outside the house, sick in her mind, wounded by savage love.

[Tutor, addressing the Nurse]
Aged loyal guardian of our mistress' person, why are you coming out of the house being so out of your mind?

[Nurse]
Desire has now seized me, poor wretch, to proclaim Medea's miseries to heaven and earth.

[Chorus?]
The ears catch a harvest of words.

[Medea, addressing the chorus of Corinthian women]
Rich and noble ladies, who have the high citadel of Corinth ... Many have managed their own business and that of their country well, while being far away from their fatherland; many who spent their lives at home have therefore been criticized.

[Medea]
For I would rather fight for my life under arms three times than give birth just once.

[Medea?]
qui ipse sibi sapiens prodesse non quit, nequiquam sapit
(*Trag.* 240 R.[3] = 271 W.)

[Creo?]
si te secundo lumine hic offendero,
moriere (*Trag.* 224-5 R.[3] = 272-3 W.)

[Medea]
nequaquam istuc istac ibit: magna inest certatio.
nam ut ego illi supplicarem tanta blandiloquentia,
ni ob rem? (*Trag.* 226-7[b] R.[3] = 274-6 W.)

ille traversa mente mi hodie tradidit repagula,
quibus ego iram omnem recludam atque illi perniciem dabo,
mihi maerores, illi luctum, exitium illi, exilium mihi
(*Trag.* 228-30 R.[3] = 278-80 W.)

[Chorus?]
utinam ne umquam, Mede Colchis, cupido corde pedem extulisses
(*Trag.* 241 R.[3] = 281 W.)

[Medea]
quo nunc me vortam? quod iter incipiam ingredi?
domum paternamne anne ad Peliae filias?   (*Trag.* 231-2 R.[3] = 284-5 W.)

[Iaso]
tu me amoris magis quam honoris servavisti gratia
(*Trag.* 233 R.[3] = 286 W.)

[?]
Sol, qui candentem in caelo sublimat facem (*Trag.* 234 R.[3] = 287 W.)

[Medea]
   salvete, optima corpora,
cette manus vestras measque accipite (*Trag.* 235-6 R.[3] = 289-90 W.)

[Chorus?]
Iuppiter tuque adeo summe Sol, qui res omnis spicis,
quique tuo <cum> lumine mare terram caelum contines,
inspice hoc facinus, prius quam fiat: prohibesseis scelus
(*Trag.* 237-9 R.[3] = 291-3 W.)

[Medea?]
The wise man who cannot care for himself is wise in vain.

[Creon?]
If I come across you here after the next sunrise, you will die.

[Medea]
In no way will this go thus: there is a great strife involved. For would I humble myself to beseech him [i.e. Creon] with such sweetness of speech, if not for some purpose?

He, with his mind turned sideways, has today entrusted the keys to me, whereby I will unlock all my wrath and cause destruction for him, sorrows for me and grief for him, ruin for him and exile for me.

[Chorus?]
If only you, Medea of Colchis, had never set foot outside with passionate heart.

[Medea]
Where shall I turn now? Which path shall I set out to take? To my paternal home or to the daughters of Pelias[4]?

[Jason]
You have saved me for the sake of love rather than for the sake of honour.

[?]
The Sun, who raises a glittering brand in heaven.

[Medea, taking leave of her children**]**
Goodbye, you best of loved ones. Stretch out your hands and take mine.

[Chorus?]
Jupiter and indeed you, highest Sun, who see all things and who cover sea, earth and sky with your light, look at this deed before it happens: you may prevent a crime.

---

1 i.e. in a forest on Pelion, a mountain in Thessaly. **2** i.e. Greek. **3** Pelias had deliberately sent Jason on the dangerous journey in quest of the Golden Fleece. **4** Medea had committed crimes in both places.

D 3. Pacuvius, *Medus* (all fragments)

The story of Medea was popular among Roman playwrights and audiences, and almost all major tragic poets produced a dramatization of the fate of this mythical heroine (cf. D 2; 5; 14). At the same time they avoided obvious overlap with already existing versions. So Pacuvius, Ennius' nephew and successor on the tragic stage (c. 220–130 BCE), wrote a Medea tragedy entitled Medus, *which covers a later section of the myth. No Greek dramatic model is known for this story; it is only attested in a Latin mythographical source (cf. Hyg. Fab. 27).*

This evidence points to the following plot: Medus, Medea's son, was shipwrecked on the coast of Colchis (Aea), where Perses, Aeetes' brother and Medea's uncle, was ruling the country. Finding himself in the power of the enemy, Medus pretended to be Hippotes, Creon's son; and the king had him taken into custody. In the meantime drought and famine occurred, and Medea arrived in her winged chariot, pretending that she was a priestess of Diana. When she heard that Hippotes was held in custody, she

[Medus]
accessi Aeaeam, et tosillam pegi laeto in litore (*Trag.* 218 R.[3] = 231 W.)

[Medus]
 te, Sol, invoco, ut mihi potestatem duis
inquirendi mei parentis (*Trag.* 219-20 R.[3] = 232-33 W.)

[Medus?]
repudio auspicium: regrediundum est ilico (*Trag.* 235 R.[3] = 236 W.)

[Perses – Custos?]
 ques sunt is? – ignoti, nescio ques ignobiles. (*Trag.* 221 R.[3] = 237 W.)

[Perses – Medus]
quae res te ab stabulis abiugat? – certum est loqui. (*Trag.* 222 R.[3] = 238 W.)

[?]
clamore et sonitu colles resonantes bount (*Trag.* 223 R.[3] = 264 W.)

[Medus?]
divorsi circumspicimus, horror percipit (*Trag.* 224 R.[3] = 265 W.)

[Perses – Medus]
quid tandem? ubi ea est? quo receptast? – exul incerta vagat.
 (*Trag.* 225 R.[3] = 239 W.)

D 3. Pacuvius, *Medus* (all fragments)

feared for her own safety and, unaware of the truth, claimed that this person was in fact Medus, sent to kill the king. She managed to have the young man given over to her for punishment. When she realized his true identity, she ordered him to take revenge for the injuries against his grandfather Aeetes. Medus killed Perses and regained power over his grandfather's kingdom. The extant fragments agree with this plot, except for a few variations: for instance, Medus sailed to Colchis on purpose and did not end up there as the result of a storm; he seems to have been in search of his mother; the play apparently included a recognition scene between Medea and her father Aeetes.

The fragments extant from this play are given in a probable order according to such a plot. The lines attested for this tragedy are supplemented by some that are not explicitly assigned to this play in the sources, but are thought to belong to it by editors.

[Medus]
I have come to the land of Aea and fixed the anchor to the pleasing beach.

[Medus]
It is you, Sun, who I invoke that you may give me the opportunity to seek out my mother.

[Medus?]
I reject the omen: one must go back immediately.

[Perses – Watchman?]
Who are those? – Unknown men, some ignoble persons.

[Perses – Medus]
What matter separates you from your dwelling-place? – I am determined to tell you.

[?]
The hills roar and resound with shouting and noise.

[Medus?]
We look around in various directions; a shuddering seizes us.

[Perses – Medus]
What then? Where is she [i.e. Medea]? Where has she withdrawn? – As an exile she roams on unknown paths.

109

[Perses?]
cedo quorsum itiner tetinisse aiunt? (*Trag.* 226 R.[3] = 246 W.)

[Medus]
si resto, pergit ut eam: si ire conor, prohibet baetere
(Trag. 227 R.[3] = 240 W.)

[Perses]
custodite istunc vos, ne vim qui attolat neve attigat
(Trag. 228 R.[3] = 241 W.)

[Nuntius?]
angues ingentes alites iuncti iugo (*Trag.* 397 R.[3] = 242 W.)

[Nuntius?]
linguae bisulcis actu crispo fulgere (*Trag.* 229 R.[3] = 243 W.)

[Nuntius?]
    mulier egregiissima
forma (*Trag.* 230-1 R.[3] = 244-5 W.)

[Chorus?]
caelitum camilla, expectata advenis: salve, hospita!
(Trag. 232 R.[3] = 247 W.)

[Medea?]
possum ego istam capite cladem averruncassere (*Trag.* 236 R.[3] = 248 W.)

[Medea?]
populoque ut faustum sempiterne sospitent (*Trag.* 234 R.[3] = 249 W.)

[Medus vel Perses?]
qua super re interfectum esse dixisti Hippotem? (*Trag.* 237 R.[3] = 250 W.)

[Medea?]
atque eccum in ipso tempore ostentum senem! (*Trag.* 238 R.[3] = 251 W.)

[Aeetes vel de Aeeta?]
vitam propagans exanimis altaribus (*Trag.* 233 R.[3] = 252 W.)

[Aeetes vel de Aeeta?]
refugere oculi; corpus macie extabuit;
lacrimae peredere umore exanguis genas;

[**Perses**?]
Tell me, where do they say that she [i.e. Medea] has turned her way?

[**Medus**]
If I stop, he confirms that I should move; if I try to go, he prevents me from making a step.

[**Perses**, to attendants]
You, guard this man, so that no one uses violence against him or touches him.

[**Messenger**, upon Medea's arrival?]
huge winged snakes, united under a yoke

[**Messenger**, upon Medea's arrival?]
two-forked tongues shining in quivering motion

[**Messenger**, upon Medea's arrival?]
a woman of most beautiful shape

[**Chorus**, greeting Medea upon arrival?]
Servant of the gods, you come as one long expected: greetings, our guest!

[**Medea**, promising help?]
I can avert that misfortune from your head.

[**Medea**?]
and so that they may preserve it everlastingly as something favourable for the people

[**Medus** or **Perses**, questioning Medea's account?]
For what reason did you say that Hippotes had been killed?

[**Medea**, upon Aeetes approaching?]
And look, the old man has shown himself at this very point in time!

[**Aeetes** or about Aeetes?]
prolonging life with lifeless offerings

[**Aeetes** or about Aeetes?]
The eyes have sunk deeply; the body has vanished in leanness; tears have eaten away the lifeless cheeks with moisture; among the dirt on

situm inter oris barba pedore horrida atque
intonsa infuscat pectus inluvie scabrum
(Trag. inc. inc. 189-92 R.[3] = Pac. Trag. 253-6 W.)

[Aeetes?]
quis tu es, mulier, quae me insueto nuncupasti nomine?
(Trag. 239 R.[3] = 257 W.)

[Medea?]
sentio, pater, te vocis calvi similitudine (<i>Trag.</i> 240 R.[3] = 258 W.)

[Aeetes?]
set quid conspicio? num me lactans calvitur
aetas? (<i>Trag.</i> 241-2 R.[3] = 259 W.)

[Medea]
    coniugem <habui>
illum, Amor quem dederat, qui plus pollet potiorque est patre
(Trag. inc. inc. 174-5 R.[3] = Pac. Trag. 260 W.)

[Medea]
cum te expetebant omnes florentissimo
regno, reliqui: nunc desertum ab omnibus
summo periclo sola ut restituam paro
(Trag. inc. inc. 186-8 R.[3] = Pac. Trag. 261-3 W.)

D 4. Pacuvius, on Fortuna (one long fragment)

*The longest consecutive piece extant from Pacuvius' tragedies is a
'philosophical' discussion of the character and role of Fortuna. In the
second century BCE interest in philosophical questions increased in Rome,
triggered by a renewed influx of Greek ways of life and thinking. This is
reflected in the contemporary dramas of Pacuvius, which also include
considerations on the structure of the universe.*

*This fragment is not explicitly ascribed to a particular drama by the
author who quotes it (Rhet. Her. 2.36), but mention of Orestes suggests an*

Fortunam insanam esse et caecam et brutam perhibent philosophi,
saxoque instare in globoso praedicant volubilei:
id quo saxum inpulerit fors, eo cadere Fortunam autumant.
insanam autem esse aiunt, quia atrox incerta instabilisque sit:
[370] caecam ob eam rem esse iterant, quia nil cernat quo sese adplicet:
brutam, quia dignum atque indignum nequeat internoscere.

the face a beard, rough in its filthiness and unshorn, darkens the breast, scruffy in uncleanness.

[**Aeetes**, addressing Medea?]
Who are you, woman, who have called me with an unaccustomed name?

[**Medea**, explaining?]
I realize, father, that you are deceived by the similarity of voice.

[**Aeetes**?]
But what do I see? It is surely not my age that dupes and deceives me?

[**Medea**]
I had him for a husband, whom Amor had given to me, who has more power and strength than a father.

[**Medea**]
When everybody sought you out with the kingdom in full bloom, I left you; now when you have been deserted by everybody, I alone, in greatest danger, am preparing to restore you.

D 4. Pacuvius, on Fortuna (one long fragment)

attribution to one of Pacuvius' dramas on Orestes, particularly to Chryses *or* Dulorestes.

The speaker juxtaposes the views on Fortuna held by two different groups of philosophers. The first group sees Fortuna as a personified entity, who stands on a revolving ball of stone; since chance moves this ball, Fortuna cannot be predicted or directed by humans. According to the second view it is not Fortuna, but accident that governs everything. Orestes' fortune is adduced as an illustrative example.

Philosophers say that Fortune is insane and blind and stupid, and they proclaim that she stands on a revolving ball of stone: in whatever direction chance has pushed this stone, there, they believe, does Fortune fall. And they say that she is insane because she is cruel, untrustworthy and unsteady; [370] they reiterate that she is blind for the reason that she does not see where she steers herself; stupid, since

113

sunt autem alii philosophi, qui contra Fortuna negant
ullam miseriam esse, temeritate omnia regi autumant.
id magis veri simile esse usus re apse experiundo edocet:
[375] velut Orestes modo fuit rex, factust mendicus modo
(*Trag.* 366-75 R.³ = *Trag. inc.* 37-46 W.)

D 5. Accius, *Medea sive Argonautae* (some fragments)

Accius, the last major tragic poet of the Republican period (170-c. 80 BCE), also wrote a tragedy about Medea, though again on a different section of the myth (cf. D 2; 3; 14). As the double title Medea sive Argonautae *('Medea or the Argonauts') suggests, his drama focuses on an earlier part of the story, preceding the stages dramatized by Ennius and Pacuvius. Accius' tragedy is set during the Argonautic voyage and covers material that was narrated in Apollonius Rhodius' Hellenistic epic* Argonautika. *The play seems to have focused on the return voyage of the Argo, carrying Medea and the Golden*

atque ille apud Accium pastor, qui navem numquam ante vidisset, ut
procul divinum et novum vehiculum Argonautarum e monte conspexit,
primo admirans et perterritus hoc modo loquitur:
 'tanta moles labitur
 fremibunda ex alto ingenti sonitu et spiritu.
 prae se undas volvit, vertices vi suscitat:
 ruit prolapsa, pelagus respargit reflat.
 [395] ita dum interruptum credas nimbum volvier,
 dum quod sublime ventis expulsum rapi
 saxum aut procellis, vel globosos turbines
 existere ictos undis concursantibus:
 nisi quas terrestris pontus strages conciet,
 [400] aut forte Triton fuscina evertens specus
 supter radices penitus undante in freto
 molem ex profundo saxeam ad caelum erigit.'
dubitat primo quae sit ea natura quam cernit ignotam, idemque iuvenibus
visis auditoque nautico cantu:
 'sicut lascivi atque alacres rostris perfremunt
 delphini –'
item alia multa:
 'Silvani melo
consimilem ad auris cantum et auditum refert'.
(*Trag.* 391-402; 403-6 R.³ = 381-96 W.)

she cannot distinguish between worthy and unworthy. There are, however, other philosophers, who, on the contrary, deny that Fortune is the cause of any misery and believe that everything is governed by accident. This is more likely, which in fact practice teaches by experience: [375] as Orestes has just been a king and has now been turned into a beggar.

D 5. Accius, *Medea sive Argonautae* (some fragments)

Fleece, when Medea and the Argonauts are being pursued by Medea's family.
The most memorable and longest fragment extant from this tragedy is the description of the approach of the Argo by a shepherd who had never seen a ship before (quoted by Cicero, Nat. deor. 2.89). Such a speech must have made the tragedy more vivid, and the prominence of ordinary characters and their experiences may be indicative of the convergence of dramatic genres towards the late Republic. The following text gives the shepherd's utterances along with Cicero's introduction.

And this shepherd in Accius, who had never seen a ship before, when he noticed from a mountain-top the divine and novel vehicle of the Argonauts in the distance, speaks in this manner, at first astonished and thoroughly terrified:

'Such a huge mass glides along, roaring from the deep sea with immense noise and blast. It rolls billows in front of itself, it stirs up eddies by its force; it rushes on, gliding forward, it splashes and blows back the sea. [395] So you might believe now that a thunder-cloud was moving, rift asunder, now that some rock thrust up on high was carried along by winds or storms, or that water whirling round was coming forth, beaten by waves clashing together: unless the sea stirs up some disaster for the land [400] or perhaps Triton, turning his cave deep below the roots upside down with his trident, raises a rocky mass in the bellowing sea from the deep to the sky.'

He is in doubt at first what kind of thing this is what he sees, something unknown, and the same man says after he has seen the young men and heard the sailors' song:

'Just as playful and lively dolphins snort with their mouths' –
and many other things of this kind:

'it brings a song, similar to the tune of Silvanus, to my ears and hearing.'

D 6. Accius, *Brutus* (some fragments)

Like all Republican tragic poets since Naevius, Accius wrote praetextae,
serious plays on events from Roman history, besides tragedies (cf. D 15).
His praetexta Brutus *is about L. Iunius Brutus, and it describes the change*
from the regal period to the Roman Republic by the expulsion of the last
king Tarquinius Superbus and the subsequent institution of Republican
offices by L. Brutus. The story of L. Brutus might have had contemporary
resonance in Accius' time; and it could be understood paradigmatically in
the late Republic, when single individuals were striving for political power
and were opposed by others trying to preserve the traditional system.

Accius' Brutus *includes the longest fragments extant from any Republi-*
can praetexta, namely a dream of Tarquinius Superbus, which he relates

sed propiora videamus. cuiusnam modi est Superbi Tarquini somnium,
de quo in Bruto Acci loquitur ipse?
   'quoniam quieti corpus nocturno impetu
   dedi, sopore placans artus languidos:
   visust in somnis pastor ad me adpellere
   [20] pecus lanigerum eximia pulchritudine,
   duos consanguineos arietes inde eligi
   praeclarioremque alterum immolare me.
   deinde eius germanum cornibus conitier,
   in me arietare, eoque ictu me ad casum dari:
   [25] exin prostratum terra, graviter saucium,
   resupinum in caelo contueri maximum ac
   mirificum facinus: dextrorsum orbem flammeum
   radiatum solis liquier cursu novo.' (*Praet.* 17-28 R.[3] = 17-28 W.)

eius igitur somnii a coniectoribus quae sit interpretatio facta, videamus:
   'rex, quae in vita usurpant homines, cogitant curant vident,
   [30] quaeque agunt vigilantes agitantque, ea si cui in somno accidunt,
   minus mirum est; sed di in re tanta haud temere inprovisa offerunt.
   proin vide, ne quem tu esse hebetem deputes aeque ac pecus,
   is sapientia munitum pectus egregie gerat
   teque regno expellat: nam id quod de sole ostentum est tibi
   [35] populo commutationem rerum portendit fore
   perpropinquam. haec bene verruncent populo! nam quod dexterum
   cepit cursum ab laeva signum praepotens, pulcherrume
   auguratum est rem Romanam publicam summam fore.'
                                (*Praet.* 29-38 R.[3] = 29-38 W.)

D 6. Accius, *Brutus* (some fragments)

himself, and its analysis by dream interpreters in response (quoted by Cicero, Div. 1.43-5). This dream foreshadows the overthrow of Tarquinius Superbus and major changes in the Roman political system initiated by someone who is regarded as stupid (an element of L. Brutus' disguise). The realization of these fears and the introduction of the consulship were presumably shown later in the play. These speeches indicate that in praetextae Roman dramatists gave incidents from Roman history a dramatic shape independent of particular Greek models, but still made use of common structural elements. In what follows the two speeches of Tarquinius Superbus and of the dream interpreteers are reproduced, along with Cicero's introductions.

But let us look at things closer at hand. Of what type is the dream of Tarquinius Superbus, about which he himself speaks in Accius' *Brutus*?

'When I gave rest to my body upon the onset of night, soothing weary limbs with deep sleep, in a dream I saw a shepherd driving towards me [20] a woolly flock of exceptional beauty; two rams, blood-relations, were selected out of them, and I sacrificed the nobler of the two. Then its brother pressed upon me with its horns and butted me, and by this blow I was brought to fall upon the ground; [25] then, thrown on the ground, heavily wounded, lying on my back, I saw an extraordinarily great and wonderful thing in the sky: the flaming and radiating orb of the sun melted away to the right in a new course.'

Now let us see what interpretation of his dream was given by the seers:

'King, what humans are concerned with in their lives, think, care for, see, [30] and what they do and are engaged in while awake, if this comes to them in their sleep, this is less surprising. But in such a great matter the gods do not offer the unexpected at random. Hence keep watch lest he whom you regard as stupid as an animal, bears a heart eminently fortified by wisdom and drives you out of your kingdom. For what has been shown to you as regards the sun [35] announces that a change of circumstances is very near for the people. May this be fortunate for the people! For as the most powerful celestial body has taken a right-hand course from the left, thereby it has been predicted exceedingly well that the affairs of Rome when in the hands of the people will be supreme.'

117

D 7. Plautus, *Amphitruo* 1-152 (prologue)

Among the surviving comedies by Plautus (c. 250-184 BCE), his Amphitruo
*stands out, since, according to the prologue, it is not a straightforward
comedy, but a mixture of comedy and tragedy; for this combination a new
term is coined and the play is described as a 'tragicomedy' (cf. T 13a). The
reason for the play's attribution to a mixed form is the status of the
dramatic characters, since these comprise both kings and slaves. Indeed,*
Amphitruo *tells the story of Jupiter and Mercury impersonating Amphitruo and his servant Sosia returning from battle to Amphitruo's wife
Alcumena, which leads to a number of misunderstandings and confusions.*

Mercurius. ut vos in vostris voltis mercimoniis
emundis vendundisque me laetum lucris
adficere atque adiuvare in rebus omnibus,
et ut res rationesque vostrorum omnium
[5] bene expedire voltis peregrique et domi,
bonoque atque amplo auctare perpetuo lucro
quasque incepistis res quasque inceptabitis,
et uti bonis vos vostrosque omnis nuntiis
me adficere voltis, ea adferam, ea ut nuntiem
[10] quae maxume in rem vostram communem sient
(nam vos quidem id iam scitis concessum et datum
mi esse ab dis aliis, nuntiis praesim et lucro):
haec ut me voltis adprobare, adnitier
lucrum ut perenne vobis semper suppetat,
[15] ita huic facietis fabulae silentium
itaque aequi et iusti hic eritis omnes arbitri.
    nunc quoiius iussu venio et quam ob rem venerim
dicam simulque ipse eloquar nomen meum.
Iovi' iussu venio: nomen Mercuriost mihi:
[20] pater huc me misit ad vos oratum meus;
tam etsi pro imperio vobis quod dictum foret
scibat facturos, quippe qui intellexerat
vereri vos se et metuere, ita ut aequom est Iovem;
verum profecto hoc petere me precario
[25] a vobis iussit leniter dictis bonis.
etenim ille quoius huc iussu venio, Iuppiter
non minu' quam vostrum quivis formidat malum:
humana matre natus, humano patre,
mirari non est aequom sibi si praetimet;
[30] atque ego quoque etiam, qui Iovis sum filius,
contagione mei patris metuo malum.

D 7. Plautus, *Amphitruo* 1-152 (prologue)

The prologue, spoken by the god Mercury, informs the audience about the unusual generic status of this play and the participation of Jupiter in the action; besides, it presents an outline of the plot, and it also includes comments on moral behaviour and remarks on practices and circumstances in the contemporary theatre. It is thus a combination of characteristic features of a narrative, expository prologue and of a theoretical, metatheatrical one, supplemented by reflections on themes of the plot, enabled by the divinity of the prologue speaker.

Mercury. As you want me to be favourable to your buying and selling of goods, to grant you gain and to help you in all things and as you want the business and transactions of all of you [5] to turn out well abroad and at home and me to continuously support with good and ample profit whatever you have started or will start and as you want me to bring good news to you and all your folks, so that I report and announce [10] what is most useful for your communal business (for you certainly have long known that this has been granted and given to me by the other gods, that I am in charge of news and gain): as you want me to favour these things and to exert myself so that perennial gain shall always be at your disposal, [15] so you will make silence for this play and will all be fair and just judges.

Now I will tell you on whose orders I come and for what reason I have come, and I will give you my name at the same time. I come on Jupiter's orders; my name is Mercury; [20] my father[1] has sent me here to intercede with you. Even though he knew that you would do what would be told to you by virtue of his power, since he had understood that you respect and fear him, so as it is appropriate for Jupiter; still, he has in fact ordered me [25] to ask this from you by way of entreaty with good words mildly spoken. For Jupiter, on whose orders I come here, fears evil[2] no less than any of you: as he was born of a human mother, of a human father, it is not appropriate to wonder that he is in fear for himself[3]. [30] And even I, who am the son of Jupiter, fear evil[4] due to contact with my father. Therefore I come here in peace and bring peace to you; I wish a just and easy matter to be asked from you, for I have been appointed a just orator for a just matter from just people. [35] For it is not right to beg unjust

propterea pace advenio et pacem ad vos fero:
iustam rem et facilem esse oratam a vobis volo,
nam iustae ab iustis iustus sum orator datus.
[35] nam iniusta ab iustis impetrari non decet,
iusta autem ab iniustis petere insipientia est;
quippe illi iniqui ius ignorant neque tenent.
    nunc iam huc animum omnes quae loquar advortite.
debetis velle quae velimus: meruimus
[40] et ego et pater de vobis et re publica;
nam quid ego memorem (ut alios in tragoediis
vidi, Neptunum, Virtutem, Victoriam,
Martem, Bellonam commemorare quae bona
vobis fecissent) quis bene factis meu' pater,
[45] deorum regnator, architectust omnibus?
sed mos numquam <ille> illi fuit patri meo
ut exprobraret quod bonis faceret boni;
gratum arbitratur esse id a vobis sibi
meritoque vobis bona se facere quae facit.
    [50] nunc quam rem oratum huc veni primum proloquar;
post argumentum huius eloquar tragoediae.
quid? contraxistis frontem quia tragoediam
dixi futuram hanc? deu' sum, commutavero.
eandem hanc, si voltis, faciam <iam> ex tragoedia
[55] comoedia ut sit omnibus isdem vorsibus.
utrum sit an non voltis? sed ego stultior,
quasi nesciam vos velle, qui divos siem.
teneo quid animi vostri super hac re siet:
faciam ut commixta sit; [sit] tragico[co]comoedia;
[60] nam me perpetuo facere ut sit comoedia,
reges quo veniant et di, non par arbitror.
quid igitur? quoniam hic servos quoque partis habet,
faciam sit, proinde ut dixi, tragico[co]moedia.
    nunc hoc me orare a vobis iussit Iuppiter
[65] ut conquistores singula in subsellia
eant per totam caveam spectatoribus,
si quoi favitores delegatos viderint,
ut is in cavea pignus capiantur togae;
sive qui ambissent palmam <his> histrionibus
[70] seu quoiquam artifici (seu per scriptas litteras
seu qui ipse ambissit seu per internuntium),
sive adeo aediles perfidiose quoi duint,
sirempse legem iussit esse Iuppiter,
quasi magistratum sibi alterive ambiverit.

things from just people, and it is unwise to try to gain just things from unjust people, since these unjust people do not know the law nor keep to it.

Now all of you turn your minds to what I am going to say. You must wish what we wish: we, [40] both myself and my father have done services for you and the republic. For why should I mention (as I have seen others in tragedies, such as Neptune, Virtue, Victory, Mars, Bellona, mention what good they had done for you) of which good deeds my father, [45] king of the gods, is architect for the benefit of all? But this father of mine never had this custom that he brought up as a reproach what good he had done to good people; he believes that you are grateful to him for this and that he does the good things for you which he does as you deserve them.

[50] Now I will first explain what matter to ask of you I have come here; then I will tell you the plot of this tragedy. What? You have wrinkled your brows because I said that this would be a tragedy? I am a god; I will have it changed. The very same play, if you wish, I will turn from a tragedy [55] into a comedy, with all verses exactly the same. Shall it be one or not: what do you wish? But I am too stupid, as if I did not know that you want it, being a god as I am. I know what your view is on this matter. I will see to it that it is mixed; it shall be a tragi-comedy; [60] for I do not think that it is right for me to turn the play into a comedy entirely, in which kings and gods take part. What then? Since a slave has a part here as well, I will turn it, as I have said, into a tragi-comedy.

Now Jupiter has ordered me to ask this of you, [65] that inspectors walk along all benches throughout the whole auditorium amid the spectators, if they see supporters assigned to anyone, so that they seize their togas in the auditorium as a surety; or if some who have canvassed for the victory palm for these actors [70] or any other artist (be it by written letters, by someone canvassing himself or by means of an intermediary), or if even the aediles grant it to someone in a perfidious way: Jupiter has ordered that the very same law should be valid as if someone has canvassed for a public office for himself or another one. [75] He has said that you live as victors by means of virtue, not by ambition nor by perjury: how should the same law that exists for the greatest man be less relevant for an actor? One must canvass by means of virtue, not through supporters. He who acts rightly always has enough supporters, [80] if there is faith in

[75] virtute dixit vos victores vivere,
non ambitione neque perfidia: qui minus
eadem histrioni sit lex quae summo viro?
virtute ambire oportet, non favitoribus.
sat habet favitorum semper qui recte facit,
[80] si illis fides est quibus est ea res in manu.
hoc quoque etiam mihi in mandatis <is> dedit
ut conquistores fierent histrionibus:
qui sibi mandasset delegati ut plauderent
quive quo placeret alter fecisset minus,
[85] eius ornamenta et corium uti conciderent.
mirari nolim vos quapropter Iuppiter
nunc histriones curet; ne miremini:
ipse hanc acturust Iuppiter comoediam.
quid? admiratin estis? quasi vero novom
[90] nunc proferatur Iovem facere histrioniam.
etiam, histriones anno quom in proscaenio hic
Iovem invocarunt, venit, auxilio is fuit.
[praeterea certo prodit in tragoedia.]
hanc fabulam, inquam, hic Iuppiter hodie ipse aget
[95] et ego una cum illo. nunc <vos> animum advortite,
dum huius argumentum eloquar comoediae.
    haec urbs est Thebae. in illisce habitat aedibus
Amphitruo, natus Argis ex Argo patre,
quicum Alcumena est nupta, Electri filia.
[100] is nunc Amphitruo praefectust legionibus,
nam cum Telobois bellum est Thebano poplo.
is priu' quam hinc abiit ipsemet in exercitum,
gravidam Alcumenam fecit uxorem suam.
nam ego vos novisse credo iam ut sit pater meus,
[105] quam liber harum rerum multarum siet
quantusque amator siet quod complacitum est semel.
is amare occepit Alcumenam clam virum
usuramque eiius corporis cepit sibi,
et gravidam fecit is eam compressu suo.
[110] nunc de Alcumena ut rem teneatis rectius,
utrimque est gravida, et ex viro et ex summo Iove.
et meu' pater nunc intus hic cum illa cubat,
et haec ob eam rem nox est facta longior,
dum <cum> illa quacum volt voluptatem capit.
[115] sed ita adsimulavit se, quasi Amphitruo siet.
nunc ne hunc ornatum vos meum admiremini,
quod ego huc processi sic cum servili schema:

those who are responsible for this matter. This too he gave me among his admonishments that there be inspectors for the actors: as for him who had arranged for himself to have people applaud on his behalf or him who had caused that another pleased less, [85] that they destroy his costume and skin. I would not want you to wonder why Jupiter now cares for actors; do not wonder: Jupiter himself is going to act this comedy. What? You wonder at that? As if indeed something new [90] was now presented when Jupiter takes part in the art of acting. Last year too, when actors on stage here called upon Jupiter, he came and brought them help. In this play, I tell you, Jupiter himself will act here today, [95] and I along with him. Now pay attention, while I explain the plot of this comedy.

This is the city of Thebes[5]. Amphitruo lives in this house[6], born in Argos from an Argive father; Alcumena, daughter of Electrus[7], is married to him. [100] This Amphitruo now commands legions, for the Theban people are having a war with the Teloboians[8]. Before he left for the campaign from here, he made his wife Alcumena pregnant. Well, I believe that you already know what my father is like, [105] how free he is in these countless things and how great a lover he is of what has pleased him once. He has started to love Alcumena in secret from her husband, and he has taken the interest from her body for himself, and he has made her pregnant by his intercourse with her. [110] Now, so that you get things about Alcumena absolutely right, she is pregnant from two sides, both from her husband and from highest Jupiter. And my father is now sleeping with her inside, and this night is therefore made longer, while he enjoys himself with her as he wishes. [115] But he has taken on such a guise as if he was Amphitruo. Now do not wonder at this my costume, since I have come here on stage with this slave outfit: I will present to you anew an old and ancient matter, therefore I have appeared dressed up in a new way. [120] For my father Jupiter is now inside right here; he has changed himself into the likeness of Amphitruo, and all the slaves who see him believe that it is him: thus does he change his skin when he likes it. I have taken on for me the likeness of the slave Sosia, [125] who has gone from here to the campaign with Amphitruo, so that I can serve my father in love, and members of the household do not ask who I am, when they see me frequently spend time in the house; now, since they

veterem atque antiquam rem novam ad vos proferam,
propterea ornatus in novom incessi modum.
[120] nam meu' pater intus nunc est eccum Iuppiter;
in Amphitruonis vertit sese imaginem
omnesque eum esse censent servi qui vident:
ita vorsipellem se facit quando lubet.
ego servi sumpsi Sosiae mi imaginem,
[125] qui cum Amphitruone abivit hinc in exercitum,
ut praeservire amanti meo possem patri
atque ut ne qui essem familiares quaererent,
vorsari crebro hic quom viderent me domi;
nunc, quom esse credent servom et conservom suom,
[130] hau quisquam quaeret qui siem aut quid venerim.
pater nunc intus suo animo morem gerit:
cubat complexus quoiius cupiens maxume est;
quae illi ad legionem facta sunt memorat pater
meus Alcumenae: illa illum censet virum
[135] suom esse, quae cum moecho est. ibi nunc meu' pater
memorat legiones hostium ut fugaverit,
quo pacto sit donis donatus plurumis.
ea dona quae illic Amphitruoni sunt data
apstulimus: facile meu' pater quod volt facit.
[140] nunc hodie Amphitruo veniet huc ab exercitu
et servos, quoiius ego hanc fero imaginem.
   nunc internosse ut nos possitis facilius,
ego has habebo usque <hic> in petaso pinnulas;
tum meo patri autem torulus inerit aureus
[145] sub petaso: id signum Amphitruoni non erit.
ea signa nemo <homo> horum familiarium
videre poterit: verum vos videbitis.
sed Amphitruonis illi[c] est servos Sosia:
a portu illic nunc <huc> cum lanterna advenit.
[150] abigam iam ego illunc advenientem ab aedibus.
adeste: erit operae pretium hic spectantibus
Iovem et Mercurium facere histrioniam.

believe that I am a slave and their fellow slave, [130] no one will ask who I am and why I have come. My father now indulges his desire inside: he sleeps embracing whom he desires most; my father tells Alcumena what has been done there on the campaign: she believes that he [135] is her husband, she who is with an adulterer. There my father now narrates how he has put the legions of the enemy to flight, in what way he was presented by a multitude of gifts. These gifts, which have been given to Amphitruo there, have been carried away by us: my father does easily what he wishes. [140] Now Amphitruo will come here today from the campaign, and the slave, whose likeness I bear.

Now, so that you can distinguish us more easily, I will have these little feathers here in my hat; and my father will have a golden tassel [145] on his hat: Amphitruo will not have this sign. No one of those in the household will be able to see these signs: yet you will see them. But here is Amphitruo's slave Sosia[9]: he is now coming here from the harbour with a lantern. [150] I will turn him away from the house straightaway when he is coming. Be alert: it will be worth the while for those watching here when Jupiter and Mercury take part in the art of acting.

---

1 i.e. Jupiter. 2 i.e. a flogging. 3 referring to the actor who will play Jupiter. 4 i.e. a flogging. 5 the actor indicating the stage area. 6 the actor indicating one of the houses at the back of the stage. 7 i.e. Electryon. 8 a people in the area of Acarnania. 9 the real Sosia is seen approaching, entering through one of the wing-entrances.

D 8. Plautus, *Miles gloriosus* 1-78 (I 1)

As Roman dramatists themselves were well aware (cf. T 13), their comedies were frequently based on standard structures and stock characters. These include the miles gloriosus, *the 'braggart warrior' or 'vainglorious soldier', who boasts of his military achievements and attractiveness to women, but is in fact a weak, cowardly and unsympathetic character, who is usually unsuccessful and punished at the end of the play. Pyrgopolynices in Plautus'* Miles gloriosus *is one of the most memorable of these soldier figures*

Pyrgopolynices. curate ut splendor meo sit clupeo clarior
quam solis radii esse olim quom sudumst solent,
ut, ubi usus veniat, contra conserta manu
praestringat oculorum aciem in acie hostibus.
[5] nam ego hanc machaeram mihi consolari volo,
ne lamentetur neve animum despondeat,
quia se iam pridem feriatam gestitem,
quae misera gestit fartem facere ex hostibus.
sed ubi Artotrogus hic est? **Artotrogus**. stat propter virum
[10] fortem atque fortunatum et forma regia,
tum bellatorem – Mars haud ausit dicere
neque aequiperare suas virtutes ad tuas.
Pyrg. quemne ego servavi in campis Curculionieis,
ubi Bumbomachides Clutomestoridysarchides
[15] erat imperator summus, Neptuni nepos?
Art. memini. nempe illum dicis cum armis aureis,
quoius tu legiones difflavisti spiritu,
quasi ventus folia aut peniculum tectorium.
Pyrg. istuc quidem edepol nihil est. **Art**. nihil hercle hoc quidemst
[20] praeut alia dicam – quae tu numquam feceris.
peiiuriorem hoc hominem si quis viderit
aut gloriarum pleniorem quam illic est,
me sibi habeto, ego me mancupio dabo;
nisi unum, epityra estur insanum bene.
[25] **Pyrg**. ubi tu es? **Art**. eccum. edepol vel elephanto in India,
quo pacto ei pugno praefregisti bracchium.
Pyrg. quid, 'bracchium'? **Art**. illud dicere volui, 'femur'.
Pyrg. at indiligenter iceram. **Art**. pol si quidem
conixus esses, per corium, per viscera
[30] perque os elephanti transmineret bracchium.
Pyrg. nolo istaec hic nunc. **Art**. ne hercle operae pretium quidemst
mihi te narrare tuas qui virtutes sciam.
venter creat omnis hasce aerumnas: auribus

D 8. Plautus, *Miles gloriosus* 1-78 (I 1)

in Roman comedy, and the comedy is aptly named after him and his characteristic trait, based on an Alazon *('Braggart') by a poet of Greek New Comedy. Such a soldier is frequently accompanied by a parasite, who praises the non-existent virtues of the soldier in exchange for free dinners.*

The initial scene of Miles gloriosus *(before a 'delayed prologue') introduces the soldier Pyrgopolynices and his parasite Artotrogus, who display the typical characteristics of their roles in an impressive way.*

Pyrgopolynices (*to servants*). Take care that the brilliance of my shield is brighter than the beams of the sun are accustomed to be at times in clear weather, so that in close combat, when it is needed, it may dazzle the pupils of the eyes of the enemy in battle line. [5] For I wish to comfort this sword of mine, so that it does not lament or lose courage, since I have been carrying it resting for a long time already, when it, the poor thing, longs to make mincemeat out of the enemy. But where is our Artotrogus?

Artotrogus. He stands next to a [10] brave man, fortunate and of royal appearance, and a real fighter – Mars would not dare to call or regard his virtues as equal to yours.

Pyrg. Whom did I save in the Curculionian[1] fields, where Bumbomachides Clutomestoridysarchides[2] [15] was the chief commander, a grandson of Neptune?

Art. I remember. You certainly mean the man with gold armour, whose legions you blew apart with your breath, just as the wind blows away leaves or a roof thatch.

Pyrg. This, by Pollux, is really nothing.

Art. By Hercules, this is indeed nothing, [20] compared with other things I might mention – (*aside*) which you never did. If anyone has seen a man who is a bigger liar or more swelled by boasting than he is, they shall have me for themselves, I will give myself up for possession; if it were not for one thing: one dines exceedingly well on his olive-dishes.

[25] **Pyrg**. Where are you?

Art. Here. By Pollux, for instance this elephant in India, in what way you have smashed its forearm with your fist.

Pyrg. What, 'arm'?

Art. This is what I wanted to say: 'foreleg'.

Pyrg. But I had struck it in a rather unskilled way.

Art. By Pollux, if you had stretched yourself, your arm would have pierced through the skin, through the flesh [30] and through the bone of the elephant.

perhaurienda sunt, ne dentes dentiant,
[35] et adsentandumst quidquid hic mentibitur.
Pyrg. quid illuc quod dico? **Art.** ehem, scio iam quid vis dicere.
factum herclest, memini fieri. **Pyrg.** quid id est? **Art.** quidquid est.
Pyrg. habes – **Art.** tabellas vis rogare? habeo, et stilum.
Pyrg. facete advortis tuom animum ad animum meum.
[40] **Art.** novisse mores tuos me meditate decet
curamque adhibere ut praeolat mihi quod tu velis.
Pyrg. ecquid meministi? **Art.** memini centum in Cilicia
et quinquaginta, centum in Scytholatronia,
triginta Sardos, sexaginta Macedones –
[45] sunt homines quos tu – occidisti uno die.
Pyrg. quanta istaec hominum summast? **Art.** septem milia.
Pyrg. tantum esse oportet. recte rationem tenes.
Art. at nullos habeo scriptos: sic memini tamen.
Pyrg. edepol memoria's optuma. **Art.** offae monent.
[50] **Pyrg.** dum tale facies quale adhuc, adsiduo edes,
communicabo semper te mensa mea.
Art. quid in Cappadocia, ubi tu quingentos simul,
ni hebes machaera foret, uno ictu occideras?
Pyrg. at peditastelli quia erant, sivi viverent.
[55] **Art.** quid tibi ego dicam, quod omnes mortales sciunt,
Pyrgopolynicem te unum in terra vivere
virtute et forma et factis invictissumis?
amant ted omnes mulieres neque iniuria,
qui sis tam pulcher; vel illae quae here pallio
[60] me reprehenderunt. **Pyrg.** quid eae dixerunt tibi?
Art. rogitabant: 'hicine Achilles est?' inquit mihi.
'immo eius frater' inquam 'est.' ibi illarum altèra
'ergo mecastor pulcher est' inquit mihi
'et liberalis. vide caesaries quam decet.
[65] ne illae sunt fortunatae quae cum isto cubant!'
Pyrg. itane aibant tandem? **Art.** quaen me ambae opsecraverint
ut te hodie quasi pompam illa praeterducerem?
Pyrg. nimiast miseria nimi' pulchrum esse hominem. **Art.** immo itast.
molestae sunt: orant, ambiunt, exopsecrant
[70] videre ut liceat, ad sese arcessi iubent,
ut tuo non liceat dare operam negotio.
Pyrg. videtur tempus esse ut eamus ad forum,
ut in tabellis quos consignavi hic heri
latrones, ibus denumerem stipendium.
[75] nam rex Seleucus me opere oravit maxumo
ut sibi latrones cogerem et conscriberem.

Pyrg. I do not want these things here now.

Art. By Hercules, it is not even worth the effort that you tell me about your brave exploits as I know them. (*aside*) The belly creates all these hardships: these things have to be gulped down with the ears, so that the teeth do not grow long, [35] and one must agree with whatever lies he tells.

Pyrg. What about the point I was about to make?

Art. Ah, I know already what you wish to say. This has been done, by Hercules, I remember that it was.

Pyrg. What is it?

Art. Whatever it is.

Pyrg. You have –

Art. You wish to ask after writing tablets? I have them, and a pen.

Pyrg. You excellently turn your mind to my mind.

[40] **Art**. It is right that I am thoroughly familiar with your character and take care that the smell of what you wish gets to me first.

Pyrg. Do you remember anything?

Art. I remember one hundred and fifty in Cilicia[3], one hundred in Scytholatronia[4], thirty people from Sardis[5], sixty men from Macedonia[6] – [45] these are people that you – have killed in a single day.

Pyrg. What is the total of these people?

Art. Seven thousand.

Pyrg. It must be that much. You are good at calculating.

Art. But I have not written down anything: even so I remember it.

Pyrg. By Pollux, you have an excellent memory.

Art. (*aside*) Appetizers admonish me.

[50] **Pyrg**. While you continue to do such things as you have done so far, you will always eat, I will always share my table with you.

Art. What about Cappadocia[7], where you would have killed five hundred all at one stroke if your sword had not been blunt?

Pyrg. But because they were wretched foot soldiers, I let them live.

[55] **Art**. Why shall I tell you, what all mortals know, that you are the one and only Pyrgopolynices living on earth, not to be surpassed at all in bravery, appearance and deeds? All women love you, and not without reason, as you are so handsome; for instance those girls who [60] caught me by my cloak yesterday.

Pyrg. What did they say to you?

Art. They kept asking: 'Is he Achilles?' she said to me. 'No, he is his brother[8]', I said. Then another one of them said to me: 'That's why, by Castor, he is handsome and gentlemanly. Look how his hair makes him good-looking. [65] Indeed, fortunate are those women who sleep with him!'

Pyrg. They really spoke like this?

regi hunc diem mihi operam decretumst dare.
Art. age eamus ergo. **Pyrg.** sequimini, satellites.

---

1 a fictitious name, suggesting fields full of corn-worms. **2** a fictitious, pompous-sounding, Greek-style name. **3** an area in southern Asia Minor. **4** a fictitious name, 'the land of Scythian brigands'. **5** a city in Asia Minor. **6** a country to the north of the Greek peninsula. **7** an area in Asia Minor, north of Cilicia. **8** this figure does not feature in any myth. **9** one member of a dynasty of kings of that name in Syria; it is unclear whether a particular one is alluded to.

D 9. Caecilius Statius, *Plocium* (Gellius, *Noctes Atticae* 2.23)

Caecilius Statius (c. 230/20-168/7 BCE) was a palliata poet active between Plautus and Terence and is often thought to represent a kind of intermediate or transitional stage. His works have only been preserved in fragments; so it is hard to come to definite conclusions about them. The remains of his comedies include a valuable piece of evidence as regards the way Roman poets used Greek models. Although Roman playwrights are known to have based their Greek-style tragedies and comedies on Greek models (cf. T 15), it is often difficult to determine the precise nature of this relationship since only in a few cases have both texts been preserved.

The archaist Gellius (writing in the second century CE) quotes passages from Caecilius Statius' Plocium ('Necklace'), along with the corresponding bits from Menander's Plokion, which enables direct comparison. Gellius

Consultatio diiudicatioque locorum facta ex comoedia Menandri et Caecilii, quae Plocium inscripta est.

[1] comoedias lectitamus nostrorum poetarum sumptas ac versas de Graecis Menandro aut Posidippo aut Apollodoro aut Alexide et quibusdam item aliis comicis. [2] neque, cum legimus eas, nimium sane displicent, quin lepide quoque et venuste scriptae videantur, prorsus ut melius posse fieri nihil censeas. [3] sed enim si conferas et componas Graeca ipsa, unde illa venerunt, ac singula considerate atque apte iunctis et alternis lectionibus committas, oppido quam iacere atque sordere incipiunt, quae Latina sunt; ita Graecarum, quas aemulari nequiverunt, facetiis atque luminibus obsolescunt.

[4] nuper adeo usus huius rei nobis venit. [5] Caecili Plocium

Art. They who both beseeched me that I should lead you past there today like a procession?

Pyrg. It is too great a misfortune if a man is too handsome.

Art. Indeed it is. The women are a nuisance: they plead, they solicit, they entreat [70] that they may see you, they ask that you be brought to them, so that it is impossible to give attention to your business.

Pyrg. It seems to be time for us to go to the Forum, so that I count their dues for those mercenaries who I registered in the lists yesterday. [75] For king Seleucus[9] has asked me most urgently that I bring together and enrol mercenaries for him. I have decided to work for the king on this day.

Art. Come on, let's go then.

Pyrg. Follow me, attendants. (*they all leave the stage*)

D 9. Caecilius Statius, *Plocium* (Gellius, *Noctes Atticae* 2.23)

thinks that Caecilius has worsened Menander's play by his changes. Irrespective of the assessment of the alterations, it is clear that Caecilius did not translate literally, but rather modified and adapted the text, which resulted in another play with a different focus. The plot of the comedy consists of standard elements: an old man complaining about his rich and ugly wife, who prevented him from enjoying a relationship with a maidservant; a girl raped by a young man, who is about to repudiate her when she is giving birth, only to recognize that it was he who raped her and to renew the betrothal.

The chapter in Gellius gives both the Caecilian and the Menandrean fragments, along with Gellius' comments.

Discussion and comparative assessment of passages from the comedy by Menander and by Caecilius that is entitled Plocium *('Necklace').*

[1] We frequently read comedies of our poets, taken and adapted from the Greeks Menander, Posidippus, Apollodorus or Alexis and equally some other comic poets. [2] And when we read these, they are indeed not too displeasing, they even seem to be written charmingly and gracefully, certainly so that one would believe that nothing better could exist. [3] But when one compares and juxtaposes the Greek material itself, where this has come from, and submits individual items to comparative parallel readings thoughtfully and appropriately, how completely do the Latin texts start to be of little value and seem paltry; to such an extent are they overshadowed by the witticisms and stylistic beauty of the Greek plays, which they could not emulate.

legebamus; hautquaquam mihi et, qui aderant, displicebat. [6] libitum et Menandri quoque Plocium legere, a quo istam comoediam verterat. [7] sed enim postquam in manus Menander venit, a principio statim, di boni, quantum stupere atque frigere quantumque mutare a Menandro Caecilius visus est! Diomedis hercle arma et Glauci non dispari magis pretio existimata sunt. [8] accesserat dehinc lectio ad eum locum, in quo maritus senex super uxore divite atque deformi querebatur, quod ancillam suam, non inscito puellam ministerio et facie haut inliberali, coactus erat venundare suspectam uxori quasi paelicem. nihil dicam ego, quantum differat; versus utrimque eximi iussi et aliis ad iudicium faciundum exponi. [9] Menander sic:

ἐπ᾽ ἀμφότερα νῦν ἡ ᾽πίκληρος ἡ κ<αλὴ>
μέλλει καθευδήσειν. κατείργασται μέγα
καὶ περιβόητον ἔργον· ἐκ τῆς οἰκίας
ἐξέβαλε τὴν λυποῦσαν, ἣν ἐβούλετο,
ἵν᾽ ἀποβλέπωσιν πάντες εἰς τὸ Κρωβύλης
πρόσωπον ἧ τ᾽ εὔγνωστος οὖσ᾽ ἐμὴ γυνὴ
δέσποινα. καὶ τὴν ὄψιν ἣν ἐκτήσατο·
ὄνος ἐν πιθήκοις, τοῦτο δὴ τὸ λεγόμενον,
ἔστιν. σιωπᾶν βούλομαι τὴν νύκτα τὴν
πολλῶν κακῶν ἀρχηγόν. οἴμοι Κρωβύλην
λαβεῖν ἔμ᾽, εἰ καὶ δέκα τάλαντ᾽ <ἠνέγκατο,
τὴν> ῥῖν᾽ ἔχουσαν πήχεως. εἶτ᾽ ἐστὶ τὸ
φρύαγμα πῶς ὑποστατόν; <μὰ τὸν> Δία
τὸν Ὀλύμπιον καὶ τὴν Ἀθηνᾶν, οὐδαμῶς.
παιδισκάριον θεραπευτικὸν δὲ καὶ λόγου
† τάχιον· ἀπαγέσθω δέ. τίς ἄρ᾽ ἂν εἰσάγοι; (fr. 296 Kassel-Austin)

[10] Caecilius autem sic:

is demum miser est, qui aerumnam suam nescit occultare
foris: ita me uxor forma et factis facit, si taceam, tamen indicium,
{145} quae nisi dotem omnia quae nolis habet: qui sapiet de me
                                                                         discet,
qui quasi ad hostis captus liber servio salva urbe atque arce.
quaen mihi quidquid placet eo privatum it me servatam
                                                                         <velim>?
dum <ego> eius mortem inhio, egomet inter vivos vivo mortuus.
ea me clam se cum mea ancilla ait consuetum. id me arguit:
{150} ita plorando orando instando atque obiurgando me optudit,
eam uti venderem. nunc credo inter suas
aequalis, cognatas sermonem serit:
'quis vostrarum fuit integra aetatula
quae hoc idem a viro

[4] Recently we happened to come across an experience of this. [5] We were reading Caecilius' *Plocium*; it did not at all displease me and those who were present. [6] We wished to read also Menander's *Plocium*, from which he had adapted this comedy. [7] But after Menander had come into our hands, right from the start suddenly, by god, how stiff and lifeless and how changed from Menander Caecilius seemed to be! The armour of Diomedes, by Hercules, and those of Glaucus have not been thought of as differing more in value[1]. [8] Our reading had then reached the passage where an old husband complained about his rich and ugly wife, since he had been forced to sell his maidservant, a girl not unskilled in her work and of not ignoble appearance, and suspected by his wife of being his mistress. I will not say anything about how great the difference is; I have ordered both sets of verses to be excerpted and to be put here for others to make a judgement.

[9] Menander thus:

'Now the beautiful heiress [i.e. the speaker's wife] is ready to go to sleep on both sides. She has done a great deed that will be talked about everywhere: she has thrown out of the house the girl she wanted to, who was annoying her, so that everyone may look at the face of Crobyle [i.e. the wife's name] and my wife will easily be seen to be my master. And the looks that she possesses: she is an ass among apes, that is how the saying goes. I will keep silent about the night that was the beginning of many evils. Ah me, that I took Crobyle, who, even if she has brought ten talents, has a nose a cubit long. Then, how is her insolence to be borne? By the Olympian Zeus and by Athena, in no way. And the little maidservant (obeys) faster than a word has been uttered[2]; but she shall be led away. Who could lead her into their house?'

[10] But Caecilius thus:

'He indeed is wretched, who does not know how to hide his hardship out of doors: so my wife still makes me betray myself by looks and actions, even if I remain silent, {145} she who, except her dowry, has everything that you do not wish: he who will be wise will learn from me, who, like a free man captured for the enemy, am a servant while city and citadel are unharmed. Would I wish long life for the woman who is going to strip me of everything that pleases me? While I yearn for her death, I myself live as a dead man among the living. She claims that I had a close relationship with my maidservant in secret from her. This is what she accuses me of: {150} by lamenting, praying, insisting and blaming she stunned my ears so much that I sold her. Now, I believe, she spreads the following tale among her friends and relatives: 'Who of you has there been who, in the bloom of youth, {155} has obtained the same from her husband, what I, an old woman, have just achieved, that I stripped my husband of his mistress?' These sorts of meetings will happen today: I will be miserably defamed by gossip.'

133

{155} impetrarit suo, quod ego anus modo
effeci, paelice ut meum privarem virum?'
haec erunt concilia hocedie: differar sermone misere.

(*Com.* 143-57 R.³ = 136-50 W.)

[11] praeter venustatem autem rerum atque verborum in duobus
libris nequaquam parem in hoc equidem soleo animum attendere,
quod, quae Menander praeclare et apposite et facete scripsit, ea
Caecilius, ne qua potuit quidem, conatus est enarrare, [12] sed quasi
minime probanda praetermisit et alia nescio qua mimica inculcavit
et illud Menandri de vita hominum media sumptum, simplex et
verum et delectabile, nescio quo pacto omisit. idem enim ille maritus
senex cum altero sene vicino colloquens et uxoris locupletis
superbiam deprecans haec ait:

ἔχω δ᾽ ἐπίκληρον Λάμιαν· οὐκ εἴρηκά σοι
τουτὶ γάρ; – οὐχί. – κυρίαν τῆς οἰκίας
καὶ τῶν ἀγρῶν καὶ † πάντων ἄντ᾽ ἐκείνης †
ἔχομεν. – Ἄπολλον, ὡς χαλεπόν. – χαλεπώτατον.
ἅπασι δ᾽ ἀργαλέα 'στίν, οὐκ ἐμοὶ μόνῳ,
υἱῷ πολὺ μᾶλλον, θυγατρί. – πρᾶγμ᾽ ἄμαχον λέγεις. –
εὖ οἶδα. (fr. 297 Kassel-Austin)

[13] Caecilius vero hoc in loco ridiculus magis, quam personae isti,
quam tractabat, aptus atque conveniens videri maluit. sic enim haec
corrupit:

sed tua morosane uxor, quaeso, est? – va! rogas? –
qui tandem? – taedet mentionis, quae mihi,
ubi domum adveni, adsedi, extemplo savium
dat ieiuna anima. – nil peccat de savio:
ut devomas volt quod foris potaveris. (*Com.* 158-62 R.³ = 151-5 W.)

[14] quid de illo quoque loco in utraque comoedia posito existimari
debeat, manifestum est, cuius loci haec ferme sententia: [15] filia
hominis pauperis in pervigilio vitiata est. [16] ea res clam patrem
fuit, et habebatur pro virgine. [17] ex eo vitio gravida mensibus
exactis parturit. [18] servus bonae frugi, cum pro foribus domus
staret et propinquare partum erili filiae atque omnino vitium esse
oblatum ignoraret, gemitum et ploratum audit puellae in puerperio
enitentis: timet, irascitur, suspicatur, miseretur, dolet. [19] hi omnes
motus eius affectionesque animi in Graeca quidem comoedia
mirabiliter acres et illustres, apud Caecilium autem pigra istaec
omnia et a rerum dignitate atque gratia vacua sunt. [20] post, ubi
idem servus percontando, quod acciderat repperit, has aput
Menandrum voces facit:

[11] And beyond the charm of subject matter and diction, which is by no means the same in the two books, I tend to pay attention to this fact: as for what Menander has written admirably, appropriately and elegantly, Caecilius has not tried to reproduce this, not even where he could, [12] but rather omitted it as if not in the least to be approved and has crammed in some other mime-like stuff and somehow missed that feature of Menander, taken directly from the life of men, simple, true and enjoyable. For this same old husband, talking to another old man, his neighbour, and deprecating the haughtiness of his rich wife, says the following [i.e. in Menander]:

'I have got an heiress who is a witch. Have I not told you this? – No. – We have got a mistress of the house, the fields and indeed of everything[3]. – By Apollo, how troublesome. – Most troublesome. She is a nuisance to everybody, not only to me, far more to my son, to my daughter. – You mention something one cannot fight against. – I know very well.'

[13] Caecilius, however, in this passage, wanted to be amusing rather than be seen as appropriate and fitting to that character with whom he was dealing. For he has spoiled the passage thus:

'But your wife is peevish, tell me please? – Oh, you ask? – How then? – It is disgusting to mention her, who, as soon as I have come home and sat down, immediately gives me a kiss with bad breath. – There is nothing wrong with the kiss: she wishes that you throw up what you have drunk elsewhere.'

[14] What one should think also about this passage used in both comedies is clear, its narrative roughly being as follows: [15] the daughter of a poor man was raped during a religious vigil. [16] This matter happened in secret from the father, and she was considered a virgin. [17] Having become pregnant as a result of this fault, she was giving birth after the months had passed. [18] A good slave, as he was standing in front of the doors of the house and did not know that the delivery of his master's daughter was approaching and generally that a rape had been committed, hears the groans and entreaties of the girl labouring in childbirth: he is in fear, in anger, he suspects, he commiserates, he is sad. [19] All these emotions and passions of his mind are wonderfully vivid and lucid in the Greek comedy, but in Caecilius all this is weak and devoid of gravity and elegance. [20] Later, when the same slave has found out by questioning what had happened, he utters these words in Menander:

'Oh thrice unhappy who, though poor, marries and has children. How foolish is the man who neither has the protection of relatives nor, when he has experienced bad luck as regards common incidents in life, can clothe this with money, but lives an unprotected and miserable life, battered by storms, having a share of all painful things, but no

ὦ τρισκακοδαίμων, ὅστις ὢν πένης γαμεῖ
καὶ παιδοποιεῖθ᾽· ὡς ἀλόγιστός ἐστ᾽ ἀνήρ,
ὃς μήτε φυλακὴν τῶν ἀναγκαίων ἔχει
μήτ᾽ ἂν ἀτυχήσας εἰς τὰ κοινὰ τοῦ βίου
ἐπαμφιέσαι δύναιτο τοῦτο χρήμασιν,
ἀλλ᾽ ἐν ἀκαλύπτῳ καὶ ταλαιπώρῳ βίῳ
χειμαζόμενος ζῇ, τῶν μὲν ἀνιαρῶν ἔχων
τὸ μέρος ἁπάντων, τῶν δ᾽ ἀγαθῶν οὐδὲν μέρος.
ὑπὲρ γὰρ ἑνὸς ἀλγῶν ἅπαντας νουθετῶ. (fr. 298 Kassel-Austin)
[21] ad horum autem sinceritatem veritatemque verborum an adspi-
raverit Caecilius, consideremus. versus sunt hi Caecili trunca quaedam ex Menandro dicentis et consarcinantis verba tragici tumoris:

is demum infortunatust homo,
pauper qui educit in egestatem liberos;
cui fortuna et res nuda est, continuo patet.
nam opulento famam facile occultat factio.

(*Com.* 169-72 R.³ = 163-6 W.)

[22] itaque, ut supra dixi, cum haec Caecilii seorsum lego, neutiquam
videntur ingrata ignavaque, cum autem Graeca comparo et contendo,
non puto Caecilium sequi debuisse, quod assequi nequiret.

D 10. Terence, *Eunuchus* 232-64 (II 2); 771-816 (IV 7)

Terence's (c. 195/4-159 BCE) Eunuchus *('The Eunuch') is thought to have
been the most successful Republican comedy: it earned the playwright an
unprecedented sum in fees, which became inscribed on the title page, and
it was soon presented in a repeat performance (as recorded in ancient
commentaries). This is often put down to the fact that this play, based on
Menander's* Eunouchos, *not only includes the more restrained characters
and serious moral messages typical of Terentian comedy, but also funny
characters and slapstick scenes as they are known from Plautus: Terence
inserted a soldier and a parasite from another Greek play, Menander's* Kolax
*('The Flatterer'), by the technique of Roman playwrights known as
contaminatio and also made use of the device of mistaken identity.
Terence's* Eunuchus *indeed has impressive and entertaining scenes, but the*

(a) Terence, *Eunuchus* 232-64 (II 2)

Gnatho. di inmortales, homini homo quid praestat? stulto intellegens
quid inter est? hoc adeo ex hac re venit in mentem mihi:
conveni hodie adveniens quendam mei loci hinc atque ordinis,
[235] hominem haud inpurum, itidem patria qui abligurrierat bona:

136

share of the good things. For when I grieve for one person, I admonish everybody.'

[21] Whether Caecilius has aspired to the sincerity and truthfulness of these words, let us consider. These are the verses of Caecilius, who says something truncated from Menander and patches together words of tragic bombast:

'This is indeed an unfortunate man, who, being poor, brings up his children to poverty; he for whom fortune and position are obvious is continuously exposed. For in the case of a rich man his people easily hide rumour.'

[22] Therefore, as I have said above, when I read this of Caecilius by itself, it does not at all seem inelegant and spiritless; but when I compare and juxtapose the Greek, I do not believe that Caecilius should have followed what he could not achieve.

---

1 one set of armour was made of bronze and the other one of gold; this alludes to an incident in the Trojan War. 2 this seems to be the sense of the corrupt Greek text. 3 this may be the sense of the corrupt Greek text.

D 10. Terence, *Eunuchus* 232-64 (II 2); 771-816 (IV 7)

impact of this comedy is not only due to farcical characteristics and the activities of the dramatic characters, but also to the ways in which their portrayals slightly diverge from the standard framework and in which clever jokes are employed.

The monologue of the parasite Gnatho at his first appearance, when he introduces himself and his profession, and a later scene in which the soldier Thraso, Gnatho and the 'army' of their servants attempt an attack on the house of the courtesan Thais (who is in the company of the young man Chremes at the time) to confront the soldier's rival and to regain the girl Pamphila illustrate both the typical and the slightly unusual features of this comedy and its dramatic characters.

(a) Terence, *Eunuchus* 232-64 (II 2)

Gnatho. Immortal gods, how does one man excel another? What is the difference between a stupid and an intelligent man? This has come to my mind precisely for this reason: on my way here today, I met someone of my rank and class, [235] not a base man, who in the same way had wasted his paternal fortune: I noticed how he was rough, filthy, sick, beset by rags and

video sentum squalidum aegrum, pannis annisque obsitum. 'oh
quid istuc' inquam 'ornatist?' 'quoniam miser quod habui perdidi, em
quo redactu' sum. omnes noti me atque amici deserunt.'
hic ego illum contempsi prae me: 'quid homo' inquam 'ignavissime?
[240] itan parasti te ut spes nulla relicua in te siet tibi?
simul consilium cum re amisti? viden me ex eodem ortum loco?
qui color nitor vestitu', quae habitudost corporis!
omnia habeo neque quicquam habeo; nil quom est, nil defit tamen.'
'at ego infelix neque ridiculus esse neque plagas pati
[245] possum.' 'quid? tu his rebu' credi' fieri? tota erras via.
olim isti fuit generi quondam quaestus apud saeclum prius:
hoc novomst aucupium; ego adeo hanc primus inveni viam.
est genus hominum qui esse primos se omnium rerum volunt
nec sunt: hos consector; hisce ego non paro me ut rideant,
[250] sed eis ultro adrideo et eorum ingenia admiror simul.
quidquid dicunt laudo; id rursum si negant, laudo id quoque;
negat quis: nego; ait: aio; postremo imperavi egomet mihi
omnia adsentari. is quaestu' nunc est multo uberrimus.'
Parmeno. scitum hercle hominem! hic homines prorsum ex stultis
insanos facit.

[255] **Gn**. dum haec loquimur, interealoci ad macellum ubi advenimus,
concurrunt laeti mi obviam cuppedenarii omnes,
cetarii, lanii, coqui, fartores, piscatores,
quibus et re salva et perdita profueram et prosum saepe:
salutant, ad cenam vocant, adventum gratulantur.
[260] ille ubi miser famelicus videt mi esse tantum honorem et
tam facile victum quaerere, ibi homo coepit me obsecrare
ut sibi liceret discere id de me: sectari iussi,
si potis est, tamquam philosophorum habent disciplinae ex ipsis
vocabula, parasiti ita ut Gnathonici vocentur.

(b) Terence, *Eunuchus* 771-816 (IV 7)

Thraso. hancin ego ut contumeliam tam insignem in me
accipiam, Gnatho?
mori me satiust. Simalio, Donax, Syrisce, sequimini.
primum aedis expugnabo. **Gnatho**. recte. **Thr**. virginem
eripiam. **Gn**. probe.
Thr. male mulcabo ipsam. **Gn**. pulchre. **Thr**. in medium huc
agmen cum vecti, Donax;
[775] tu, Simalio, in sinistrum cornum; tu, Syrisce, in dexterum.
cedo alios: ubi centuriost Sanga et manipulus furum? **Sanga**. eccum
adest.

years. 'Oh', I said, 'what sort of apparel is this?' 'Since I, poor wretch, have
lost what I had, look, to what status I have been reduced. All acquaintances
and friends have deserted me.' I looked down upon him with contempt, in
comparison with me: 'What, you most sluggish man?' I said. [240] 'Have you
arranged your life in such a way that no hope in yourself is left for you? Have
you lost your wits together with your fortune? Do you see me, born of the same
rank? What complexion, what elegance of clothing, what condition of body! I
have got everything, and I have nothing; although there is nothing, nothing
is lacking nevertheless.' 'But I, unhappy as I am, can neither be ridiculous nor
bear a beating.' [245] 'What? Do you think that it is done by these things? You
are entirely on the wrong track. A long time ago, among an earlier generation,
that once was the way of making a living for this type of people: this is a new
way of catching prey; I have indeed been the first to find this way. There is a
type of men who wish to be the first in all things, but are not: I pursue these;
for these I do not arrange that they laugh at me, [250] but I smile at them of
my own accord and at the same time admire their genius. Whatever they say,
I praise it; if they then say the opposite, I praise this too; they say no: I say no;
they say yes: I say yes; in short I have ordered myself to agree with everything.
This way of making a living now is by far the most profitable.'

Parmeno. (*aside*) By Hercules, a smart man! He actually makes insane
men out of stupid ones.

[255] **Gn**. While we were discussing this, in the course of it, as soon as we
had come to the meat market, all confectioners came together happy to see
me, fishmongers, butchers, cooks, poulterers, fishermen, to whom I had been
useful in both good and bad times and often still am: they greeted me, they
invited me to dinner, they congratulated me on my arrival. [260] As soon as
this starving wretch saw that I received such a great honour and earned a
living so easily, there the fellow started to beseech me that he should be
permitted to learn this from me: I ordered him to follow me as a pupil, so
that, if possible, just as the schools of philosophers have their names after
these very men, so parasites may be called 'Gnathonici'.

(b) Terence, *Eunuchus* 771-816 (IV 7)

Thraso. That I should put up with such a great insult against me,
Gnatho? It would be better for me to die. Simalio, Donax, Syriscus [i.e.
his servants], follow me. First I will storm the house.

Gnatho. Right. **Thr**. I will snatch away the girl. **Gn**. Very good.

Thr. I will badly thrash the mistress. **Gn**. Excellent.

Thr. In the middle of this battle line over here with the crowbar,
Donax; [775] you, Simalio, on the left wing; you, Syriscus, on the right
one. Now the others: where is centurion Sanga and the troop of thieves?

Sanga. Look, he is here.

139

Thr. quid ignave? peniculon pugnare, qui istum huc portes,
cogitas?

Sa. egon? imperatoris virtutem noveram et vim militum;
sine sanguine hoc non posse fieri: qui abstergerem volnera?
[780] **Thr**. ubi alii? **Gn**. qui malum "alii"? solu' Sannio servat
domi.

Thr. tu hosce instrue; ego hic ero post principia: inde omnibus
signum dabo.

Gn. illuc est sapere: ut hosce instruxit, ipsu' sibi cavit loco.
Thr. idem hoc iam Pyrru' factitavit. **Chremes**. viden tu, Thais,
quam hic rem agit?

nimirum consilium illud rectumst de occludendis aedibus.
[785] **Thais**. sane quod tibi nunc vir videatur esse hic, nebulo
magnus est:

ne metuas. **Thr**. quid videtur? **Gn**. fundam tibi nunc nimi' vellem
dari,

ut tu illos procul hinc ex occulto caederes: facerent fugam.
Thr. sed eccam Thaidem ipsam video. **Gn**. quam mox inruimus?
Thr. mane:

omnia prius experiri quam armis sapientem decet.
[790] qui scis an quae iubeam sine vi faciat? **Gn**. di vostram
fidem,

quantist sapere! numquam accedo quin abs te abeam doctior.
Thr. Thai', primum hoc mihi responde: quom tibi do istam
virginem,

dixtin hos dies mihi soli dare te? **Th**. quid tum postea?
Thr. rogitas? quae mi ante oculos coram amatorem adduxti
tuom ...

[795] **Th**. quid cum illoc agas? **Thr**. et cum eo clam te subduxti
mihi?

Th. lubuit. **Thr**. Pamphilam ergo huc redde, nisi vi mavis eripi.
Chr. tibi illam reddat aut tu eam tangas, omnium ...? **Gn**. ah
quid agis? tace.

Thr. quid tu tibi vis? ego non tangam meam? **Chr**. tuam autem,
furcifer?

Gn. cave sis: nescis quoi maledicas nunc viro. **Chr**. non tu hinc
abis?

[800] scin tu ut tibi res se habeat? si quicquam hodie hic turbae
coeperis,

faciam ut huius loci dieique meique semper memineris.
Gn. miseret tui me qui hunc tantum hominem facias inimicum
tibi.

Thr. What, you coward? You intend to fight with a sponge, as you are carrying one over here?

Sa. Me? I knew the bravery of the commander and the force of the soldiers; this could not happen without blood: how should I wipe the wounds?

[780] **Thr**. Where are the others?

Gn. What 'others', damn? Sannio on his own guards the house.

Thr. You draw up these; I will be here behind the front lines: from this position I will give the signal to everybody.

Gn. (*aside*) This is being wise: as he has drawn up these, he has guarded himself by this position.

Thr. Pyrrhus[1] already used to do the very same thing[2].

Chremes. (*to Thais*) Do you see, Thais, what action this man is taking? It is certainly the right decision to bolt the door.

[785] **Thais**. (*to Chremes*) Indeed, as for him now seeming a real man to you, he is a great worthless fellow: do not be afraid.

Thr. (*to Gnatho*) What is your advice?

Gn. I would very much wish that a sling was now given to you, so that you could strike those from afar out of hiding: they would take to flight.

Thr. But look, I see Thais herself.

Gn. How soon are we going to attack?

Thr. Wait: it is right for a wise man to try everything first before arms. [790] How do you know that she will not do what I order without force?

Gn. By god, what value has being wise! I never come near you without going away from you the wiser.

Thr. (*to Thais*) Thais, first give me an answer to this: when I gave this girl to you, did you say that you would give those days to me alone?

Th. What then?

Thr. You ask? You who have brought your lover openly before my very eyes ...

[795] **Th**. What is your business with him?

Thr. And with him you have withdrawn yourself from me in secret?

Th. It was my pleasure.

Thr. Then return Pamphila [i.e. the girl] here, if you do not prefer her to be snatched away by force.

Chr. (*to Thraso*) She shall return her to you, or you will touch her, you complete ...?

Gn. (*to Chremes*) Ah, what are you doing? Hold your tongue.

Thr. (*to Chremes*) What do you want? I shall not touch what is mine?

Chr. Yours indeed, rascal?

Gn. (*to Chremes*) Be careful: you do not know what man you are abusing.

Chr. (*to Gnatho*) You are not going away from here? [800] (*to Thraso*)

141

Chr. diminuam ego caput tuum hodie, nisi abis. **Gn**. ain vero,
canis?

sicin agis? **Thr**. quis tu homo es? quid tibi vis? quid cum illa rei
tibist?

[805] **Chr**. scibi': principio eam esse dico liberam. **Thr**. hem.
Chr. civem Atticam. **Thr**. hui.

Chr. meam sororem. **Thr**. os durum. **Chr**. miles, nunc adeo
edico tibi

ne vim facias ullam in illam. Thais, ego eo ad Sophronam
nutricem, ut eam adducam et signa ostendam haec. **Thr**. tun me
prohibeas

meam ne tangam? **Chr**. prohibebo inquam. **Gn**. audin tu? hic
furti se adligat.

[810] **Chr**. sat hoc tibist? **Thr**. idem hoc tu, Thai'? **Th**. quaere
qui respondeat. –

Thr. quid nunc agimu'? **Gn**. quin redeamu': iam haec tibi aderit
supplicans

ultro. **Thr**. credin? **Gn**. immo certe: novi ingenium mulierum:
nolunt ubi velis, ubi nolis cupiunt ultro. **Thr**. bene putas.
Gn. iam dimitto exercitum? **Thr**. ubi vis. **Gn**. Sanga, ita ut fortis
decet

[815] milites, domi focique fac vicissim ut memineris.
Sa. iamdudum animus est in patinis. **Gn**. frugi es. **Thr**. vos me
hac sequimini.

---

1 a king of Epirus in north-west Greece. 2 this is not attested in the historical record. 3 these will identify the girl beyond doubt.

Do you know how the matter stands for you? If you start any kind of trouble here today, I will see to it that you will always remember this place, this day and myself.

Gn. (*to Chremes*) I am sorry for you, who are turning such a great man into your enemy.

Chr. (*to Thraso*) I will dash your head to pieces today, if you do not go away.

Gn. (*to Chremes*) Do you indeed say so, you creature? Are you acting thus?

Thr. (*to Chremes*) Who do you think you are? What do you want for you? What business do you have with her?

[805] **Chr**. You will learn it: first of all I say that she is free.

Thr. Ah.

Chr. An Athenian citizen.

Thr. Oh.

Chr. My sister.

Thr. Harsh impudence.

Chr. Soldier, now I definitely give the order to you that you do not use any force against her. (*to Thais*) Thais, I am going to the nurse Sophrona, so that I fetch her and show her these tokens[3].

Thr. You are preventing me from touching my own girl?

Chr. I say I will prevent you.

Gn. (*to Thraso*) Do you hear? This man shows himself guilty of theft.

[810] **Chr**. Is this enough for you? (*exits*)

Thr. Do you say the same, Thais?

Th. Look for someone who shall answer you. (*exits*)

Thr. (*to Gnatho*) What do we do now?

Gn. Why don't we go back: she will soon be with you as a suppliant of her own accord.

Thr. Do you think so?

Gn. Absolutely. I know the character of women: they do not want when you want; when you do not want, they yearn for it of their own accord.

Thr. Excellent view.

Gn. Do I now dismiss the army?

Thr. When you wish.

Gn. Sanga, as it is right for brave [815] soldiers, see to it that you now call home and hearth to mind.

Sa. My mind has been on the pans for a long time.

Gn. You are excellent.

Thr. (*to his attendants*) You follow me hither. (*they all leave the stage*)

143

D 11. Terence, *Adelphoe* 26-81 (I 1); 81-154 (I 2)

Terence's Adelphoe *('The brothers'), based on Menander's* Adelphoi, *was first performed at the funeral games for L. Aemilius Paullus in 160 BCE, organized by his natural sons. The comedy deals with the question of education, which has been seen as fitting the occasion and has made this play well known in more recent times. The drama features two elderly brothers, Demea and Micio, who each bring up one of Demea's natural sons, Ctesipho and Aeschinus. Demea is presented as a strict father, who keeps his son Ctesipho in the countryside, while Micio, a town-dweller,*

(a) Terence, *Adelphoe* 26-81 (I 1)

Micio. Storax! – non rediit hac nocte a cena Aeschinus
neque servolorum quisquam qui advorsum ierant.
profecto hoc vere dicunt: si absis uspiam
aut ibi si cesses, evenire ea satius est,
[30] quae in te uxor dicit et quae in animo cogitat
irata quam illa quae parentes propitii.
uxor, si cesses, aut te amare cogitat
aut tete amari aut potare atque animo obsequi
et tibi bene esse soli, quom sibi sit male.
[35] ego quia non rediit filius quae cogito et
quibu' nunc sollicitor rebu'! ne aut ille alserit
aut uspiam ceciderit aut praefregerit
aliquid. vah quemquamne hominem in animum instituere aut
parare quod sit carius quam ipsest sibi!
[40] atque ex me hic natu' non est sed ex fratre. is adeo.
dissimili studiost iam inde ab adulescentia:
ego hanc clementem vitam urbanam atque otium
secutu' sum et, quod fortunatum isti putant,
uxorem numquam habui. ille contra haec omnia:
[45] ruri agere vitam; semper parce ac duriter
se habere; uxorem duxit; nati filii
duo; inde ego hunc maiorem adoptavi mihi;
eduxi a parvolo; habui amavi pro meo;
in eo me oblecto, solum id est carum mihi.
[50] ille ut item contra me habeat facio sedulo:
do praetermitto, non necesse habeo omnia
pro meo iure agere; postremo, alii clanculum
patres quae faciunt, quae fert adulescentia,
ea ne me celet consuefeci filium.
[55] nam qui mentiri aut fallere institerit patrem aut
audebit, tanto magis audebit ceteros.

D 11. Terence, *Adelphoe* 26-81 (I 1); 81-154 (I 2)

is more liberal and allows Aeschinus more freedom to enjoy his life. In the course of the play it looks as if Micio's principles are superior, but eventually Demea decides to act more liberally than Micio, so that it is he who ultimately appears successful.

The opening of the play (after the prologue) first shows Micio on his own delivering a monologue and then the two old men in conversation; these scenes introduce the brothers and their contrasting methods for dealing with the young men as the starting point for the plot.

(a) Terence, *Adelphoe* 26-81 (I 1)

Micio. Storax [i.e. one of his slaves]! – Aeschinus has not come back from the dinner party last night, nor any of the slaves who had gone to fetch him. Indeed they say this correctly: if you should be away somewhere or if you should loiter there, this is the better outcome [30] what an angry wife says to you and what she thinks in her mind than what loving parents do. If you should be late, a wife thinks that you either are in love or are being loved or drink and enjoy yourself and are fine on your own while she is feeling bad. [35] In my case, since my son has not come back, what do I think and by what matters am I now upset! I fear that he has caught a cold or has fallen over somewhere or broken something. Oh, that any human resolves upon or acquires what is dearer to him than he himself!

[40] And this young man was not fathered by me, but by my brother. So far, so good. He [i.e. the brother] has been of a dissimilar inclination right from early manhood: I pursued this gentle urban life and leisure, and, what some consider fortunate, I never had a wife. He has been the opposite in all these respects: [45] he spent his life in the country; he always lived parsimoniously and austerely; he led home a wife; two sons were born; of these I adopted the elder one; I brought him up since he was a little boy; I have treated him and loved him like my own; in him I find delight, this is the only thing that is dear to me. [50] I work hard so that he on his part equally has affection for me: I give generously, I overlook, I do not regard it as necessary to do everything on the basis of my authority; in short, what others do in secret from their fathers, what youth brings about, I have accustomed my son not to hide this from me. [55] For he who has set about or will dare to lie to or cheat his father, will dare all the more when dealing with others. I believe it is better to keep children within bounds by respect and generosity rather than by fear.

On this my brother does not agree with me, and it does not please him. [60] He often comes to me, shouting: 'What are you doing, Micio?

pudore et liberalitate liberos
retinere satius esse credo quam metu.
   haec fratri mecum non conveniunt neque placent.
[60] venit ad me saepe clamitans 'quid agi', Micio?
quor perdis adulescentem nobis? quor amat?
quor potat? quor tu his rebu' sumptum suggeris,
vestitu nimio indulges? nimium ineptus es.'
nimium ipse durust praeter aequomque et bonum,
[65] et errat longe mea quidem sententia
qui imperium credat gravius esse aut stabilius
vi quod fit quam illud quod amicitia adiungitur.
mea sic est ratio et sic animum induco meum:
malo coactu' qui suom officium facit,
[70] dum id rescitum iri credit, tantisper cavet;
si sperat fore clam, rursum ad ingenium redit.
ill' quem beneficio adiungas ex animo facit,
studet par referre, praesens absensque idem erit.
hoc patriumst, potiu' consuefacere filium
[75] sua sponte recte facere quam alieno metu:
hoc pater ac dominus interest. hoc qui nequit
fateatur nescire imperare liberis.
   sed estne hic ipsu' de quo agebam? et certe is est.
nescioquid tristem video: credo, iam ut solet
[80] iurgabit. salvom te advenire, Demea,
gaudemus.

(b) Terence, *Adelphoe* 81-154 (I 2)

   Demea. ehem opportune: te ipsum quaerito.
Micio. quid tristis es? **De**. rogas me ubi nobis Aeschinus
siet? quid tristis ego sum? **Mi**. dixin hoc fore?
quid fecit? **De**. quid ille fecerit? quem neque pudet
[85] quicquam nec metuit quemquam neque legem putat
tenere se ullam. nam illa quae antehac facta sunt
omitto: modo quid dissignavit? **Mi**. quidnam id est?
De. fores effregit atque in aedis inruit
alienas; ipsum dominum atque omnem familiam
[90] mulcavit usque ad mortem; eripuit mulierem
quam amabat: clamant omnes indignissume
factum esse. hoc advenienti quot mihi, Micio,
dixere! in orest omni populo. denique,
si conferendum exemplumst, non fratrem videt
[95] rei dare operam, ruri esse parcum ac sobrium?

146

Why do you destroy our young man? Why does he have love affairs? Why does he drink? Why do you bankroll these things and allow him so much clothing? You are too stupid.' He himself is too harsh beyond what is just and good, [65] and he errs gravely, in my opinion at any rate, he who believes that authority that is achieved by force is stronger and steadier than that which is created by friendship. This is my argument, and thus do I firmly believe: he who does his duty forced by punishment, [70] is cautious as long as he believes that this might be found out; if he hopes that he will remain in secret, he returns again to his inclination. He whom you attach to yourself by kindness acts from the heart, is eager to repay in kind and will be the same, present or absent. This is the duty of a father to accustom his son [75] to acting rightly out of his own accord rather than out of fear for others: this is the difference between a father and a master. He who cannot do this shall admit that he does not know how to manage children.

(*seeing Demea approaching*) But isn't this the very man I was talking about? And certainly it is him. I see him somewhat gloomy: I suppose, as he always does, [80] he will quarrel. (*to Demea*) We are glad that you have arrived all right, Demea.

(b) Terence, *Adelphoe* 81-154 (I 2)

Demea. Oh, how opportunely: I have been looking precisely for you.

Micio. Why are you gloomy?

De. You ask me when we have got Aeschinus? Why am I gloomy?

Mi. (*aside*) Didn't I say that this was going to happen? (*to Demea*) What has he done?

De. What he has done? He who is not ashamed of [85] anything, does not fear anybody and does not believe that he is governed by any law. For I pass over those things that have been done earlier: what has he committed just now?

Mi. What is it then?

De. He has broken a door and forced his way into someone else's house; he has [90] beaten the master himself and the whole household virtually to death; he has snatched away the woman whom he was in love with: everyone declares that this was done in the most disgraceful manner. How many people, Micio, have mentioned this to me as I was coming into town! It is on the lips

nullum huiu' simile factum. haec quom illi, Micio,
  dico, tibi dico: tu illum corrumpi sinis.
Mi. homine imperito numquam quicquam iniustiust,
qui nisi quod ipse fecit nil rectum putat.
[100] **De**. quorsum istuc? **Mi**. quia tu, Demea, haec male iudicas.
non est flagitium, mihi crede, adulescentulum
scortari neque potare: non est; neque fores
effringere. haec si neque ego neque tu fecimus,
non siit egestas facere nos. tu nunc tibi
[105] id laudi duci' quod tum fecisti inopia?
iniuriumst; nam si esset unde id fieret,
faceremus. et tu illum tuom, si esses homo,
sineres nunc facere dum per aetatem decet
potius quam, ubi te exspectatum eiecisset foras,
[110] alieniore aetate post faceret tamen.
De. pro Iuppiter, tu homo adigi' me ad insaniam!
non est flagitium facere haec adulescentulum? **Mi**. ah
ausculta, ne me optundas de hac re saepius:
tuom filium dedisti adoptandum mihi;
[115] is meus est factu': siquid peccat, Demea,
mihi peccat; ego illi maxumam partem fero.
opsonat potat, olet unguenta: de meo;
amat: dabitur a me argentum dum erit commodum;
ubi non erit fortasse excludetur foras.
[120] fores effregit: restituentur; discidit
vestem: resarcietur; et – dis gratia –
e<s>t unde haec fiant, et adhuc non molesta sunt.
postremo aut desine aut cedo quemvis arbitrum:
te plura in hac re peccare ostendam. **De**. ei mihi,
[125] pater esse disce ab illis qui vere sciunt.
Mi. natura tu illi pater es, consiliis ego.
De. tun consulis quicquam? **Mi**. ah, si pergis, abiero.
De. sicin agis? **Mi**. an ego totiens de eadem re audiam?
De. curaest mihi. **Mi**. et mihi curaest. uerum, Demea,
[130] curemus aequam uterque partem: tu alterum,
ego item alterum; nam ambos curare propemodum
reposcere illumst quem dedisti. **De**. ah Micio!
Mi. mihi sic videtur. **De**. quid istic? tibi si istuc placet,
profundat, perdat, pereat; nil ad me attinet.
[135] iam si uerbum unum posthac ... **Mi**. rursum, Demea,
irascere? **De**. an non credi'? repeto quem dedi?
aegrest; alienu' non sum; si obsto ... em desino.
unum vis curem: curo; et est dis gratia,

148

of the entire populace. Finally, if an example is needed for comparison, does he not see that his brother [95] devotes himself to work and lives in the countryside, parsimonious and sober? No action similar to this. When I say this about him, Micio, I am saying this about you: you allow him to be misled.

Mi. There is nothing more unreasonable than a man without experience, who considers right only what he himself has done.

[100] **De**. What is this leading up to?

Mi. Because you, Demea, are making a bad judgement in this. It is not a disgraceful act for young men, believe me, to have love affairs or to drink: it really is not; nor to break a door. If neither I nor you have done this, poverty did not allow us to do it. Do you now [105] count as laudable what you did not do then out of poverty? This is wrong; for if there had been any means that enabled it, we would have done it. And if you were a human being, you would allow your son to do it now as long as it is appropriate due to his age, rather than, as soon as he had thrown you out of the house as expected [i.e. after your death], [110] have him do it all the same later at a more inappropriate age.

De. By Jupiter, you, man, are driving me to insanity! It is not a disgraceful act for young men to do this?

Mi. Ah, listen, do not batter me about this matter again and again: you gave me your son to adopt; [115] he has become mine: if he does anything wrong, Demea, this wrongdoing concerns me; I bear the greatest share for him. He feasts, he drinks, he smells of perfume: out of my pocket; he has a love affair: money will be given by me as long as it will suit me; when there will be none, he will be kept out of doors. [120] He has broken a door: it will be replaced; he has torn a garment: it will be mended; and – thanks to the gods – there are funds from which this can be done, and so far it has not been troublesome. Finally, either stop or suggest an arbitrator of your choice: I will show that in this matter you are the greater sinner.

De. O dear, [125] learn to be a father from those who really know it.

Mi. You are his father by nature, I by counsel.

De. You counsel anything?

Mi. Ah, if you continue, I will go away.

De. You are behaving in such a way?

Mi. Or will I hear about the same matter so often?

De. I am concerned for him.

Mi. I too am concerned for him. But, Demea, [130] let either of us take an equal share of concern: you for one of them, and I equally for the other one; for to be concerned for both is almost demanding back him whom you have given to me.

De. Ah, Micio!

Mi. Thus it seems right to me.

De. What then? If this pleases you, let him squander, waste, pine away;

149

quom ita ut volo est. iste tuos ipse sentiet
[140] posteriu' ... nolo in illum graviu' dicere. –
Mi. nec nil neque omnia haec sunt quae dicit: tamen
non nil molesta haec sunt mihi; sed ostendere
me aegre pati illi nolui. nam itast homo:
quom placo, advorsor sedulo et deterreo;
[145] tamen vix humane patitur; verum si augeam
aut etiam adiutor si<e>m eius iracundiae,
insaniam profecto cum illo. etsi Aeschinus
non nullam in hac re nobis facit iniuriam.
quam hic non amavit meretricem? aut quoi non dedit
[150] aliquid? postremo nuper (credo iam omnium
taedebat) dixit velle uxorem ducere.
sperabam iam defervisse adulescentiam:
gaudebam. ecce autem de integro! nisi, quidquid est,
volo scire atque hominem convenire, si apud forumst.

D 12. Afranius, *Divortium* (all fragments)

Afranius (fl. c. 160-120 BCE) wrote togatae, light dramas set in a Roman environment, soon after Terence. Togatae are similar to palliatae in terms of dramatic characters, plots and atmosphere, but, in addition to the setting, they differ by being somewhat more serious and more down to earth and by focusing on 'more normal' love affairs and interhuman relationships within the family. The largest number of extant togata fragments comes from Afranius, but no play has been preserved in its entirety.

Afranius' Divortium ('Divorce') seems to be a rather typical example of

      qui conere noctu clanculum
rus ire, dotem ne retro mittas, vafer,
honeste ut latites et nos ludas diutius (*Tog.* 47-9 R.³)

cum testamento patria partisset bona (*Tog.* 50 R.³)

quod vult diserte pactum aut dictum (*Tog.* 51 R.³)

o dignum facinus! adulescentis optumas
bene convenientes, <bene> concordes cum viris
repente viduas factas spurcitia patris. (*Tog.* 52-4 R.³)

it does not concern me. [135] But if only one word later on ...

Mi. Are you, Demea, getting angry again?

De. Don't you believe me? I demand back him whom I have given to you? This is hard; I am not unrelated; if I am in your way, ... well, I will stop. You would like me to be concerned for one: I am concerned; and I am grateful to the gods that he is as I want him to be. This one of yours will realize [140] later ... I do not wish to say anything too harsh against him. (*exits*)

Mi. Neither is this nothing nor everything that he says: nevertheless, this is in no way not annoying to me; but I did not wish to show him that I was bearing it with difficulty. For he is a man like this: when I am calming him down, I work hard to oppose and discourage him; [145] nevertheless he reacts in hardly human fashion; but if I supported it or even functioned as an assistant to his irascibility, I would indeed be insane with him. All the same Aeschinus has done us some injustice in this matter. Which courtesan has he not had a love affair with? Or to whom has he not given [150] something? Finally, he has recently said (I believe he was fed up with them all) that he wished to take a wife home. I hoped that the passion of youth had already boiled down: I was delighted. But look, all over again! Well, whatever it is, I want to know it and to find the man, if he is near the Forum. (*exits*)

D 12. Afranius, *Divortium* (all fragments)

its dramatic genre: the extant fragments suggest that it deals with an unhappy relationship between a husband and a wife, in which the woman's parents somehow play a role; the play alludes to both the emotional and the practical, juridical consequences of breaking up the marriage, but a happy ending with the couple reunited is likely. Since details of the plot are unclear, no possible speakers have been assigned to the preserved fragments; but their content on its own conveys an idea of the individuals involved and the topics treated.

you, who try to go to the countryside in secret at night, so that you do not send back the dowry, you cunning person, so that you hide honestly and continue to fool us

when he had divided the paternal fortune in his will

what he wants to be clearly arranged or said

O worthy deed! The best young ladies, in perfect harmony and well unanimous with their husbands, have suddenly been made widows by the outrageous behaviour of their father.

151

letiferum genus
cognationes morborum cognomines (*Tog.* 55-6 R.[3])

mulier, novercae nomen huc adde impium,
spurca gingiuast, gannit, hau dici potest (*Tog.* 57-8 R.[3])

quam perspicace, quam benigne, quam cito,
quam blande, quam materno visast pectore (*Tog.* 59-60 R.[3])

vigilans ac sollers, sicca sana sobria:
virosa non sum, et si sum, non desunt mihi
qui ultro dent: aetas integra est, formae satis. (*Tog.* 61-3 R.[3])

et ponito! avorruncent cum syrma simul (*Tog.* 64 R.[3])

disperii, perturbata sum, iam flaccet fortitudo (*Tog.* 65 R.[3])

o diem scelerosum, indignum (*Tog.* 66 R.[3])

immo olli mitem faxo faciant fustibus (*Tog.* 67 R.[3])

<clam> nobis dictes, quaeso, ne ille indaudiat (*Tog.* 68 R.[3])

---

1 presumably referring to elements of tragedy in a light drama.

D 13. Decimus Laberius and Publilius Syrus (Macrobius, *Saturnalia* 2.7.1-10)

In addition to Greek-style tragedy and comedy as well as their Roman counterparts, further dramatic genres emerged in literary form towards the end of the Republican period. These included mimes, written by Decimus Laberius and Publilius Syrus in the mid-first century BCE. Ancient writers tend to look down on mimes and to regard them as low, crude and vulgar. Nevertheless, mimes could have serious and noteworthy well-phrased content and feature topical political comment.

The most famous incident in the history of the mime is a display of the two main mime writers before the dictator Caesar, which is described most extensively in the late-antique author Macrobius: Laberius, a poet of equestrian status, was forced by Caesar to appear on stage in his own

a death-bringing type, a family of illnesses with the same name

a woman, add to this the impious name of stepmother, she has got filthy gums, she pesters, it cannot be described

how acutely, how kindly, how quickly, how caressingly, how she is seen to have the heart of a mother

I am vigilant and skilful, vigorous, sane, sober; I am not longing after men, and if I am, I do not lack men who present themselves out of their own accord; my age is fresh, and my appearance is sufficiently beautiful.

And put it down! The gods may avert it together with the tragic cloak[1].

I am undone, I am disturbed; my courage is already faint.

o abominable and unworthy day

Indeed I will see to it that they make him mellow by cudgels.

If you would tell us secretly, I pray, so that he will not hear it.

D 13. Decimus Laberius and Publilius Syrus (Macrobius, *Saturnalia* 2.7.1-10)

mimes, jeopardizing his social position at the age of 60; Laberius obeyed and reacted with lines including obvious comments on the present situation; Caesar then turned his support to Publilius Syrus. This mime writer challenged all contemporary poets writing for the stage to a poetic contest, in which he defeated them all, including Laberius. Thereupon Caesar awarded Publilius Syrus the prize and Laberius the equestrian ring and the fortune required for the equestrian property qualification (thus reaffirming his social status). The verses spoken by Laberius at his initial appearance on stage constitute the longest consecutive piece extant from the Roman mime and illustrate its potential for political and topical application. Macrobius' narrative provides the necessary context.

[1] sed quia et paulo ante Aurelius Symmachus et ego nunc Laberii fecimus mentionem, si aliqua huius atque Publilii dicta referemus, videbimur et adhibendi convivio mimos vitasse lasciviam et tamen celebritatem quam, cum adsunt, illi excitare pollicentur, imitari. [2] Laberium asperae libertatis equitem Romanum Caesar quingentis milibus invitavit ut prodiret in scaenam et ipse ageret mimos quos scriptitabat. sed potestas non solum si invitet sed et si supplicet cogit, unde se et Laberius a Caesare coactum in prologo testatur his versibus:
[3] 'Necessitas, cuius cursus transversi impetum
voluerunt multi effugere, pauci potuerunt,
{100} quo me detrusti paene extremis sensibus!
quem nulla ambitio, nulla umquam largitio,
nullus timor, vis nulla, nulla auctoritas
movere potuit in iuventa de statu:
ecce in senecta ut facile labefecit loco
{105} viri excellentis mente clemente edita
summissa placide blandiloquens oratio!
etenim ipsi di negare cui nihil potuerunt,
hominem me denegare quis posset pati?
ego bis tricenis annis actis sine nota
{110} eques Romanus e Lare egressus meo
domum revertar mimus. nimirum hoc die
uno plus vixi mihi quam vivendum fuit.
Fortuna, inmoderata in bono aeque atque in malo,
si tibi erat libitum litterarum laudibus
{115} florens cacumen nostrae famae frangere,
cur cum vigebam membris praeviridantibus,
satis facere populo et tali cum poteram viro,
non me flexibilem concurvasti ut carperes?
nuncine me deicis? quo? quid ad scaenam adfero?
{120} decorem formae an dignitatem corporis,
animi virtutem an vocis iucundae sonum?
ut hedera serpens vires arboreas necat,
ita me vetustas amplexu annorum enecat:
sepulcri similis nil nisi nomen retineo.' (*Mim.* 98-124 R.³)
[4] in ipsa quoque actione subinde se, qua poterat, ulciscebatur, inducto habitu Syri, qui velut flagris caesus praeripientique se similis exclamabat: 'porro, Quirites, libertatem perdimus' (*Mim.* 125 R.³); et paulo post adiecit: 'necesse est multos timeat quem multi timent' (*Mim.* 126 R.³). [5] quo dicto universitas populi ad solum Caesarem oculos et ora convertit, notantes impotentiam eius hac dicacitate lapidatam. ob haec in Publilium vertit favorem.
[6] is Publilius natione Syrus cum puer ad patronum domini esset

[1] But since both Aurelius Symmachus a little earlier and I¹ just now have mentioned Laberius [i.e. Decimus Laberius], if we are quoting some utterances of his and of Publilius [i.e. Publilius Syrus], we will seem both to have avoided the irresponsibility of introducing mimes at a dinner party and still to imitate the festival atmosphere that they promise to arouse when they are present. [2] Caesar invited Laberius, a Roman equestrian of fiercely free speech, for a fee of 500,000 sesterces, to appear on stage and act himself the mimes that he was accustomed to writing. But power exerts force, not only when it invites, but also when it pleads; hence, Laberius also provides evidence of the fact that he was forced by Caesar, in a prologue with the following verses:

[3] 'Necessity – many have wished to flee from the onslaught of your opposing course, but few were able to – {100} where have you thrust me down, almost at the end of my senses! Whom no canvassing, no bribery, no fear, no force, no authority could ever move from my position in my youth: look, in old age how easily {105} the flattering speech of an excellent man, delivered with mild mind and uttered calmly, has shaken me from my place! For who could bear that I, a human being, deny anything to him to whom the gods themselves have not been able to deny anything? Having lived twice thirty years without censorial mark, {110} I have left my home as a Roman equestrian and shall return home as a mime actor. Surely, on this day I have lived one day longer than I should have lived. Fortune, immoderate in good equally as in evil, if you wished to {115} break the height of our fame, flourishing through renown in literature, why, when I was thriving with very vigorous limbs, when I could satisfy the people and such a man, did you not bend me then when I was flexible so that you could strike me down? Are you hurling me down now? For what purpose? What can I bring to the stage? {120} Elegance of appearance or dignity of body, the powers of the mind or the sound of a sweet voice? Just as twining ivy kills strong trees, thus does old age kill me by an embrace of years: similar to a tomb, I retain nothing but the name.'

[4] Even in the performance itself that followed he constantly took his revenge where he could, dressed as a Syrian, who, as if beaten by whips and like one trying to escape, exclaimed: 'Now, Men of Rome, we are losing our liberty.' And a little later he added: 'It is necessary that he whom many fear fears many.' [5] When this had been said, the entire populace turned their eyes and faces to Caesar alone, recognizing that his despotism had received a blow by this scathing remark. That is why he [i.e. Caesar] shifted his support to Publilius.

[6] This Publilius, a Syrian national, had been brought to his master's patron as a boy and then won his favour no less by his wit and talent than by his appearance. For when he [i.e. the patron] had happened to see a

adductus, promeruit eum non minus salibus et ingenio quam forma. nam forte cum ille servum suum hydropicum iacentem in area vidisset increpuissetque quid in sole faceret respondit: 'aquam calefacit'. ioculari deinde super cena exorta quaestione quodnam esset molestum otium, aliud alio opinante, ille 'podagrici pedes' dixit. [7] ob haec et alia manu missus et maiore cura eruditus, cum mimos componeret ingentique adsensu in Italiae oppidis agere coepisset, productus Romae per Caesaris ludos, omnes qui tunc scripta et operas suas in scaenam locaverant provocavit ut singuli secum posita in vicem materia pro tempore contenderent. nec ullo recusante superavit omnes, in quis et Laberium. [8] unde Caesar adridens hoc modo pronuntiavit: 'favente tibi me victus es, Laberi, a Syro'; statimque Publilio palmam et Laberio anulum aureum cum quingentis sestertiis dedit. tunc Publilius ad Laberium recedentem ait: 'quicum contendisti scriptor, hunc spectator subleva'. [9] sed et Laberius sequenti statim commissione mimo novo interiecit hos versus:

'non possunt primi esse omnes omni in tempore.
summum ad gradum cum claritatis veneris,
consistes aegre, et citius quam ascendas cades.
cecidi ego, cadet qui sequitur: laus est publica' (*Mim.* 127-30 R.³).

[10] Publilii autem sententiae feruntur lepidae et ad communem usum accommodatissimae, ex quibus has fere memini singulis versibus circumscriptas:

'beneficium dando accepit qui digno dedit.'
'feras, non culpes quod mutari non potest.'
'cui plus licet quam par est, plus vult quam licet.'
'comes facundus in via pro vehiculo est.'
'frugalitas miseria est rumoris boni.'
'heredis fletus sub persona risus est.'
'furor fit laesa saepius patientia.'
'improbe Neptunum accusat, qui iterum naufragium facit.'
'nimium altercando veritas amittitur.'
'pars benefici est quod petitur si cito neges.'
'ita amicum habeas, posse ut fieri hunc inimicum putes.'
'veterem ferendo iniuriam invites novam.'
'numquam periclum sine periclo vincitur.'
(*Sent.* 55; 176; 106; 104; 193; 221; 178; 264; 416; 469; 245; 645; 383 R.²)

---

1 Avienus, the speaker; both he and Aurelius Symmachus are interlocutors in the dialogue. 2 i.e. therefore liable to change.

---

slave of his, suffering from dropsy, lying in the courtyard and had reproached him, asking what he was doing in the sun, he [i.e. Publilius Syrus] answered: 'he is heating water'. On another occasion, when the humorous question had arisen over dinner what troublesome idleness was, each one having a different opinion, he said: 'feet suffering from gout'. [7] Because of this and other things he was freed and educated with greater care; when he was composing mimes and had begun to produce them in the towns of Italy to great acclaim, he was brought forth in Rome during the games of Caesar, and he challenged all those who had then entered contractual arrangements to give their scripts and performance activities to the stage to compete with him, one on one, with themes being proposed in turns in line with the occasion. And when no one refused, he surpassed all, including also Laberius. [8] Whereupon, smiling, Caesar declared the following: 'Although I favoured you, you, Laberius, have been defeated by Syrus.' And immediately he gave Publilius the victory palm and Laberius the golden ring with 500,000 sesterces. Then Publilius said to Laberius, as he was withdrawing: 'Him with whom you have competed as a writer, support now as a spectator.' [9] But Laberius too inserted these verses into a new mime in a contest that followed immediately:

'All cannot be the first at all times. When you have reached the highest step of fame, you will remain there with difficulty, and you will fall more quickly than you could climb. I have fallen; he who follows will fall: praise is a common good[2].'

[10] And sententious statements by Publilius are in everyone's mouth, witty and very appropriate for general use; out of those I happen to remember the following ones, contained in single verses:

'He who gives to a worthy person receives a benefit by giving.'
'Endure and do not blame what cannot be changed.'
'He to whom is granted more than is right wants more than is allowed.'
'A good companion on a journey is like a vehicle.'
'Sobriety is the misfortune of good report.'
'The tears of an heir are laughter behind a mask.'
'Fury arises when patience has been hurt too frequently.'
'He who is shipwrecked for a second time accuses Neptune unjustly.'
'By too much arguing truth is lost.'
'It is somewhat of a benefit if you deny quickly what is requested.'
'Treat a friend in such a way that you bear in mind that he might become an enemy.'
'By putting up with an old wrong your may invite a new one.'
'Never is danger overcome without danger.'

D 14. Seneca, *Medea* 150-78; 893-977

After the pieces of Ennius, Pacuvius and Accius (cf. D 2; 3; 5) the popularity of the Medea story continued among dramatists; plays of this title are attested for several Roman playwrights whose writings have not been preserved. The next extant Medea play and the only classical Latin Medea drama surviving in full is the tragedy by Seneca (c. 1 BCE-65 CE).

When Seneca wrote his dramas in the early imperial period, conditions in the theatre as well as political and social circumstances had changed since the time of the Republican dramatists. It is unclear whether Seneca intended his plays to be performed in full in big theatres. Modern stagings have shown that his dramas can be performed; yet they differ in various ways from what can be inferred for Republican plays. For instance, the formal structure in Seneca is closer to Greek tragedies in that he uses a

(a) Seneca, *Medea* 150-78 (dialogue between Medea and Nutrix)

[150] **Nutrix**. sile, obsecro, questusque secreto abditos
manda dolori. gravia quisquis vulnera
patiente et aequo mutus animo pertulit,
referre potuit: ira quae tegitur nocet;
professa perdunt odia vindictae locum.
[155] **Medea**. levis est dolor, qui capere consilium potest
et clepere sese: magna non latitant mala.
libet ire contra. **Nut**. siste furialem impetum,
alumna: vix te tacita defendit quies.
Med. fortuna fortes metuit, ignavos premit.
[160] **Nut**. tunc est probanda, si locum virtus habet.
Med. numquam potest non esse virtuti locus.
Nut. spes nulla rebus monstrat adflictis viam.
Med. qui nil potest sperare, desperet nihil.
Nut. abiere Colchi, coniugis nulla est fides
[165] nihilque superest opibus e tantis tibi.
Med. Medea superest: hic mare et terras vides
ferrumque et ignes et deos et fulmina.
Nut. rex est timendus. **Med**. rex meus fuerat pater.
Nut. non metuis arma? **Med**. sint licet terra edita.
[170] **Nut**. moriere. **Med**. cupio. **Nut**. profuge. **Med**. paenituit fugae.
Nut. Medea – **Med**. fiam. **Nut**. mater es. **Med**. cui sim vide.
Nut. profugere dubitas? **Med**. fugiam, at ulciscar prius.
Nut. vindex sequetur. **Med**. forsan inveniam moras.
Nut. compesce verba, parce iam, demens, minis
[175] animosque minue: tempori aptari decet.

158

D 14. Seneca, *Medea* 150-78; 893-977

more regular form of the iambic metre and punctuates the action by choral odes, while the chorus members are not directly involved in the action.

Seneca's Medea *covers the same section of the myth as Euripides' and Ennius' versions: in Corinth Medea is confronted with the infidelity of her husband Jason and plans to take revenge on him, his new bride Creusa and Creon, his bride's father, before going into exile. Like other characters in Seneca's tragedies, Medea is subject to her emotions and passions and is well aware of what is expected of her as 'Medea'; she is both intent on taking revenge and cannot bring herself to kill her children straightaway; she is both a human character and has supernatural, magical powers. Her monologues and her dialogues with her nurse reveal the psychological processes Medea undergoes.*

(a) Seneca, *Medea* 150-78 (dialogue between Medea and her Nurse)

[150] **Nurse**. Be silent, I beg you, and entrust your complaints to hidden grief in secret. Whoever bears severe wounds silently and with a patient and composed mind is able to repay them: anger that is covered causes harm; hatred that is confessed destroys the opportunity for revenge.

[155] **Medea**. The pain is light that can take counsel and hide itself: great hardships do not remain hidden. My wish is to attack.

Nur. Check your furious impulse, child: silently keeping quiet hardly protects you.

Med. Fortune fears the brave and overwhelms cowards.

[160] **Nur**. Bravery is to be approved only when it is in place.

Med. There can never be no place for bravery.

Nur. No hope shows a way for desperate circumstances.

Med. He who can hope for nothing would despair of nothing.

Nur. The Colchians have gone[1]; there is no faith in the husband [i.e. Jason], [165] and nothing is left for you out of your great riches.

Med. Medea is left: here you see sea and land, steel and fire, gods and thunderbolts.

Nur. The king [i.e. Creon] must be feared.

Med. My father [i.e. Aeetes] was a king.

Nur. You do not fear weapons?

Med. Not even if they were brought forth from the earth[2].

[170] **Nur**. You will die.

Med. I long to.

Nur. Flee.

Med. Flight displeases me.

159

Med. fortuna opes auferre, non animum potest.
sed cuius ictu regius cardo strepit?
ipse est Pelasgo tumidus imperio Creo.

---

1 i.e. there is no longer support from her fellow citizens in her native land.
2 alludes to the earth-born warriors in Colchis.

(b) Seneca, *Medea* 893-977 (monologue of Medea)

Medea. egone ut recedam? si profugissem prius,
ad hoc redirem. nuptias specto novas.
[895] quid, anime, cessas? sequere felicem impetum.
pars ultionis ista, qua gaudes, quota est!
amas adhuc, furiose, si satis est tibi
caelebs Iason. quaere poenarum genus
haut usitatum iamque sic temet para:
[900] fas omne cedat, abeat expulsus pudor;
vindicta levis est quam ferunt purae manus.
incumbe in iras teque languentem excita
penitusque veteres pectore ex imo impetus
violentus hauri. quidquid admissum est adhuc,
[905] pietas vocetur. hoc age! en faxo sciant
quam levia fuerint quamque vulgaris notae
quae commodavi scelera. prolusit dolor
per ista noster: quid manus poterant rudes
audere magnum, quid puellaris furor?
[910] Medea nunc sum; crevit ingenium malis:
iuvat, iuvat rapuisse fraternum caput,
artus iuvat secuisse et arcano patrem
spoliasse sacro, iuvat in exitium senis
armasse natas. quaere materiam, dolor:
[915] ad omne facinus non rudem dextram afferes.
quo te igitur, ira, mittis, aut quae perfido
intendis hosti tela? nescioquid ferox

Nur. Medea –
Med. I shall become.
Nur. You are a mother.
Med. See for whom.
Nur. You hesitate to flee?
Med. I will flee, but I will take revenge first.
Nur. An avenger will pursue you.
Med. Perhaps I shall find some kind of delay.
Nur. Hold your words in check; refrain from threats now, you mad woman, [175] and subdue your spirits: it is right to adapt to circumstances.
Med. Fortune can take away riches, but not the spirit. But by whose pushing does the hinge of the royal door creak? It is he himself, Creon, swollen with Pelasgian power.

(b) Seneca, *Medea* 893-977 (monologue of Medea)

Medea. I should withdraw? If I had fled earlier, I would come back for this. I am watching a new marriage[1]. [895] Why do you hesitate, my spirit? Follow up the successful attack. How small a part of your revenge is this about which you rejoice! You are still in love, mad spirit, if Jason without a wife is enough for you. Look for a type of punishment that is unprecedented and make yourself ready now in this way: [900] all moral obligations shall withdraw, feelings of shame shall be thrust out and go away; revenge is light when pure hands carry it out. Devote yourself to your anger and rouse yourself who are languishing and draw the accustomed violent impulse from deep within your breast. Whatever has been committed so far, [905] this shall be called piety. Come on! Look, I will make them realize how light and of what a common type the crimes have been that I have committed as a favour to others. My pain has done some practising with those: what great thing could unskilled hands dare to do, what the madness of a girl?

[910] Now I am Medea; my inborn talent has grown with evils: it is a delight, it is a delight to have torn off my brother's head, it is a delight to have cut up his limbs and to have robbed my father of a secret relic, it is a delight to have armed the daughters for the killing of the old man [i.e. Pelias]. Look for a field of action, my pain: [915] you will bring a right hand not untrained to every deed.

Where are you then directing yourself, my anger, or what missiles are you aiming at the treacherous enemy? The mind within me has decided on something terrible and does not yet dare to admit it to itself. I, a fool,

decrevit animus intus et nondum sibi
audet fateri. stulta properavi nimis:
[920] ex paelice utinam liberos hostis meus
aliquos haberet – quidquid ex illo tuum est,
Creusa peperit. placuit hoc poenae genus,
meritoque placuit: ultimum magno scelus
animo parandum est: liberi quondam mei,
[925] vos pro paternis sceleribus poenas date.

   cor pepulit horror, membra torpescunt gelu
pectusque tremuit. ira discessit loco
materque tota coniuge expulsa redit.
egone ut meorum liberum ac prolis meae
[930] fundam cruorem? melius, a, demens furor!
incognitum istud facinus ac dirum nefas
a me quoque absit; quod scelus miseri luent?

   scelus est Iason genitor et maius scelus
Medea mater – occidant, non sunt mei;
[935] pereant, mei sunt. crimine et culpa carent,
sunt innocentes, fateor: et frater fuit.
quid, anime, titubas? ora quid lacrimae rigant
variamque nunc huc ira, nunc illuc amor
diducit? anceps aestus incertam rapit;
[940] ut saeva rapidi bella cum venti gerunt,
utrimque fluctus maria discordes agunt
dubiumque fervet pelagus, haut aliter meum
cor fluctuatur: ira pietatem fugat
iramque pietas – cede pietati, dolor.

   [945] huc, cara proles, unicum afflictae domus
solamen, huc vos ferte et infusos mihi
coniungite artus. habeat incolumes pater,
dum et mater habeat – urguet exilium ac fuga:
iam iam meo rapientur avulsi e sinu,
[950] flentes, gementes – osculis pereant patris,
periere matris. rursus increscit dolor
et fervet odium, repetit invitam manum
antiqua Erinys – ira, qua ducis, sequor.
utinam superbae turba Tantalidos meo
[955] exisset utero bisque septenos parens
natos tulissem! sterilis in poenas fui –
fratri patrique quod sat est, peperi duos.
quonam ista tendit turba Furiarum impotens?
quem quaerit aut quo flammeos ictus parat,
[960] aut cui cruentas agmen infernum faces

162

have been too hasty: [920] if only my enemy had some children from the mistress – whatever you have from him, Creusa is the mother. This kind of punishment pleases, and rightly it pleases: the ultimate crime must be prepared with great heart: children, once mine, [925] pay a penalty for your father's crimes.

Shudders have shaken my heart, my limbs are growing stiff with cold, and my breast has trembled. Anger has retreated from its post, and the mother has returned completely after the wife has been driven out. I should shed the blood of my children [930] and my offspring? Better, a, mad fury, for this unknown misdeed and dire crime to be far even from me; what crime will the poor ones atone?

The crime is the father Jason, and a greater crime is the mother Medea – let them die, they are not mine; [935] let them perish, they are mine. They are free from crime and guilt, they are innocent, I admit it: and so was my brother. Why, my spirit, are you vacillating? Why are tears watering my cheeks, and why does now anger in this direction and now love in that direction tear me apart as I waver? An undecided tide hurries me along in my uncertainty; [940] just as, when violent winds wage fierce wars, the billows in disharmony drive the sea in two directions and the ocean rages in uncertainty, not differently does my heart fluctuate: anger puts piety to flight, and piety anger – surrender to piety, my pain.

[945] Here, dear offspring, only consolation of a ruined house, move here and embrace me with your arms around me. Let your father have you unharmed, as long as your mother has you too – exile and flight beset me: soon, soon they will be snatched away and removed from my bosom, [950] crying, groaning – let them be lost to the kisses of their father, they are lost to those of their mother.

Pain increases again and hatred boils up, the old Erinys² demands again my unwilling hand – anger, where you lead, I follow. If only the band of Tantalus' proud daughter [955] had left my womb and I had produced twice seven children as a parent³! I have been infertile as regards punishment – what is enough for a brother and a father: I have given birth to two. Where is this unbridled group of Furies heading? Whom is it looking for or whereto does it prepare fiery blows, [960] or against whom does the infernal crowd direct its bloody torches? An immense snake hisses and twists with a whip cracking. Whom is Megaera⁴ seeking with a menacing club? Whose hazy shade is coming, with limbs scattered? It is my brother, he seeks revenge: [965] we will provide it, but all of us. Drive the torches into my eyes, cut them to pieces, burn through, see, my breast is open to the Furies.

Order, brother, the goddesses of revenge to move away from me and go to the deepest shades reassured: leave me to myself and use this hand,

intentat? ingens anguis excusso sonat
tortus flagello. quem trabe infesta petit
Megaera? cuius umbra dispersis venit
incerta membris? frater est, poenas petit:
[965] dabimus, sed omnes. fige luminibus faces,
lania, perure, pectus en Furiis patet.
  discedere a me, frater, ultrices deas
manesque ad imos ire securas iube:
mihi me relinque et utere hac, frater, manu
[970] quae strinxit ensem – uictima manes tuos
placamus ista. quid repens affert sonus?
parantur arma meque in exitium petunt.
excelsa nostrae tecta conscendam domus
caede incohata. perge tu mecum comes.
[975] tuum quoque ipsa corpus hinc mecum aveham.
nunc hoc age, anime: non in occulto tibi est
perdenda virtus; approba populo manum.

D 15. Pseudo-Seneca, *Octavia* 377-592

The drama Octavia *has been transmitted in the corpus of Seneca's tragedies, but the vast majority of scholars now believe that it was not written by Seneca himself, but rather later in the first century CE, after Seneca's (and Nero's) death, by someone influenced by Seneca. The play dramatizes an event from Nero's reign, which is also recorded in historiographical sources: Nero's divorce from his legitimate wife Octavia, Claudius' daughter, and his marriage with his beloved Poppaea. As the play's subject matter is an event from Roman history, it belongs to the Roman dramatic genre of praetexta; indeed it is the only fully preserved example of this dramatic genre (cf. D 6).*

Like tragedies, praetextae continued to be written in the imperial period, though not necessarily for full-scale productions in big theatres.

Seneca. quid, impotens Fortuna, fallaci mihi
blandita vultu, sorte contentum mea
alte extulisti, gravius ut ruerem edita
[380] receptus arce totque prospicerem metus?
melius latebam procul ab invidiae malis
remotus inter Corsici rupes maris,
ubi liber animus et sui iuris mihi
semper vacabat studia recolenti mea.
  [385] o quam iuvabat, quo nihil maius parens
Natura genuit, operis immensi artifex,

brother, [970] that has drawn the sword – with this victim we placate your shade[5]. What does this sudden noise mean? Arms are being made ready, and they seek me for my destruction. I will climb to the lofty roof of our house, with the slaughter begun. You[6], come with me as a companion. [975] Your[7] body too I myself shall carry with me away from here. Now come on, my spirit: you should not waste your bravery in secret; have your work approved by the people.

---

1 between Jason and Creon's daughter Creusa. 2 i.e. a spirit of punishment and revenge. 3 alludes to the fourteen children of Niobe. 4 an Erinys. 5 Medea kills the first child. 6 addressed to the one surviving child. 7 addressed to the dead child.

D 15. Pseudo-Seneca, *Octavia* 377-592

Also, while praetextae in the Republican period were typically supportive of Roman ideology, they tended to be critical by imperial times. The most telling scene for the political message of Octavia *comes in the middle of the drama: Seneca, who is a character in the play, delivers a monologue about his own circumstances and the situation of the universe; when Nero joins him, a dialogue between the emperor and his advisor develops, in which they discuss qualities of a ruler and principles of appropriate governance and, specifically, Nero's plan to marry Poppaea in order to establish his own dynasty and secure his position. Seneca seems to support a 'constitutional monarchy' with a responsible ruler, while Nero is convinced that a ruler's power allows him to do anything he wishes and to use force if necessary.*

Seneca. Why, headstrong Fortune, did you, with a deceiving and flattering face, exalt me, who was content with my lot, to a great height, only that I would crash down the harder, [380] having been admitted to an elevated citadel, and look out on so many kinds of fear? It was much better when I was hidden far from the evils of envy, in a remote spot among the rocks of Corsica's sea[1], where my spirit, free and independent, was always at liberty for me to reflect again upon my studies.

[385] O, how enjoyable it was to watch these things, greater than which mother Nature, the creator of this immense work, has brought forth nothing, the sky, the sacred course of the sun, the movements of the world,

165

caelum intueri, solis et cursus sacros
mundique motus, noctis alternas vices
orbemque Phoebes, astra quam cingunt vaga,
[390] lateque fulgens aetheris magni decus;
qui si senescit, tantus in caecum chaos
casurus iterum, tunc adest mundo dies
supremus ille, qui premat genus impium
caeli ruina, rursus ut stirpem novam
[395] generet renascens melior, ut quondam tulit
iuvenis, tenente regna Saturno poli.
    tunc illa virgo, numinis magni dea,
Iustitia, caelo missa cum sancta Fide
terra regebat mitis humanum genus.
[400] non bella norant, non tubae fremitus truces,
non arma gentes, cingere assuerant suas
muris nec urbes: pervium cunctis iter,
communis usus omnium rerum fuit;
et ipsa Tellus laeta fecundos sinus
[405] pandebat ultro, tam piis felix parens
et tuta alumnis. alia sed suboles minus
conspecta mitis * * *
* * * tertium sollers genus
novas ad artes extitit, sanctum tamen,
mox inquietum quod sequi cursu feras
[410] auderet acres, fluctibus tectos gravi
extrahere pisces rete vel calamo levi,
decipere volucres crate * * *
tenere laqueo, premere subiectos iugo
tauros feroces, vomere immunem prius
sulcare terram, laesa quae fruges suas
[415] interior alte condidit sacro sinu.
    sed in parentis viscera intravit suae
deterior aetas; eruit ferrum grave
aurumque, saevas mox et armavit manus;
partita fines regna constituit, novas
[420] exstruxit urbes, tecta defendit sua
aliena telis aut petit praedae imminens.
neglecta terras fugit et mores feros
hominum, cruenta caede pollutas manus
Astraea virgo, siderum magnum decus.
[425] cupido belli crevit atque auri fames
totum per orbem, maximum exortum est malum
luxuria, pestis blanda, cui vires dedit

166

the alternation of nights, the circuit of Phoebe, whom wandering stars encircle, [390] and the far-shining splendour of the great ether. If it gets old, about to fall again into blind chaos in its entirety, then this final day has arrived for the world, the day that will crush the impious race by the collapse of the sky, so that, [395] reborn in better shape, it will bring forth new offspring, just as it once did in its youth, when Saturn held the kingdom of the sky.

Then did this virgin, a goddess of great divinity, Justice, sent from heaven with holy Faith, gently govern the human race on earth. [400] The people did not know wars nor the fierce sound of the war-trumpet nor arms, and they were not used to surrounding their cities with walls: paths were open to all, communal was the use of all things; and joyful Earth herself opened her fruitful lap [405] of her own accord, so happy and safe a parent to pious foster-children. But another, less gentle stock was seen * * *². A third race appeared with skills for new arts, though pious, soon restless, which dared to pursue [410] ferocious wild beasts in the chase, to drag out fish covered by water with heavy nets or light rods, to trick birds with wicker * * *³, to catch them with snares, to subdue fierce bulls under the yoke, to furrow with the plough the earth, previously unharmed by wounds, which, hurt, hid her fruits [415] deep inside her holy womb.

But a worse age intruded into the flesh of its parent; it dug out heavy iron and gold, and soon it equipped savage hands with weapons; it created kingdoms with divisions marked by borders, [420] built cities as a new development, defended its own houses or attacked those of others with javelins, eager for booty. The maiden Astraea⁴, great glory of the stars, neglected, fled the earth and the wild customs of men, hands polluted with cruel slaughter. [425] The desire for war and the hunger for gold increased all over the world; the greatest evil arose, luxury, a seductive pest, to whom a long time and grave error have given power and strength.

Vices, gathered for a long time through so many ages, [430] are overwhelming us: we are burdened by an oppressive age, in which crimes reign, mad impiety rages, powerful lust rules with disgraceful love affairs, and victorious luxury has long seized the immense riches of the world with greedy hands so as to waste them.

[435] But look, with agitated step and savage mien Nero approaches. I shudder at the intentions he will bring.

roburque longum tempus atque error gravis.
    collecta vitia per tot aetates diu
[430] in nos redundant: saeculo premimur gravi,
quo scelera regnant, saevit impietas furens,
turpi libido Venere dominatur potens,
luxuria victrix orbis immensas opes
iam pridem avaris manibus, ut perdat, rapit.
    [435] sed ecce, gressu fertur attonito Nero
trucique vultu. quid ferat mente horreo.

Nero. perage imperata: mitte, qui Plauti mihi
Sullaeque caesi referat abscisum caput.
Praefectus. iussa haud morabor: castra confestim petam. –
[440] **Sen**. nihil in propinquos temere constitui decet.
Ner. iusto esse facile est cui vacat pectus metu.
Sen. magnum timoris remedium clementia est.
Ner. extinguere hostem maxima est virtus ducis.
Sen. servare cives maior est patriae patri.
[445] **Ner**. praecipere mitem convenit pueris senem.
Sen. regenda magis est fervida adolescentia.
Ner. aetate in hac satis esse consilii reor.
Sen. ut facta superi comprobent semper tua.
Ner. stulte verebor, ipse cum faciam, deos.
[450] **Sen**. hoc plus verere quod licet tantum tibi.
Ner. Fortuna nostra cuncta permittit mihi.
Sen. crede obsequenti parcius: levis est dea.
Ner. inertis est nescire quid liceat sibi.
Sen. id facere laus est quod decet, non quod licet.
[455] **Ner**. calcat iacentem vulgus. **Sen**. invisum opprimit.
Ner. ferrum tuetur principem. **Sen**. melius fides.
Ner. decet timeri Caesarem. **Sen**. at plus diligi.
Ner. metuant necesse est – **Sen**. quidquid exprimitur grave est.
Ner. iussisque nostris pareant. **Sen**. iusta impera.
[460] **Ner**. statuam ipse. **Sen**. quae consensus efficiat rata.
Ner. destrictus ensis faciet. **Sen**. hoc absit nefas.
Ner. an patiar ultra sanguinem nostrum peti,
inultus et contemptus ut subito opprimar?
exilia non fregere summotos procul
[465] Plautum atque Sullam, pertinax quorum furor
armat ministros sceleris in caedem meam,
absentium cum maneat etiam ingens favor
in urbe nostra, qui fovet spes exulum.
tollantur hostes ense suspecti mihi,

Nero. (*to prefect*) Carry out the orders: send someone who shall bring back to me the severed heads of slaughtered Plautus and Sulla[5].

Prefect. I shall not delay your orders: I will swiftly make my way to the camp. (*exits*)

[440] **Sen**. It is good practice never to decide anything against relatives rashly.

Ner. To be just is easy for someone whose heart is free from fear.

Sen. A great remedy for fear is mercy.

Ner. To destroy an enemy is the greatest virtue of a leader.

Sen. To preserve one's citizens is a greater one for a father of the fatherland.

[445] **Ner**. It is appropriate for a gentle old man to admonish boys.

Sen. Fervid youth has to be directed all the more.

Ner. I believe that there is enough counsel in this age.

Sen. So that the gods always approve of your deeds.

Ner. I would be stupid to fear gods, when I make them myself[6].

[450] **Sen**. Fear them the more since so much is allowed to you.

Ner. Our Fortune allows me everything.

Sen. Trust the indulgent goddess more cautiously: she is fickle.

Ner. It is a sign of a feeble man not to know what is allowed to him.

Sen. It is praiseworthy to do what is right, not what is possible.

[455] **Ner**. The mob tramples on him who lies on the ground.

Sen. They overthrow a hated man.

Ner. The sword guards the king.

Sen. Faith does it better.

Ner. It is right that the emperor should be feared.

Sen. But rather be respected.

Ner. It is necessary that they fear –

Sen. Whatever is extorted is burdensome.

Ner. And that they obey our orders.

Sen. Give just orders.

[460] **Ner**. I shall decide myself.

Sen. What consensus may return as ratified.

Ner. The unsheathed sword will do it.

Sen. This outrage be far.

Ner. Or shall I suffer our blood targeted, so that I shall be crushed suddenly, not avenged and scorned? Exile has not broken those who had been far removed, [465] Plautus and Sulla, whose persevering rage arms agents of their crime for my assassination, since immense favour for the absent still remains in our city, which encourages the hopes of the exiled. These suspected enemies shall be removed by the sword, [470] my hated wife shall perish and follow her beloved brother[7]. Whatever is high shall fall.

169

[470] invisa coniunx pereat et carum sibi
fratrem sequatur. quidquid excelsum est cadat.
Sen. pulchrum eminere est inter illustres viros,
consulere patriae, parcere afflictis, fera
caede abstinere, tempus atque irae dare,
[475] orbi quietem, saeculo pacem suo.
haec summa virtus, petitur hac caelum via.
sic ille patriae primus Augustus parens
complexus astra est, colitur et templis deus.
illum tamen Fortuna iactavit diu
[480] terra marique per graves belli vices,
hostes parentis donec oppressit sui:
tibi numen incruenta summisit suum
et dedit habenas imperi facili manu
nutuque terras maria subiecit tuo;
[485] invidia tristis, victa consensu pio,
cessit; senatus, equitis accensus favor;
plebisque votis atque iudicio patrum
tu pacis auctor, generis humani arbiter
electus orbem spiritu sacro regis
[490] patriae parens: quod nomen ut serves petit
suosque cives Roma commendat tibi.
Ner. munus deorum est, ipsa quod servit mihi
Roma et senatus quodque ab invitis preces
humilesque voces exprimit nostri metus.
[495] servare cives principi et patriae graves,
claro tumentes genere quae dementia est,
cum liceat una voce suspectos sibi
mori iubere? Brutus in caedem ducis,
a quo salutem tulerat, armavit manus:
[500] invictus acie, gentium domitor, Iovi
aequatus altos saepe per honorum gradus
Caesar nefando civium scelere occidit.
quantum cruoris Roma tum vidit sui,
lacerata totiens! ille qui meruit pia
[505] virtute caelum, divus Augustus, viros
quot interemit nobiles, iuvenes senes
sparsos per orbem, cum suos mortis metu
fugerent penates et trium ferrum ducum,
tabula notante deditos tristi neci!
[510] exposita rostris capita caesorum patres
videre maesti, flere nec licuit suos,
non gemere dira tabe polluto foro,

Sen. It is glorious to be conspicuous among distinguished men, to look after the fatherland, to spare those in distress, to abstain from cruel bloodbath, to give time to anger, [475] quiet to the world and peace to one's age. This is greatest virtue; on this path heaven is gained. In this way has this first father of the fatherland, Augustus, grasped the stars, and he is worshipped as a god in temples. Yet Fortune tossed him about [480] on land and sea for a long time through the grievous vicissitudes of war, until he crushed his father's enemies: to you she has yielded her divinity unstained and has given the reigns of the empire with light hand and has subjected lands and sea to your nod. [485] Morose envy, overcome by pious consensus, has receded; the favour of the senate and the equestrians has been kindled; and by the wishes of the people and the judgement of the senators elected as provider of peace and arbiter of the human race, you govern the world with holy spirit, [490] as father of the fatherland: that you keep this title is what Rome asks for, and she entrusts her citizens to you.

Ner. It is a gift from the gods that Rome herself and the senate are servants to me and that fear of us forces prayers and humble utterances from the unwilling. [495] What madness is it to preserve citizens, burdensome for emperor and country, puffed up by illustrious descent, when it is possible to order by one word that those one suspects should die? Brutus armed his hands for the assassination of the leader from whom he had won salvation: [500] undefeated in battle, conqueror of nations, frequently made equal to Jove through high levels of honours, Caesar perished by an abominable crime of citizens. How much of her blood Rome saw then, so often torn to pieces! He who earned the sky by pious [505] virtue, divine Augustus, how many noblemen did he kill, young men and old men, scattered throughout the world, when they fled their homes and the steel of the three leaders[8] out of fear of death, given over to grim death by the branding tablet[9]! [510] In grief did the fathers see the heads of those killed exhibited upon the Rostra, and they were not at liberty to cry over their people nor groan while the Forum was polluted by awful gore and dreadful filth dripping over rotting faces. And this was not the end of blood and bloodshed: [515] gloomy Philippi fed birds and animals of prey for a long time * * *[10], and the Sicilian sea drowned fleets and men frequently killing their kin, the world was shaken by the great forces of the leaders[11]. Defeated in battle he [i.e. Mark Antony] made for the Nile with ships [520] ready for flight, himself to perish shortly: incestuous Egypt once again drank the blood of a Roman leader[12], and it now covers weightless shades. There civil war was buried, long carried on impiously. Eventually [525] the victor [i.e. Octavian], already exhausted, sheathed his sword, blunted by savage wounds, and fear maintained the empire. He was safe by his weapons and the soldiers' loyalty, he was made a god by the outstanding

stillante sanie per putres vultus gravi.
nec finis hic cruoris aut caedis stetit:
[515] pavere volucres et feras saevas diu
tristes Philippi, * * *
* * * hausit et Siculum mare
classes virosque saepe caedentes suos,
concussus orbis viribus magnis ducum.
superatus acie puppibus Nilum petit
[520] fugae paratis, ipse periturus brevi:
hausit cruorem incesta Romani ducis
Aegyptus iterum, nunc leves umbras tegit.
illic sepultum est impie gestum diu
civile bellum. condidit tandem suos
[525] iam fessus enses victor hebetatos feris
vulneribus, et continuit imperium metus.
armis fideque militis tutus fuit,
pietate nati factus eximia deus,
post fata consecratus et templis datus.
[530] nos quoque manebunt astra, si saevo prior
ense occuparo quidquid infestum est mihi
dignaque nostram subole fundaro domum.
Sen. implebit aulam stirpe caelesti tuam
generata divo, Claudiae gentis decus,
[535] sortita fratris more Iunonis toros.
Ner. incesta genetrix detrahit generi fidem,
animusque numquam coniugis iunctus mihi.
Sen. teneris in annis haud satis clara est fides,
pudore victus cum tegit flammas amor.
[540] **Ner**. hoc equidem et ipse credidi frustra diu,
manifesta quamvis pectore insociabili
vultuque signa proderent odium mei,
tandem quod ardens statuit ulcisci dolor –
dignamque thalamis coniugem inveni meis
[545] genere atque forma, victa cui cedet Venus
Iovisque coniunx et ferox armis dea.
Sen. probitas fidesque coniugis, mores pudor
placeant marito: sola perpetuo manent
subiecta nulli mentis atque animi bona;
[550] florem decoris singuli carpunt dies.
Ner. omnes in unam contulit laudes deus
talemque nasci fata voluerunt mihi.
Sen. recedat a te (temere ne credas) amor.
Ner. quem summovere fulminis dominus nequit,

piety of the son[13], hallowed after his death and enshrined in temples. [530] The stars will also be awaiting us if I have first attacked everything hostile to me with ferocious sword and have founded our house on worthy offspring.

Sen. She [i.e. Octavia] will fill your palace with celestial offspring, she, born from a god, an ornament of the Claudian race, [535] having won her brother's marriage-bed after the model of Juno[14].

Ner. An incestuous mother [i.e. Messalina] diminishes faith in the line, and my wife's soul was never united with me.

Sen. In tender years loyalty is not clear enough, when love, overcome by modesty, covers the flames.

[540] **Ner**. I myself have also believed this for a long time in vain, even though clear signs from an unsociable heart and face betrayed the hatred for me, which eventually the burning grief has decided to avenge – and I have found a wife worthy of my marriage chamber [545] in descent and appearance [i.e. Poppaea], to whom Venus will yield defeated and the wife of Jupiter and the goddess brave in arms[15].

Sen. Honesty and a wife's loyalty, character and modesty should delight a husband: the gifts of mind and heart alone remain forever, subject to nothing; [550] the flower of beauty is diminished by each individual day.

Ner. A god has assembled all merits in her alone, and the fates wished that such a person was born for me.

Sen. Love will withdraw from you (do not put your trust in this rashly).

Ner. He whom the master of the thunderbolt [i.e. Jupiter] cannot remove, [555] this tyrant of heaven, who penetrates the savage seas and the realm of Dis [i.e. the underworld] and who draws gods down from the heavens?

Sen. An error of mortals turns Love into a winged, harsh god, arms his sacred hands with shafts and bow, equips him with a fierce torch [560] and believes that he was born by Venus, fathered by Vulcan: Love is a great force of the mind and a seductive fire of the heart; it is created in youth, it is nourished by luxury and ease among the joyful gifts of Fortune. If you stop favouring and nurturing it, it falls, [565] and in a short time it is exhausted and loses its powers.

Ner. I believe that this is the greatest source of life, by which pleasure is created; the human race lacks death, since it continuously reproduces itself by pleasing Love, who soothes savage beasts. [570] This god shall carry nuptial torches for me and join Poppaea to our marriage-bed with his fire.

Sen. The people's grief might hardly be able to bear seeing this marriage, and holy piety would not grant it.

Ner. Will it be forbidden to me alone to do what is allowed to everyone?

[555] caeli tyrannum, saeva qui penetrat freta
Ditisque regna, detrahit superos polo?
Sen. volucrem esse Amorem fingit immitem deum
mortalis error, armat et telis manus
arcuque sacras, instruit saeva face
[560] genitumque credit Venere, Vulcano satum:
vis magna mentis blandus atque animi calor
Amor est; iuventa gignitur, luxu otio
nutritur inter laeta Fortunae bona.
quem si fovere atque alere desistas, cadit
[565] brevique vires perdit extinctus suas.
Ner. hanc esse vitae maximam causam reor,
per quam voluptas oritur; interitu caret,
cum procreetur semper humanum genus
Amore grato, qui truces mulcet feras.
[570] hic mihi iugales praeferat taedas deus
iungatque nostris igne Poppaeam toris.
Sen. vix sustinere possit hos thalamos dolor
videre populi, sancta nec pietas sinat.
Ner. prohibebor unus facere quod cunctis licet?
[575] **Sen**. maiora populus semper a summo exigit.
Ner. libet experiri, viribus fractus meis
an cedat animis temere conceptus furor.
Sen. obsequere potius civibus placidus tuis.
Ner. male imperatur, cum regit vulgus duces.
[580] **Sen**. nihil impetrare cum valet, iuste dolet.
Ner. exprimere ius est, ferre quod nequeunt preces?
Sen. negare durum est. **Ner**. principem cogi nefas.
Sen. remittat ipse. **Ner**. fama sed victum feret.
Sen. levis atque vana. **Ner**. sit licet, multos notat.
[585] **Sen**. excelsa metuit. **Ner**. non minus carpit tamen.
Sen. facile opprimetur. merita te divi patris
aetasque frangat coniugis, probitas pudor.
Ner. desiste tandem, iam gravis nimium mihi,
instare: liceat facere quod Seneca improbat.
[590] et ipse populi vota iam pridem moror,
cum portet utero pignus et partem mei.
quin destinamus proximum thalamis diem.

[575] **Sen**. The people always ask more from the greatest.

Ner. I should like to check whether, broken by my might, the rashly gathered fury may withdraw from their minds.

Sen. Rather oblige your citizens peacefully.

Ner. Government is bad when the mob rules the leaders.

[580] **Sen**. If they are not able to achieve anything, they grieve justly.

Ner. Is it right to extort what appeals cannot obtain?

Sen. To refuse is harsh.

Ner. It is a crime to force an emperor.

Sen. He should give way himself.

Ner. But rumour will report him conquered.

Sen. It is fickle and void.

Ner. Even if it is, it brands many.

[585] **Sen**. It fears heights.

Ner. But it carps nevertheless.

Sen. It will be crushed easily. Let the merits of a divine father [i.e. Claudius] and the wife's age, her honesty and modesty break you.

Ner. Stop finally to insist, this is already too annoying to me: it shall be allowed to do what Seneca disapproves. [590] And I myself have already been delaying the wishes of the people for a long time, when she [i.e. Poppaea] carries a pledge and a part of me in her womb. Why don't we fix the next day for the wedding?

---

1 during Seneca's exile on the island of Corsica in the Mediterranean Sea. 2 here something has presumably been lost in the Latin. 3 here again something seems to be corrupt in the Latin. 4 the goddess of Justice. 5 Rubellius Plautus and Faustus Cornelius Sulla Felix, distant relations of Nero and potential rivals to the throne. 6 i.e. by deifying his predecessor Claudius. 7 Britannicus, already killed by Nero. 8 the members of the so-called Second Triumvirate: Mark Antony, Octavian and Lepidus. 9 i.e. the proscription lists. 10 here again something is presumably missing or corrupt in the Latin. 11 alludes to the civil wars at the end of the Republican period. 12 of Mark Antony, after Pompey. 13 Tiberius, Augustus' adopted son and successor. 14 since Octavia is also Nero's sister, as Juno is both Jupiter's sister and wife. 15 Venus, Juno and Minerva, the three goddesses involved in the judgement of Paris.

Nachleben of Roman Drama

N 1. Nicholas Udall (1552), *Roister Doister* (Prologue; IV 7-8)

Nicholas Udall (1504-1556) was educated at Winchester College and then Corpus Christi College, Oxford, where he became Fellow and Lecturer in Logic and Greek. Later he was headmaster at Eton; then he undertook scholarly work for the royal court and finally returned to being headmaster of Westminster School. He wrote poetry and plays and translated religious writings; for instance, he produced the standard biblical commentary and widely used textbooks. His Roister Doister *is regarded as the first regular English comedy and was probably first performed at Windsor Castle in September 1552 before the young King Edward VI. The play is a full-length comedy of Roman type, indebted to Plautus and Terence, but adapted for education and entertainment of boys in contemporary English schools and written in English. It is thus a logical step forward from Udall's earlier annotated translation of 'the best bits from Terence'.*

Roister Doister is modelled upon the basic structure of Roman comedies and also draws upon two particular comedies, namely Plautus' Miles gloriosus *and Terence's* Eunuchus *(D 8; 10). However, although the drama uses a similar plot, a significant difference is that the entire action has been transferred to a morally higher level; vulgarity, base jokes or any unacceptable behaviour have been eliminated. The most obvious sign of these changes is that a chaste, dignified Christian lady, with a name illustrating her virtues (Christian Custance), has been substituted for the original courtesan; and the soldier's rival is betrothed to Dame Custance.*

The prologue, indicating the writer's intentions, and scenes that are indebted to the attack by the soldier and his 'army' on the courtesan's house in Terence's Eunuchus *(cf. D 10b) illustrate similarities and differences in relation to Roman comedies.*

The text (with its additional stage directions) has been taken from Three Sixteenth-Century Comedies: Gammer Gurton's Needle, Roister Doister, The Old Wife's Tale, *edited by Charles Walters Whitworth, London/New York 1984 (The New Mermaids). It has been reprinted here by kind permission of the editor, who has also slightly revised the text for this reprint.*

Dramatis personae
Prologue – Matthew Merrygreek *(a mischievous flatterer and parasite, Roister Doister's agent)* – Ralph Roister Doister *(a foolish would-be soldier*

and lover) – Dobinet, Doughty, Harpax *(Roister Doister's servants)* – Dame Christian Custance *(a widow, betrothed to Gawin Goodluck)* – Madge (or Margery) Mumblecrust *(Dame Custance's old nurse)* – Tibet Talkapace, Annot Alyface *(Dame Custance's maids)* – Tom Truepenny *(Dame Custance's servant)* – Scrivener – Gawin Goodluck *(a merchant, betrothed to Christian Custance)* – Sim Suresby *(Goodluck's servant)* – Tristram Trusty *(Goodluck's friend)* – The Parish Clerk – Servants, Musicians *(members of Roister Doister's household)*

(a) Prologue

The Prologue.
What creature is in health, either young or old,
But some mirth with modesty will be glad to use,
As we in this interlude shall now unfold?
Wherein all scurrility we utterly refuse,
[5] Avoiding such mirth wherein is abuse;
Knowing nothing more commendable for a man's recreation
Than mirth which is used in an honest fashion.
For mirth prolongeth life and causeth health,
Mirth recreates our spirits and voideth pensiveness,
[10] Mirth increases amity, not hindering our wealth,
Mirth is to be used both of more and less,
Being mixed with virtue in decent comeliness,
As we trust no good nature can gainsay the same;
Which mirth we intend to use, avoiding all blame.
[15] The wise poets long time heretofore
Under merry comedies secrets did declare,
Wherein was contained very virtuous lore,
With mysteries and forewarnings very rare.
Such to write, neither Plautus nor Terence did spare,
[20] Which among the learned at this day bears the bell;
These, with such other, therein did excel.
Our comedy or interlude which we intend to play
Is named *Roister Doister* indeed,
Which against the vainglorious doth inveigh,
[25] Whose humour the roisting sort continually doth feed.
Thus by your patience we inted to proceed
In this our interlude, by God's leave and grace;
And here I take my leave for a certain space.

(b) Act IV, Scenes 7-8

[*Enter* Roister Doister, Merrygreek, Doughty, Harpax, *and other servants, armed, with drum, ensign, etc.*]
Roister Doister. Now, sirs, keep your 'ray, and see your hearts be
stout!

But where be these caitiffs[1]? Methink they dare not rout[2]!
How sayst thou, Merrygreek? What doth Kit Custance say?
Merrygreek. I am loath to tell you. **Ro.Do.** Tush! Speak, man – yea
or nay?

[5] **Mer**. Forsooth, sir, I have spoken for you all that I can.
But if ye win her, ye must e'en play the man;
E'en to fight it out, ye must a man's heart take.
Ro.Do. Yes, they shall know, and thou knowest I have a stomach.
Mer. 'A stomach', quod you? Yea, as good as e'er man had!
[10] **Ro.Do.** I trow they shall find and feel that I am a lad.
Mer. By this cross, I have seen you eat your meat as well
As any that e'er I have seen of or heard tell!
'A stomach', quod you? He that will that deny
I know was never at dinner in your company!
[15] **Ro.Do.** Nay, the stomach of a man it is that I mean!
Mer. Nay, the stomach of an horse or a dog, I ween!
Ro.Do. Nay, a man's stomach with a weapon, mean I!
Mer. Ten men can scarce match you with a spoon in a pie!
Ro.Do. Nay, the stomach of a man to try in strife!
[20] **Mer.** I never saw your stomach cloyed[3] yet in my life.
Ro.Do. Tush, I mean in strife or fighting to try.
Mer. We shall see how ye will strike now being angry.
Ro.Do. Have at thy pate[4] then, and save thy head if thou may!
[*Strikes at him*]

Mer. Nay, then have at your pate again, by this day! [*Strikes back*]
[25] **Ro.Do.** Nay, thou may not strike at me again in no wise.
Mer. I cannot in fight make to you such warrantise;
But as for your foes here, let them the bargain 'by.
Ro.Do. Nay, as for they, shall every mother's child die!
And in this my fume, a little thing might make me
[30] To beat down house and all, and else the devil take me!
Mer. If I were as ye be, by Gog's dear mother,
I would not leave one stone upon another
Though she would redeem it with twenty thousand pounds.
Ro.Do. It shall be even so, by his lily wounds[5]!
[35] **Mer**. Be not at one with her upon any amends!
Ro.Do. No, though she make to me never so many friends!

179

Not if all the world for her would undertake;
No, not God himself neither shall not her peace make!
On, therefore! March forward! Soft! Stay awhile yet!
[40] **Mer.** On! **Ro.Do.** Tarry! **Mer.** Forth! **Ro.Do.** Back!
                        Mer. On! **Ro.Do.** Soft! Now forward set!
[*Enter* Dame Custance]
Dame Custance. What business have we here? Out, alas! Alas!
                                                    [*Exit*]

Ro.Do. Ha, ha, ha, ha, ha!
Didst thou see that, Merrygreek? How afraid she was?
Didst thou see how she fled apace out of my sight?
Ah, good sweet Custance! I pity her, by this light!
[45] **Mer.** That tender heart of yours will mar altogether;
Thus will ye be turned with wagging of a feather!
Ro.Do. On, sirs! Keep your 'ray! **Mer.** On! Forth, while this gear is
                                                            hot!

Ro.Do. Soft! The arms of Calais[6]! I have one thing forgot!
Mer. What lack we now? **Ro.Do.** Retire, or else we be all slain!
[50] **Mer.** Back, for the pash[7] of God! Back, sirs! Back again!
What is the great matter? **Ro.Do.** This hasty forth going
Had almost brought us all to utter undoing!
It made me forget a thing most necessary.
Mer. Well remembered of a captain, by Saint Mary!
[55] **Ro.Do.** It is a thing must be had. **Mer.** Let us have it then.
Ro.Do. But I wot not where nor how. **Mer.** Then wot not I when.
But what is it? **Ro.Do.** Of a chief thing I am to seek.
Mer. Tut, so will ye be when ye have studied a week.
But tell me what it is. **Ro.Do.** I lack yet an headpiece.
[60] **Mer.** The kitchen collocavit[8] – the best hence to Greece!
Run fet it, Dobinet and come at once withal,
And bring with thee my potgun hanging by the wall. [*Exit* Doughty]
I have seen your head with it full many a time,
Covered as safe as it had been with a scrine.
[65] And I warrant it save your head from any stroke,
Except perchance to be amazed with the smoke.
I warrant your head therewith, except for the mist,
As safe as if it were fast locked up in a chest.
And lo, here our Dobinet cometh with it now!
[*Enter* Doughty *with a pail and a pistol*]
[70] **Doughty**. It will cover me to the shoulders well enow.
Mer. Let me see it on. **Ro.Do.** In faith, it doth meetly well.
Mer. There can be no fitter thing. Now ye must us tell
What to do. **Ro.Do.** Now, forth in 'ray, sirs, and stop no more!

Mer. Now Saint George to borrow! Drum, 'dub-a-dub' afore!
[*Enter* Trusty]
[75] **Trusty.** What mean you to do sir? Commit manslaughter?
Ro.Do. To kill forty such is a matter of laughter!
Tru. And who is it, sir, whom ye intend thus to spill?
Ro.Do. Foolish Custance here forceth me against my will.
Tru. And is there no mean your extreme wrath to slake?
[80] She shall some amends unto your good ma'ship make.
Ro.Do. I will none amends. **Tru.** Is her offence so sore?
Mer. And he were a lout, she could have done no more.
She hath called him fool, and dressed him like a fool,
Mocked him like a fool, used him like a fool.
[85] **Tru**. Well, yet the sheriff, the justice or constable
Her misdemeanour to punish might be able.
Ro.Do. No, sir! I mine own self will in this present cause
Be sheriff and justice and whole judge of the laws;
This matter to amend, all officers be I shall,
[90] Constable, bailiff, sergeant – **Mer.** And hangman and all.
Tru. Yet a noble courage and the heart of man
Should more honour win by bearing with a woman.
Therefore take the law, and let her answer thereto.
Ro.Do. Merrygreek, the best way were even so to do.
[95] What honour should it be with a woman to fight?
Mer. And what then? Will ye thus forego and lose your right?
Ro.Do. Nay, I will take the law on her withouten grace!
Tru. Or if your ma'ship could pardon this one trespass –
I pray you, forgive her. **Ro.Do.** Ho! **Mer.** Tush, tush, sir, do not!
[100] **Tru.** Be good master to her. **Ro.Do.** Ho! **Mer.** Tush, I say, do
not!
And what, shall your people here return straight home?
Ro.Do. Yea, levy the camp, sirs, and hence again, each one.
But be still in readiness if I hap to call;
I cannot tell what sudden chance may befall.
[105] **Mer.** Do not off your harness, sirs, I you advise,
At the least for this fortnight, in no manner wise.
Perchance in an hour when all ye think least,
Our master's appetite to fight will be best.
But, soft! Ere ye go, have once at Custance's house!
[110] **Ro.Do.** Soft! What wilt thou do? **Mer.** Once discharge my
harquebouse,
And for my heart's ease, have once more with my potgun.
Ro.Do. Hold thy hands! Else is all our purpose clean fordone!
Mer. And it cost me my life – **Ro.Do.** I say thou shalt not!

Mer. By the matte[9], but I will! Have once more with hail shot!
[115] I will have some pennyworth, I will not lose all!

Scene 8

[*Enter* Dame Custance]
Dame Custance. What caitiffs[1] are those that so shake my house
wall?

Merrygreek. Ah, sirrah! Now, Custance, if ye had so much wit,
I would see you ask pardon and yourselves submit.
Da.Cu. Have I still this ado with a couple of fools?
[5] **Mer**. Hear ye what she saith? **Da.Cu.** Maidens, come forth with
your tools!
[*Enter* Tibet Talkapace, Annot Alyface, Madge Mumblecrust *and* Tom
Truepenny, *armed, with drum, ensign, etc.*]
Roister Doister. [*To his men*] In array! **Mer.** 'Dub-a-dub',
sirrah! **Ro.Do**. In array!
They come suddenly on us! **Mer.** 'Dub-a-dub'! **Ro.Do**. In array!
That ever I was born! We are taken tardy!
Mer. Now, sirs, quit ourselves like tall men and hardy!
[10] **Da.Cu.** On afore, Truepenny! Hold thine own, Annot!
On toward them, Tibet, for 'scape us they cannot!
Come forth, Madge Mumblecrust! So stand fast together.
Mer. God send us a fair day! **Ro.Do.** See, thy march on hither!
Tibet. But, mistress – **Da.Cu.** What sayst thou? **Tib.** Shall I go fet
our goose?
[15] **Da.Cu.** What to do? **Tib.** To yonder captain I will turn her loose.
And she gape and hiss at him as she doth at me,
I durst jeopard my hand she will make him flee!
Da.Cu. On! Forward! **Ro.Do.** They come! **Mer.** Stand!
Ro.Do. Hold! **Mer.** Keep! **Ro.Do.** There! **Mer.** Strike!
Ro.Do. Take heed!
Da.Cu. Well said, Truepenny! **True**. Ah, whoresons! **Da.Cu.** Well
done, indeed!
[20] **Mer.** Hold thine own, Harpax! Down with them, Dobinet!
Da.Cu. Now, Madge! There, Annot! Now stick them, Tibet!
Tib. All my chief quarrel is to this same little knave
That beguiled me last day – nothing shall him save!
Doughty. Down with this little quean[10] that hath at me such
spite!
[25] Save you from her, master! It is a very sprite!
Da.Cu. I myself will Monsieur Grand Capitaine undertake!
Ro.Do. They win ground! **Mer.** Save yourself, sir, for God's sake!

182

Ro.Do. Out, alas! I am slain! Help! **Mer.** Save yourself!

Ro.Do. Alas!

Mer. Nay then, have at you, mistress! **Ro.Do.** Thou hittest me, alas!

[30] **Mer.** I will strike at Custance here! **Ro.Do.** Thou hittest

me! **Mer.** So I will!

Nay, Mistress Custance! **Ro.Do.** Alas, thou hittest me still!

Hold! **Mer.** Save yourself, sir! **Ro.Do.** Help! Out, alas! I am slain!

Mer. Truce! Hold your hands! Truce, for a pissing while or twain!

Now, how say you, Custance? For saving of your life,

[35] Will ye yield and grant to be this gent'man's wife?

Da.Cu. Ye told me he loved me! Call ye this love?

Mer. He loved a while, even like a turtledove.

Da.Cu. Gay love, God save it! So soon hot, so soon cold!

Mer. I am sorry for you. He could love you yet, so he could.

[40] **Ro.Do.** Nay, by Cock's precious, she shall be none of mine!

Mer. Why so? **Ro.Do.** Come away! By the matte⁹, she is mankine¹¹!

I durst adventure the loss of my right hand

If she did not slay her other husband!

And see if she prepare not again to fight!

[45] **Mer.** What then? Saint George to borrow, our Lady's knight!

Ro.Do. Slay else whom she will, by Gog, she shall not slay me!

Mer. How then? **Ro.Do.** Rather than to be slain, I will flee!

Da.Cu. To it again, my knightesses! Down with them all!

Ro.Do. Away, away, away! She will else kill us all!

[50] **Mer.** Nay, stick to it, like an hardy man and a tall!

Ro.Do. Oh, bones! Thou hittest me! Away, or else die we shall!

Mer. Away, for the pash⁷ of our sweet Lord Jesus Christ!

Da.Cu. Away, lout and lubber, or I shall be thy priest!

Exeunt [Roister Doister, Merrygreek *and their men*]

So, this field is ours; we have driven them all away.

[55] **Tib.** Thanks to God, mistress, ye have had a fair day.

Da.Cu. [*To her servants*] Well, now go ye in and make yourself some

good cheer.

All. We go. [*Exeunt* Tibet, Annot, Madge *and* Truepenny, *their drum,*

ensign, etc.]

Trusty. Ah sir, what a field we have had here!

Da.Cu. Friend Tristram, I pray you be a witness with me.

[60] **Tru.** Dame Custance, I shall depose for your honesty.

And now fare ye well, except something else ye would

Da.Cu. Not now, but when I need to send, I will be bold.

I thank you for these pains. *Exit* [**Tru.**] And now I will get me in.

Now Roister Doister will no more wooing begin! *Exit.*

183

1 i.e. villains. 2 i.e. assemble. 3 i.e. satiated. 4 i.e. head. 5 by Christ's lovely wounds. 6 i.e. the location of a large arsenal. 7 i.e. passion. 8 i.e. kitchen pail or tub. 9 i.e. mass. 10 i.e. whore. 11 i.e. furious, mad.

N 2. William Shakespeare (early 1590s), *The Comedy of Errors* (III 1)

Although Ben Jonson famously described William Shakespeare's (1564-1616) education as consisting of 'small Latin and less Greek', he also acknowledged that Shakespeare equalled and perhaps even surpassed ancient Greek and Roman dramatists. Indeed it is beyond doubt that many of Shakespeare's plays (tragedies, comedies and history plays) have been influenced by ancient examples, in both motifs and structural elements, since Shakespeare was familiar with classical texts (cf. also Hamlet *II 2: Polonius: 'Seneca cannot be too heavy, nor Plautus too light.'). His* Comedy of Errors *(early 1590s, before 1594) uses classical, romantic and biblical sources, but a major inspiration comes from two famous and much imitated pieces by Plautus:* Menaechmi *as the main model and* Amphitruo *(cf. D 7) as a secondary source. Both ancient plays deal with mistaken identity, as they include two characters of the same name, who are identified wrongly by others and are confused when they meet each other.*

With two pairs of identical characters (twins) on the level of both the masters and the slaves Shakespeare has emphasized the element of confusion and error. A lively encounter between one of the Antipholuses and the two Dromios, full of misunderstandings due to confused identities, takes place in the first scene of the third act. This scene also features common comedy themes (such as desire for food and women or the fate of slaves) and formal structures (such as verbal puns and banter). And, as characters demand entry into a house, it is reminiscent of the attack on the courtesan's house in Terence's Eunuchus *(cf. D 10b), but also of a scene in Plautus'* Amphitruo, *since it is the husband (Antipholus of Ephesus) who cannot get into his own house. He therefore goes off to seek entertainment elsewhere.*

The text is taken from The New Cambridge Shakespeare: The Comedy of Errors, *edited by T.S. Dorsch, Cambridge / New York / New Rochelle / Melbourne / Sydney 1988. © Cambridge University Press 1988, reproduced with permission.*

Dramatis personae
Solinus, *Duke of Ephesus* – Egeon, *a merchant of Syracuse* – Antipholus of Ephesus, Antipholus of Syracuse, *twin sons of Egeon and Æmilia* –

Dromio of Ephesus, Dromio of Syracuse, *twin slaves of the Antipholuses* –
Balthasar, *a merchant* – Angelo, *a goldsmith* – Doctor Pinch, *a school-master (or conjurer)* – First Merchant – Second Merchant – *An* Officer –
A Jailer – *A* Messenger – Æmilia, *wife of Egeon and Abbess of the Priory in Ephesus* – Adriana, *wife of Antipholus of Ephesus* – Luciana, *Adriana's sister* – Luce (*or* Nell), *her maid* – *A* Courtesan – *Officers, Headsman, Attendants*

Act III, Scene 1

Enter Antipholus of Ephesus, *his man* Dromio, Angelo *the goldsmith, and* Balthasar *the merchant.*
Antipholus E. Good Signior Angelo, you must excuse us all.
My wife is shrewish when I keep not hours.
Say that I lingered with you at your shop
To see the making of her carcanet[1],
[5] And that tomorrow you will bring it home.
But here's a villain that would face me down
He met me on the mart, and that I beat him,
And charged[2] him with a thousand marks in gold,
And that I did deny my wife and house.
[10] Thou drunkard, thou, what didst thou mean by this?
Dromio E. Say what you will, sir, but I know what I know:
That you beat me at the mart I have your hand to show.
If the skin were parchment and the blows you gave were ink,
Your own handwriting would tell you what I think.
Ant.E. I think thou art an ass.
[15] **Dro.E.**   Marry, so it doth appear
By the wrongs I suffer and the blows I bear.
I should kick, being kicked, and, being at that pass[3],
You would keep from my heels, and beware of an ass.
Ant.E. You're sad[4], Signior Balthasar. Pray God our cheer[5]
[20] May answer my good will, and your good welcome here.
Balthasar. I hold your dainties cheap, sir, and your welcome dear.
Ant.E. O, Signior Balthasar, either at flesh or fish
A table full of welcome makes scarce one dainty dish.
Bal. Good meat, sir, is common. That every churl affords.
[25] **Ant.E**. And welcome more common, for that's nothing but words.
Bal. Small cheer and great welcome makes a merry feast.
Ant.E. Ay, to a niggardly host and more sparing guest.
But though my cates[6] be mean, take them in good part.
Better cheer may you have, but not with better heart.
[30] But soft, my door is locked. Go bid them let us in.

185

Dro.E. Maud, Bridget, Marian, Cicely, Gillian, Ginn!
Dromio S. [*Within*] Mome[7], malthorse[8], capon, coxcomb, idiot, patch[9],
Either get thee from the door or sit down at the hatch.
Dost thou conjure for[10] wenches, that thou callest for such store,
[35] When one is one too many? Go, get thee from the door.
Dro.E. What patch is made our porter? My master stays in the
street.
Dro.S. [*Within*] Let him walk from whence he came, lest he catch
cold on's feet.
Ant.E. Who talks within, there? Ho, open the door.
Dro.S. [*Within*] Right, sir, I'll tell you when and you'll tell me where-
fore.
[40] **Ant.E.** Wherefore? For my dinner. I have not dined today.
Dro.S. [*Within*] Nor today here you must not. Come again when you
may.
Ant.E. What art thou that keepest me out from the house I owe[11]?
Dro.S. [*Within*] The porter for this time, sir, and my name is Dromio.
Dro.E. O, villain, thou hast stolen both mine office and my name.
[45] The one ne'er got me credit, the other mickle[12] blame.
If thou hadst been Dromio today in my place,
Thou wouldst have changed thy face for a name, or thy name for an
ass.

Enter Luce [*above*]
Luce. What a coil[13] is there, Dromio! Who are those at the gate?
Dro.E. Let my master in, Luce.
Luce.   Faith, no, he comes too late,
And so tell your master.
[50] **Dro.E.**   O lord, I must laugh.
Have at you with a proverb: 'Shall I set in my staff?'
Luce. Have at you with another. That's 'When? Can you tell?'
Dro.S. [*Within*] If thy name be called Luce, Luce, thou hast answered
him well.
Ant.E. Do you hear, you minion[14]? You'll let us in, I trow.
Luce. I thought to have asked you.
[55] **Dro.S.** [*Within*]   And you said no.
Dro.E. So come – help. Well struck! There was blow for blow.
Ant.E. Thou baggage, let me in.
Luce.   Can you tell for whose sake?
Dro.E. Master, knock the door hard.
Luce.   Let him knock till it ache.
Ant.E. You'll cry for this, minion, if I beat the door down.
[60] **Luce.** What needs all that, and a pair of stocks in the town?

Enter Adriana [*above*]

Adriana. Who is that at the door that keeps all this noise?

Dro.S. [*Within*] By my troth, your town is troubled with unruly boys.

Ant.E. Are you there, wife? You might have come before.

Adr. Your wife, sir knave? Go get you from the door. [*Exit with Luce*]

[65] **Dro.E.** If you went in pain, master, this knave would go sore.

Angelo. Here is neither cheer, sir, nor welcome. We would fain have
either.

Bal. In debating which was best, we shall part[15] with neither.

Dro.E. They stand at the door, master. Bid them welcome hither.

Ant.E. There is something in the wind, that we cannot get in.

[70] **Dro.E.** You would say so, master, if your garments were thin.

Your cake is warm within. You stand here in the cold.

It would make a man mad as a buck to be so bought and sold[16].

Ant.E. Go fetch me something. I'll break ope the gate.

Dro.S. [*Within*] Break any breaking here, and I'll break your knave's
pate.

[75] **Dro.E.** A man may break a word with you, sir, and words are but
wind;

Ay, and break it in your face, so he break it not behind.

Dro.S. [*Within*] It seems thou wantest breaking. Out upon thee,
hind[17]!

Dro.E. Here's too much 'Out upon thee.' I pray thee, let me in.

Dro.S. [*Within*] Ay, when fowls have no feathers, and fish have no
fin.

[80] **Ant.E.** Well, I'll break in. Go borrow me a crow.

Dro.E. A crow without feather, master? Mean you so?

For a fish without a fin, there's a fowl without a feather.

If a crow help us in, sirrah, we'll pluck a crow together[18].

Ant.E. Go, get thee gone. Fetch me an iron crow.

[85] **Bal**. Have patience, sir. O, let it not be so.

Herein you war against your reputation,

And draw within the compass of suspect[19]

The'unviolated honour of your wife.

Once this[20]: your long experience of her wisdom,

[90] Her sober virtue, years, and modesty,

Plead on her part some cause to you unknown.

And doubt not, sir, but she will well excuse[21]

Why at this time the doors are made[22] against you.

Be ruled by me. Depart in patience,

[95] And let us to the Tiger[23] all to dinner,

And about evening come yourself alone

To know the reason of this strange restraint.

If by strong hand you offer to break in
Now in the stirring passage[24] of the day,
[100] A vulgar[25] comment will be made of it,
And that supposed by the common rout
Against your yet ungalled estimation[26]
That may with foul intrusion enter in
And dwell upon your grave when you are dead.
[105] For slander lives upon succession,
For ever housed where it gets possession.
Ant.E. You have prevailed. I will depart in quiet,
And in despite of mirth mean to be merry.
I know a wench of excellent discourse,
[110] Pretty and witty; wild and yet, too, gentle.
There will we dine. This woman that I mean,
My wife (but, I protest, without desert)
Hath oftentimes upbraided me withal.
To her will we to dinner. [*To Angelo*] Get you home
[115] And fetch the chain[27]. By this, I know, 'tis made.
Bring it, I pray you, to the Porpentine[28],
For there's the house. That chain will I bestow –
Be it for nothing but to spite my wife –
Upon mine hostess there. Good sir, make haste.
[120] Since mine own doors refuse to entertain me,
I'll knock elsewhere, to see if they'll disdain me.
Ang. I'll meet you at that place some hour hence.
Ant.E. Do so. – This jest shall cost me some expense. *Exeunt.*

---

1 i.e. a jewelled necklace. 2 i.e. entrusted. 3 i.e. in such a predicament. 4 i.e. serious. 5 i.e. fare. 6 i.e. provisions. 7 i.e. blockhead. 8 i.e. stupid fellow. 9 i.e. fool. 10 i.e. bring into being by magic incantations. 11 i.e. own. 12 i.e. much. 13 i.e. commotion. 14 i.e. hussy. 15 i.e. depart. 16 i.e. tricked. 17 i.e. boorish fellow. 18 i.e. settle our quarrel. 19 i.e. suspicion. 20 i.e. in short. 21 i.e. explain. 22 i.e. shut. 23 i.e. presumably an inn. 24 i.e. bustling traffic. 25 i.e. public. 26 i.e. unsullied reputation. 27 i.e. the carcanet, mentioned above (cf. n. 1). 28 i.e. Porcupine, the Courtesan's house.

N 3. Matthew Gwinne (1603), *Nero* (II 3)

The English translation of the Tenne Tragedies *ascribed to Seneca, published in 1581 included the pseudo-Senecan praetexta* Octavia, *rendered into English by Thomas Nuce.* Octavia *was performed at Christ Church, Oxford, in 1588, at a time when the chronicle play had become popular in the wake of Thomas Legge's* Richardus Tertius *(performed at St John's*

College, Cambridge, in 1579), the first representative of its kind and one of the first history plays in England more generally. Matthew Gwinne's (c. 1558-1627) Nero (1603), a slightly later university drama, a tragoedia nova *written in Latin (full title:* Nero. Tragædia nova. Matthæo Gwinne Med. Doct. Collegij Diui Joannis Præcursoris apud Oxonienses Socio collecta è Tacito, Suetonio, Dione, Seneca*), then applied the interest in historical drama to the Nero theme, the only event from Roman history that could build on a classical dramatic precedent. Gwinne's drama was soon followed by tragedies on Nero in English. The topic then became popular in opera as well, the most famous version being* L'incoronazione di Poppea *of 1642/43 (libretto by Giovanni Francesco Busenello and music attributed to Claudio Monteverdi).*

Gwinne's play is based on all relevant ancient sources, both historiographical and dramatic; it covers a much longer period and hence a more varied action than the pseudo-Senecan Octavia, *and it is couched in a highly rhetorical Latin. The play consists of five very long acts; each of the first four acts dramatizes a conspiracy that leads up to a murder, and the ghost of the victim introduces the following act. Nero is the main character, an intriguing villain, who, after becoming emperor, changes from a moderate young man to a murderous and ferocious adult. Hence a scene about principles of Nero's reign in the second act, taking place soon after Nero's accession to the throne, conveys a portrait of Seneca and Nero that is reminiscent of their dialogue in the classical* Octavia *(cf. D 15), but also differs in a number of ways, including Nero's attitude, the setting and the number of characters involved.*

The Latin text (followed by an English translation) is taken from a reproduction of the copy of the original edition in the Bodleian Library, Oxford (with some conventions of seventeenth-century spelling of Latin texts eliminated): Matthew Gwinne. Nero *(printed 1603), prepared with an Introduction by Heinz-Dieter Leidig, Hildesheim/New York 1983 (Renaissance Latin Drama in England 13). This edition has been used by kind permission of Olms Verlag.*

Act. II, Sc. 3

Nero e castris in curiam. Senatores. L. Antistius Consul. Burrhus praefectus Praetorianus. Seneca.
[770] **Nero**. postquam inter homines desiit divus Nero
morari, avitis Claudiis clarus Nero,
suis triumphis clarus, illorum inclytus,
Graecae et Latinae scriptor historiae Nero,
patriae pater, curator annonae Nero,
[775] sub quo regente triste nil, tuta omnia,
providus (id acta vita sub Caio docet)

sapiens (id ipsum nomen imperii probat)
Caesar, Tiberius, Drusus, Augustus, Nero;
pietatis ergo, Claudium in caelos, patres,
[780] unco trahamus, Divus ubi fungos edat,
cibos deorum: funus Augustum apparo.
nunc quia Deorum gratia, voto meo,
virtute matris, militum assensu omnium,
filius, et haeres Claudii, imperium gero,
[785] auctoritatem postulo vestram, Patres,
summam, auspicatam, liberam, unanimem, gravem.
unam esse Lunam, luceant stellae licet,
solum esse Solem, Luna licet orbem impleat,
unum esse superis, inferis, mediis Iovem,
[790] unum esse Romae, monstra nisi gignat, caput,
pax, ordo, lex, vis, usus, utilitas iubent.
ille unus ecce Iupiter, pastor, pater,
adsum, iuvando Iupiter, amando pater,
et alendo pastor adsum, ut Augusti pia
[795] subinde referam regna, licet impar feram.
Augustus, ecce denuo Augustus, redit.
nec mihi iuventus civicis armis furit
imbuta, nec sunt, quas alam, lites domi.
nulla odia, nullae iniuriae, nulla ultio.
[800] vestra odia, vestrae iniuriae, vestra ultio
mihi vindicanda: mitis in reliquos ero,
in me severus: esse vos tales volo,
qualis videbor, nec ero quam videor minor.
talis ero vobis, mihi Deos quales velim:
[805] exempla vitae recta quasi leges dabo.
documenta legum sancta mihi vitam instruent.
hominem meminero, non Deum, sed nec feram,
praeesse hominibus, non feris, sed nec Deis.
non unus omnes arbiter causas agam;
[810] ne reus et actor, una cum capiat domus,
paucos potentes, pauperes sese eiulent.
venale nihil est in domo nostra: nihil,
nihil impetrandum est ambitu, merito omnia.
mea domus aliud, aliud est Romae status.
[815] id cupio, non me, sed mihi timeant mei.
antiqua teneat munia Senatus volo.
Italia lectos Consules tota audeat,
provinciaeque pareant: illi Patres
vocent: gerenda bella mandantur mihi.

[820] pace moderabor milites, bello instruam.
sic Caesar astrum, sic fit Augustus Deus.
L. Antistius. o nos sub isto principe beatos Patres.
perpetua Deus haec servet Aeneadis bona.
vivat Domitius, Claudius, Caesar, Nero,
[825] Augustus, Imperator, Invictus, Pius,
Plebis tribunus, Pontifex, Patriae Pater:
concinite, 'vivat'.
Omnes.   vivat, o vivat Nero.
   Tubae concinunt.
L. Antist. iurandum in acta Caesaris nostis, Patres.
Nero. collega, noli vel Patris Patriae mihi
[830] induere nomen, quod mihi iuventus neget:
vel tute in acta nostra iurare: haud decet
esse beneficiis imparem, officiis parem.
tu Seneca iuris verba iurandi doce.
   Genu flectant Senatores.
Seneca. Tarpeie Stator, rector in coelo soli,
[835] Romule Quirine, de solo coeli incola,
Auguste Caesar, hominum amor, superum comes,
audite falsos, vindices; testes, pios.
quae Nero iubebit sancta, quae faciet rata,
facienda quae vult ille, quae non vult nefas,
[840] nisi reputemus, Iupiter sic nos foras
proiiciat, ut nos iacimus hos lapides foras:
tantoque iaciat gravius, ut gravius potest.
   Singuli Senatores ovum aut aliquid simile tinctum et aqua rosacea
   repletum proiiciant: tubis concinentibus.
Burrhus. quodnam excubantes milites signum ferent?
Nero. signum excubantes 'optimae matris' ferant.
[845] **Bur**. nunc huic tabellae Caesar apponas manum,
qua destinantur in crucem fures duo.
Nero. urgere noli Burrhe: nam membrum mihi
resecare videor, cum reseco civem mihi:
nec ad secandum medicus accedo lubens.
[850] **Sen**. medicum severum intemperans aeger facit.
quicunque parcit improbis perdit probos.
probi tenentur praemio, poena improbi.
impune facinus provocat crimen recens.
aliena vitia si feres, facies tua.
[855] qui parcit omni ac nemini, est aeque ferus.
Nero. qui cito libenter qui nimis, inique iubet.
nescire vellem literas.

191

Sen.   vocem, Patres,
audite, dignam tota quam Roma audiat.
dignam innocente saeculo, dignam Deo.
habeamus ergo gratias.
[860] **Nero**.   illas Patres
habete cum meruero: nunc actum nihil,
quin melius actum debeam, et melius velim.
    Procedunt hinc legati Armenii; inde Agrippina cum Pallante.
sed ecce gressus inde Legati ferunt
Armenii; et inde mater Augusta advenit.
[865] **Sen**. quin Imperator, potius Augustae obvius
procede, ne sit faeminae in solio locus.
Nero. Augusta mater, alius Armenios erit
locus audiendi: petere nunc aedes placet.
Agrippina. mihi me relinque Caesar, ubi visum sequar.
    Nero descendit de tribunali. Exeunt Nero, Senatores, Seneca,
    Burrhus, caeteri praeter Agrippinam et Pallantem.

Act II, Scene 3

Nero is on the way from the camp to the Senate. Senators. Lucius Antistius, Consul. Burrhus, Prefect of the Praetorian Guards. Seneca.
[770] **Nero**. After the divine Nero[1] has ceased to be about among humans, Nero, renowned for his Claudian ancestors, renowned for his triumphs, famous because of them, Nero, the writer of history in Greek and Latin, the father of the fatherland, Nero, the guardian of the grain supply, [775] during whose reign nothing was sad and everything safe, circumspect (his life led under Gaius[2] proved this), wise (the very name of the empire confirmed this), Tiberius Drusus Caesar Augustus Nero; as a result of piety, let us, Senators, draw Claudius up into the heavens [780] on a hook, now that the Divine has eaten mushrooms, food of the gods[3]: I am preparing an Augustan[4] funeral. Now since by favour of the Gods, by my own wishes, by the virtue of my mother and by the approval of all soldiers, I govern the empire as son and heir of Claudius, [785] I demand, Senators, your approving decree, supreme, auspicious, free, unanimous and weighty. That there should be one Moon, even though the stars shine, there should be one Sun, even though the Moon fills the orb of the world, that there should be one Jupiter for those in the heavens, for those in the underworld and for those in the middle, [790] that there should be one head in Rome, if it does not bring forth monsters, is commanded by peace, order, law, force, custom and utility. Look, this one Jupiter is shepherd and father; here I am, a Jupiter by aiding, a father by loving and a shepherd by nourishing, here I am, so that I [795] immediately restore the

pious reign of Augustus, even though I bear it not as his equal. Augustus, look, Augustus returns once more. And neither does my youth, infected, rage in civic arms, nor are there quarrels at home, which I nourish. No hatred, no injury, no vendetta. [800] Your hatred, your injury, your vendetta are to be avenged by me: I will be mild against everyone else, but strict against me: I wish you to be such as I shall be seen, nor will I be less than I appear. I shall be such towards you as I wish the Gods to be towards me: [805] I shall give right examples of life like laws. Hallowed documents of the laws shall form my life. I shall remember that I am a human being, not a God, but not a wild beast either, that I rule over human beings, not wild beasts, but not Gods either. I shall not carry through all cases as sole judge, [810] accused and plaintiff, as one house holds them, shall not lament that a few are powerful and they are poor. Nothing is for sale in our house: nothing, nothing is to be gained by canvassing, everything by merit. My house is one thing, the condition of Rome another. [815] This I desire, that my people should be afraid not of me, but for me. The Senate should retain its ancient duties, I wish. The whole of Italy shall venture to have elected Consuls, and the provinces shall obey them: they shall summon the Senators: wars to wage are entrusted to me. [820] In peace I shall restrain the soldiers, in war I shall draw them up. Thus Caesar becomes a star, thus Augustus becomes a God.

L. Antistius. Oh, we happy Senators under such an emperor. The God shall preserve perpetual good for the descendants of Aeneas. Long live Domitius Nero Claudius Caesar [825] Augustus, Emperor, Invincible, Pious, Tribune of the People, Pontifex, Father of the Fatherland: shout together 'long live'.

All. Long live, oh, long live Nero.

Trumpets sound together.

L. Antist. You know, Senators, that oaths must be sworn to Caesar's acts.

Nero. My colleague, neither impose upon me the title 'Father of the Fatherland', [830] which my youth denies me, nor swear to my acts: it is not fitting for me to be not equal in kindnesses and equal in offices. You, Seneca, announce the words for the oath.

The Senators fall to their knees.

Seneca. Tarpeian Supporter, governor of the sun in heaven, [835] Romulus Quirinus, inhabitant of the heavens, coming from the earth, Augustus Caesar, beloved by humans, companion of gods, listen to false avengers and pious witnesses. If we do not consider as sacred what Nero will order, as ratified what he will do, as ordered what he wishes, as a crime what he does not wish, [840] Jupiter shall thrust us out of doors, just as we throw these stones out of doors: and he shall throw us so much more vehemently, as he can do it more vehemently.

193

Individual Senators may throw an egg or something similar bathed in and filled with rose water, as trumpets sound together.

Burrhus. What password will the soldiers on nightwatch use?

Nero. The watchmen shall use the password 'the best mother'.

[845] **Bur**. Now, Caesar, please put your hand to this tablet, whereby two thieves are given over to the cross.

Nero. Do not press me, Burrhus: for I seem to cut off one of my limbs when I cut off a fellow citizen: and I do not approach the duty of cutting off as a willing surgeon.

[850] **Sen**. Someone immoderately ill makes the doctor severe. Whoever spares the dishonest, destroys the honest. The honest are governed by rewards, the dishonest by punishment. A misdeed unpunished provokes a fresh crime. If you bear vices of others, you will make them your own. [855] Those who spare everybody and nobody are equally fierce.

Nero. He who orders such things quickly, gladly and excessively, orders unjustly. I wish that I did not know the alphabet.

Sen. Listen to this statement, Senators, worthy for the whole of Rome to hear, worthy of an innocent age, worthy of a God. [860] Hence let us be full of gratitude.

Nero. Be full of this gratitude, Senators, when I have deserved it: now nothing has been done but what I ought and wish to have done better.

Thereupon Armenian ambassadors appear, and then Agrippina with Pallas.

But, look, the Armenian Ambassadors are making their way over here; and then Augusta, my mother[5], arrives.

[865] **Sen**. Why don't you rather go forth and meet the Augusta[6], Emperor, so that there be no room on the throne for a woman.

Nero. Augusta, my mother, there will be another occasion for hearing the Armenians: now it pleases me to head for the palace.

Agrippina. Leave me to myself, Caesar[7]; I shall follow when I decide to.

Nero descends from the tribunal. Nero, the Senators, Seneca, Burrhus and the others leave except for Agrippina and Pallas.

---

1 i.e. Emperor Claudius, Nero's predecessor. 2 i.e. Caligula. 3 Claudius was allegedly killed by poisoned mushrooms. 4 i.e. splendid and royal. 5 i.e. Agrippina; Augusta used as a title. 6 i.e. Agrippina. 7 i.e. Nero.

N 4. John Dryden (1690), *Amphitryon; or The Two Sosias* (I 1)

Jean Giraudoux called his dramatic treatment of the Amphitruo story Amphitryon 38, indicating that thirty-seven earlier versions already existed (1929). Irrespective of whether this precise number is correct, this choice

*of title shows the popularity of the topic and the awareness of a long tra-
dition on the part of later poets. Although the Amphitruo story is already
attested in Greek literature, the first extant damatic version is Plautus'*
Amphitruo; *since the Renaissance this has inspired a large number of imi-
tations, adaptations and further developments. Famous versions include
Molière's (i.e. Jean-Baptiste Poquelin, 1622-1673)* Amphitryon *(1668),
John Dryden's (1631-1700)* Amphitryon; or The Two Sosias *(1690), Hein-
rich von Kleist's (1777-1811)* Amphitryon *(1807) and, of course, Jean Giraudoux's (1882-1944)* Amphitryon 38 *(1929).*

*As John Dryden says in the dedicatory letter for his play, his version of
the story takes its starting point from Plautus and Molière, 'the two greatest names of ancient and modern comedy'; this connection is seen as justi-
fying and ennobling his drama. At the same time he claims 'that more than
half of it is mine, and that the rest is rather a lame imitation of their ex-
cellencies than a just translation'; while adopting a conventional stance of
modesty, the poet certainly made deliberate changes to create his own version.*

The first scene of the first act (after the prologue) of John Dryden's Amphitryon *is a good example of the impact of Plautus'* Amphitruo *(cf. D 7)
on later generations of poets; it also shows how Dryden has adapted the
story to his own time, as he was writing at the beginning of the neo-classical
period in English literature and right after the Glorious Revolution.*

The edition used is Four Restoration Marriage Plays (Thomas Otway,
The Soldiers' Fortune; Nathaniel Lee, The Princess of Cleves; John Dryden, Amphitryon; or The Two Sosias; Thomas Southerne, The Wives' Excuse; or Cuckolds Make Themselves), *edited by Michael Cordner with
Ronald Clayton, Oxford/New York 1995 (The World's Classics). The extract has been reprinted by permission of Oxford University Press.*

Dramatis personae
Jupiter – Mercury – Phoebus – Amphitryon – Sosia – Gripus – Polydas –
Tranio – Alcmena – Phaedra – Bromia – Night – Musicians and Dancers

Act I, Scene 1

Thebes. Mercury and Phoebus descend in several machines.
Phoebus. Know you the reason of this present summons?
'Tis neither council-day, nor is this heaven.
What business has our Jupiter on earth?
Why more at Thebes than any other place?
And why we two of all the herd of gods
Are chosen out to meet him in consult?
They call me god of wisdom;

But Mars and Vulcan, the two fools of heaven,
Whose wit lies in their anvil and their sword,
Know full as much as I.

Mercury. And Venus may know more than both of us,
For 'tis some petticoat affair, I guess.

I have discharged my duty, which was to summon you, Phoebus. We shall know more anon, when the Thunderer comes down. 'Tis our part to obey our father; for, to confess the truth, we two are little better than sons of harlots; and if Jupiter had not been pleased to take a little pains with our mothers, instead of being gods, we might have been a couple of link-boys.

Phoeb. But know you nothing farther, Hermes? What news in court?

Merc. There has been a devilish quarrel, I can tell you, betwixt Jupiter and Juno. She threatened to sue him in the spiritual court for some matrimonial omissions; and he stood upon his prerogative. Then she hit him on the teeth of all his bastards; and your name and mine were used with less reverence than became our godships. They were both in their cups[1]; and at the last the matter grew so high, that they were ready to have thrown stars at one another's heads.

Phoeb. 'Twas happy for me that I was at my vocation, driving daylight about the world; but I had rather stand my father's thunderbolts than my stepmother's railing.

Merc. When the tongue-battle was over, and the championess had harnessed her peacocks to go for Samos and hear the prayers that were made to her —

Phoeb. By the way, her worshippers had a bad time on't. She was in a damnable humour for receiving petitions.

Merc. Jupiter immediately beckons me aside, and charges me, that as soon as ever you had set up[2] your horses, you and I should meet him here at Thebes. Now, putting the premises together, as dark as it is, methinks I begin to see daylight.

Phoeb. As plain as one of my own beams. She has made him uneasy at home, and he is going to seek his diversion abroad. I see heaven itself is no privileged place for happiness, if a man must carry his wife along with him.

Merc. 'Tis neither better nor worse, upon my conscience. He is weary of hunting in the spacious forest of a wife, and is following his game incognito in some little purlieu[3] here at Thebes. That's many an honest man's case on earth too, Jove help 'em — as indeed he does, to make 'em cuckolds.

Phoeb. But so, Mercury, then I, who am a poet, must indite his love-letter; and you, who are by trade a porter, must convey it.

Merc. No more. He's coming down souse upon us, and hears as far as

he can see too. He's plaguy⁴ hot upon the business; I know it by his hard
driving.
Jupiter descends.
Jupiter. What, you are descanting upon my actions?
Much good may do you with your politics.
All subjects will be censuring their kings.
Well, I confess I am in love. What then?
Phoeb. Some mortal, we presume, of Cadmus' blood,
Some Theban beauty, some new Semele,
Or some Europa.
Merc. I'll say that for my father – he's constant to an handsome family.
He knows when they have a good smack with 'em, and snuffs up incense
so savourly, when 'tis offered him by a fair hand.
Jup. Well, my familiar sons, this saucy carriage
I have deserved; for he who trusts a secret
Makes his own man his master.
I read your thoughts;
Therefore you may as safely speak as think.
Merc. Mine was a very homely thought. I was considering into what
form your almightyship would be pleased to transform yourself tonight.
Whether you would fornicate in the shape of a bull, or a ram, or an eagle,
or a swan. What bird or beast you would please to honour, by transgress-
ing your own laws in his likeness. Or, in short, whether you would recre-
ate yourself in feathers or in leather?
Phoeb. Any disguise to hide the king of gods.
Jup. I know your malice, Phoebus. You would say
That when a monarch sins it should be secret,
To keep exterior show of sanctity,
Maintain respect, and cover bad example;
For kings and priests are in a manner bound,
For reverence sake, to be close hypocrites.
Phoeb. But what necessitates you to this love,
Which you confess a crime, and yet commit?
For to be secret makes not sin the less.
'Tis only hidden from the vulgar view –
Maintains, indeed, the reverence due to princes,
But not absolves the conscience from the crime.
Jup. I love, because 'twas in the fates I should.
Phoeb. With reverence be it spoke, a bad excuse.
Thus every wicked act in heaven or earth
May make the same defence. But what is fate?
Is it a blind contingence of events?
Or sure necessity of causes linked

That must produce effects? Or is't a power
That orders all things by superior will,
Foresees his work, and works in that foresight?
Jup. Fate is, what I
By virtue of omnipotence have made it;
And power omnipotent can do no wrong –
Not to myself, because I willed it so;
Nor yet to men, for what they are is mine.
This night I will enjoy Amphitryon's wife;
For, when I made her, I decreed her such
As I should please to love. I wrong not him
Whose wife she is; for I reserved my right
To have her while she pleased me. That once past,
She shall be his again.

Merc. Here's omnipotence with a vengeance – to make a man a cuckold, and yet not to do him wrong. Then I find, father Jupiter, that when you made fate, you had the wit to contrive a holiday for yourself now and then. For you kings never enact a law, but you have a kind of an eye to your own prerogative.

Phoeb. If there be no such thing as right and wrong,
Of an eternal being, I have done;
But if there be –
Jup.   Peace, thou disputing fool.
Learn this. If thou couldst comprehend my ways,
Then thou wert Jove, not I. Yet, thus far know,
That, for the good of humankind, this night
I shall beget a future Hercules,
Who shall redress the wrongs of injured mortals,
Shall conquer monsters, and reform the world.

Merc. Ay, brother Phoebus; and our father made all those monsters for Hercules to conquer, and contrived all those vices on purpose for him to reform too. There's the jest on't.

Phoeb. Since arbitrary power will hear no reason, 'tis wisdom to be silent.

Merc. Why, that's the point. This same arbitrary power is a knockdown argument. 'Tis but a word and a blow. Now methinks our father speaks out like an honest barefaced god, as he is. He lays the stress in the right place – upon absolute dominion. I confess, if he had been a man, he might have been a tyrant, if his subjects durst have called him to account. But you, brother Phoebus, are but a mere country gentleman, that never comes to court, that are abroad all day on horseback, making visits about the world, are drinking all night and in your cups are still railing at the government. O these patriots, these bumpkin patriots, are a very silly sort of animal.

198

Jup. My present purpose and design you heard –
T'enjoy Amphitryon's wife, the fair Alcmena.
You two must be subservient to my love.
Merc. (*to Phoebus*) No more of your grumbletonian[5] morals, brother.
There's preferment coming. Be advised and pimp dutifully.
Jup. Amphitryon, the brave Theban general,
Has overcome his country's foes in fight,
And in a single duel slain their king.
His conquering troops are eager on their march,
Returning home; while their young general,
More eager to review his beauteous wife,
Posts on before, winged with impetuous love,
And, by tomorrow's dawn, will reach this town.
Merc. That's but short warning, father Jupiter. Having made no former
advances of courtship to her, you have need of your omnipotence, and all
your godship, if you mean to be beforehand with him.
Phoeb. Then how are we to be employed this evening?
Time's precious, and these summer nights are short.
I must be early up to light the world.
Jup. You shall not rise; there shall be no tomorrow.
Merc. Then the world's to be at an end, I find.
Phoeb. Or else a gap in nature, of a day.
Jup. A day will well be lost to busy man:
Night shall continue sleep, and care shall cease.
So, many men shall live, and live in peace,
Whom sunshine had betrayed to envious[6] sight,
And sight to sudden rage, and rage to death.
Now, I will have a night for love and me,
A long luxurious night, fit for a god
To quench and empty his immortal heat.
Merc. I'll lay on[7] the woman's side for all that, that she shall love
longest tonight, in spite of your omnipotence.
Phoeb. I shall be cursed by all the labouring trades
That early rise; but you must be obeyed.
Jup. No matter for the cheating part of man;
They have a day's sin less to answer for.
Phoeb. When would you have me wake?
Jup. Why, when Jove goes to sleep. When I have finished,
Your brother Mercury shall bring you word.
Exit Phoebus on his chariot.
Jup. (*to Mercury*) Now, Hermes, I must take Amphitryon's form,
T'enjoy his wife.
Thou must be Sosia, this Ampitryon's slave,

199

Who, all this night, is travelling to Thebes
To tell Alcmena of her lord's approach
And bring her joyful news of victory.
Merc. But why must I be Sosia?
Jup. Dull god of wit, thou statue of thyself!
Thou must be Sosia, to keep out Sosia,
Who, by his entrance, might discover[8] Jove,
Disturb my pleasures, raise unruly noise,
And so distract Alcmena's tender soul,
She would not meet my warmth, when I dissolve
Into her lap, nor give down half her love.
Merc. Let me alone; I'll cudgel him away.
But I abhor so villainous a shape.
Jup. Take it; I charge thee on thy duty, take it.
Nor dare to lay it down, till I command.
I cannot bear a moment's loss of joy.
Night appears above in her chariot.
Look up. The night is in her silent chariot,
And rolling just o'er Thebes. Bid her drive slowly,
Or make a double turn about the world,
While I drop Jove and take Amphitryon's dress,
To be the greater, while I seem less.
Exit Jupiter.
Merc. (*to Night*) Madam Night, a good even to you. Fair and softly, I
beseech you, madam. I have a word or two to you, from no less a god than
Jupiter.
Night. O my nimble-fingered god of theft, what make you here on earth
at this unseasonable hour? What banker's shop is to be broken open
tonight? Or what clippers, and coiners, and conspirators have been invok-
ing your deity for their assistance?
Merc. Faith, none of those enormities; and yet I am still in my vocation,
for you know I am a kind of jack-of-all-trades. At a word, Jupiter is in-
dulging his genius tonight with a certain noble sort of recreation called
wenching. The truth on't is, adultery is its proper name.
Night. Jupiter would do well to stick to his wife Juno.
Merc. He has been married to her above these hundred years; and
that's long enough in conscience to stick to one woman.
Night. She's his sister too, as well as his wife – that's a double tie of
affection to her.
Merc. Nay, if he made bold with his own flesh and blood, 'tis likely he
will not spare his neighbours'.
Night. If I were his wife, I would raise a rebellion against him for the
violation of my bed.

Merc. Thou art mistaken, old Night; his wife could raise no faction. All the deities in heaven would take the part of the cuckold-making god, for they are all given to the flesh most damnably. Nay, the very goddesses would stickle in the cause of love; 'tis the way to be popular – to whore and love. For what dost thou think old Saturn was deposed, but that he was cold and impotent, and made no court to the fair ladies. Pallas and Juno themselves, as chaste as they are, cried shame on him. I say unto thee, old Night, woe be to the monarch that has not the women on his side.

Night. Then by your rule, Mercury, a king who would live happily must debauch his whole nation of women.

Merc. As fas as his ready money will go, I mean; for Jupiter himself can't please all of 'em. But this is beside my present commission. He has sent me to will and require you to make a swingeing long night for him, for he hates to be stinted in his pleasures.

Night. Tell him plainly, I'll rather lay down my commission. What, would he make a bawd of me?

Merc. Poor ignorant! Why, he meant thee for a bawd when he first made thee. What art thou good for, but to be a bawd? Is not daylight better for mankind, I mean as to any other use, but only for love and fornification? Thou hast been a bawd too, a reverend, primitive, original bawd, from the first hour of thy creation! And all the laudable actions of love have been committed under thy mantle. Prithee for what dost thou think that thou art worshipped?

Night. Why, for my stars and moonshine.

Merc. That is, for holding a candle to[9] iniquity. But if they were put out, thou wouldst be double worshipped by the willing, bashful virgins.

Night. Then for my quiet, and the sweetness of my sleep.

Merc. No, for they sweet waking all the night, for sleep comes not upon lovers till thou art vanished.

Night. But it will be against nature, to make a long winter's night at midsummer.

Merc. Trouble not yourself for that. Phoebus is ordered to make a short summer's day tomorrow; so in four-and-twenty hours all will be at rights again.

Night. Well, I am edified by your discourse; and my comfort is, that whatever work is made, I see nothing.

Merc. About your business then. Put a spoke into your chariot-wheels, and order the seven stars a halt, while I put myself into the habit of a servingman and dress up a false Sosia to wait upon a false Amphitryon. Good-night, Night.

Night. My service to Jupiter. Farewell, Mercury.

Night goes backward. Exit Mercury.

1 i.e. drunk. 2 i.e. stabled. 3 i.e. outlying area. 4 i.e. excessively. 5 a contemptuous epithet, applied to certain members of the so-called 'Country' opposition to the Court. 6 i.e. malicious. 7 i.e. wager on, lay odds on. 8 i.e. unmask. 9 i.e. assisting.

N 5. Tony Harrison (1985), *Medea: a sex-war opera* (openings of acts 1 and 2)

The myth of Medea has been an extremely popular one in both ancient and more recent times. The two surviving classical dramatic versions, Euripides' Medea (431 BCE) and Seneca's Medea (cf. D 14), along with other ancient narratives of Medea have triggered a large number of modern versions. Famous ones include, for instance, Pierre Corneille's (1606-1684) Médée (1635), Franz Grillparzer's (1791-1872) Medea (1820) or Jean Anouilh's (1910-1987) Médée (1946). One of the more recent attempts, which, rather like Jean Giraudoux's Amphitryon 38 (1929; cf. N 4), builds on a long preceding Medea tradition and is composed in full awareness of it, is Tony Harrison's (b. 1937) Medea: a sex-war opera (1985).

Tony Harrison is well known for a wide range of plays creatively taking up ancient motifs and referring back to particular ancient dramas. The incorporation of a preceding mythical and literary tradition is obvious in Medea: a sex-war opera *not only by attempts to include the whole Medea story, but also by literal quotations from earlier Medea versions by other poets in the original languages, as at the beginning of the play, which appropriately starts with a quotation from Euripides' Medea (and will eventually end with further quotations from Euripides' Medea, followed by quotations of contemporary newspaper headlines about mothers killing children). The second act opens with Medea's reactions to the wedding of Jason and his new bride, a situation that also defines the beginning of Seneca's Medea. This wedding contrasts with Medea's own previous wedding with Jason, and she develops her plans of revenge in a conversation with her Nurse against this background.*

The edition used is: Tony Harrison, Theatre Works 1973-1985, Harmondsworth 1985 (Penguin). The extract has been reprinted by kind permission of the author.

Act One

The OVERTURE *spills over on to the stage where we see a circle of threatening* MEN, *chanting their hostility to a murderer of children as yet unidentified. They express their horror and hostility in words culled from the world's drama and opera on the subject of* MEDEA, *the murderer of her own children.*

CHORUS [M].
παιδολέτορ [Euripides, *Medea* 1393]
παιδοφόνου [Euripides, *Medea* 1407]

nefanda liberorum carnifex [Buchanan 515]
natorum caede cruenta [Buchanan 516]

exécrable tigresse [Corneille V.vi]
furie exécrable [Corneille V.vii]

mrzká, hnusná, zhubitelko dêti!
[*Euripidova Medeia*, tr. Dr Petr Durdik (Prague, 1878)]

tu, tu, malorum machinatrix facinorum [Seneca 226]

O madre iniqua e perfida! [Mayr]

Crudel! Feroce! Barbara! [Cherubini]

Hechizera! [Calderón, *Los Tres Mayores Prodigios*]

This bedlem Wight, and divelysh despret dame
[John Studeley/Seneca, 1566]

O vile malitious mynded wretich [*ibid*]

'The murd'rous witch ...' [*Medea; or the Best of Mothers*, 1856]

As the CHORUS [M] *chant their multi-lingual hatred, which becomes more and more intense, a vast female figure rises from the stage and this becomes the focus of male hatred. It is a vast effigy of the murderous* MEDEA *and as it becomes more gigantic we see that in its hand is a knife and hidden in its skirts frightened children. When the chant of the* CHORUS [M] *reaches a climax of hatred the knife plunges down, and the hostile circle of chanting men is dispersed and scattered in fear and panic, and the giant effigy collapses like a deflated blimp.*

Act Two

The Wedding Hymn is heard loud, clear, joyful, where the Wedding Hymn of the marriage of JASON *and* MEDEA *was quiet, subdued, secretive. Where we heard only the male voices of the* ARGONAUTS *in the previous Wedding Hymn, we now hear a rich, harmonious complement of male and female voices, hymning the true, potentially peaceful, union between man and woman. As the curtain rises we see the* WEDDING PROCESSION *grouped as before, with the addition of women, but as near as possible to the concluding spectacles of Act One. Whereas on Macris the procession was conducted in the dark with torches that had to be doused, this procession is in the full light of day. The elements of the ritual are identical and we should feel we are watching a continuation of the same procession we saw at the end of Act One. Once more we see the bridegroom* JASON *come into view with his bride, only this time the bride is not* MEDEA *but* CREUSA, *daughter of* CREON, *King of Corinth.*

The WEDDING PROCESSION *should begin to establish itself both as 'real' and as in the mind of the raging* MEDEA *we now see with the* NURSE.

MEDEA. (*With the hymn still audible, to Nurse.*)
    I wish now my father had got me back!
    The terrors of torture, the pains of the rack,
    the scars of the whip and the *scourge*,
    the flesh stripped bare to the bloodied bone,
    the gamut of agonies and cruel hurts
    are nothing to the pains that sear and *surge*
    through the heart of a woman a man deserts
    for another, leaving her alone
    in a hostile land, with her children, *alone*,
    for the mad mob who hate her to stab and to *stone*.

NURSE.
    Call the Virgin! Call the Mother! Call the Crone!

MEDEA.
    In Colchis at least I'd have died before I knew
    that a man who loved you could be untrue.
    Though love took me wholly by surprise
    I'm more surprised now that his love dies
    and his faithless heart is a nest of lies.
    It's taken ten years for the truth to *emerge:*
    he doesn't want his children or their *mother*
    he wants to bind himself to another
    and all to possess a paltry *throne*.

NURSE.
    Call the Virgin! Call the Mother! Call the Crone!

204

The sounds of the Wedding Hymn continue to return.

MEDEA. (*To Nurse.*)
    I should have let him be burnt to death,
    his flesh set aflame by the bull's fierce breath,
    I should have let them trample him dead
    cracking his bones and crushing his head
    I should have let the men hack him piece by piece,
    I should have let him die, but instead,
    deceived by love my magic can't check
    I put a noose round my own neck
    and let him win the Golden Fleece,
    and all for these ten years in his bed,
    wandering with him from place to place
    being abused for my foreign face,
    only to be thrown aside
    once he found himself a 'better' bride!

    I'll turn their wedding hymn into a *dirge*.
    I'll *smother* the torches in the smoke of death,
    and change their joy-chants to a dismal *drone*.

NURSE.
    Call the *Virg*in! Call the *Mother*! Call the *Crone*!

MEDEA.
    I'll turn their wedding hymn into a *dirge*.
    I'll *smother* their torches in the smoke of death,
    and change their joy-chants to a dismal *drone*.

NURSE.
    Call the *Virg*in! Call the *Mother*! Call the *Crone*!

This leads the two women into an invocation of the GODDESS, *one of the 'quotations' from a previous opera, the* Medea *of Cherubini. The Invocation is heard against the sound of the Wedding Hymn as the* WEDDING PROCESSION *re-enters. The* WEDDING PROCESSION *should be felt as a continuous presence, a perpetual goad to the rage of* MEDEA, *and present on stage, either as 'real' or still tormentingly imagined by* MEDEA, *stung that* JASON *and* CREUSA *are marrying to the same ritual by which he married her on Macris 10 years ago, a ritual hurried, hushed and suppressed. Its musical presence should also be continuous, giving us a hymn to the potential union of man and woman and something which continually enrages the mind and heart of* MEDEA.

The WEDDING PROCESSION *in all its glory 'delivers' JASON to MEDEA and possibly continues and then re-emerges to 'pick up' JASON after his confrontation with* MEDEA, *or stays in a 'freeze' which is re-animated each time JASON rejoins his bride.*

M.   Your marriage torch will be a funeral brand.
J.   You are meddling in things you don't understand.
M.   Deceit and fraud I don't understand, no!
J.   Don't cause trouble. Creon wants you to go.
M.   I don't want to stay here. *We*'ll go away!
J.   Creon may allow the children to stay.
M.   Our sons will go where their mother goes.
J.   They'll stone you, you witch in barbaric clothes.
M.   I have my magic! I can get by!
J.   Corinth doesn't want you, nor do I!
M.   Once you couldn't wait to drag me to bed.
J.   That part of me will never be dead.
M.   Then why take some little virgin instead?
J.   To be able to wear a crown on my head.
     King Creon's daughter gives me power in this land.
M.   Your marriage torch will be a funeral brand.

As if to prove her wrong JASON raises his wedding torch and rejoins the WEDDING PROCESSION *which resumes, the Wedding Hymn loud and dominant.*

MEDEA.
    I'll turn their wedding hymn into a *dirge*.
    I'll *smother* their torches in the smoke of death
    and change their joy-chants to a dismal *drone*.

NURSE.
    Call the *Vir*gin! Call the *Mother*! Call the *Crone*!

Bibliography and Further Reading

B 1. Editions, translations, commentaries

(1) Collections of fragments

Blänsdorf, J. (ed.) [*FPL*³] (1995) *Fragmenta poetarum Latinorum epicorum et lyricorum praeter Ennium et Lucilium, post W. Morel novis curis adhibitis ed. C. Büchner*. Editionem tertiam auctam curavit (Stuttgart).

Bonaria, M. (ed.) (1965) *Romani Mimi* (Rome) (Poetarum Latinorum reliquiae: Aetas rei publicae VI 2); originally: M. Bonaria (1955/6), *Mimorum Romanorum fragmenta*. Collegit, disposuit, recensuit. 2 vols (Genoa) (Università di Genova, Facoltà di Lettere, Pubblicazioni dell'Istituto di Filologia Classica 5).

Daviault, A. (ed.) (1981) *Comoedia Togata. Fragments*. Texte établi, traduit et annoté (Paris) (CUF lat.).

de Durante, G. (ed.) (1966) *Le fabulae praetextae* (Rome) (Testi e studi per la scuola universitaria. Testi 1).

Frassinetti, P. (ed.) (1967) *Atellanae fabulae* (Rome) (Poetarum Latinorum reliquiae: Aetas rei publicae, vol. VI 1); originally: P. Frassinetti (ed.) (1955) *Fabularum Atellanarum fragmenta* (Torino/Milan/Padua/Florence/Pescara/Rome/Naples/Catania/Palermo) (Corpus Scriptorum Latinorum Paravianum).

Pedroli, L. (ed.) (1954) *Fabularum praetextarum quae extant. Introduzione – Testi – Commenti* (Genoa) (Pubblicazioni dell'Istituto di filologia classica dell'Università di Genova).

Ribbeck, O. (ed.) [R.²] (1871) *Scaenicae Romanorum poesis fragmenta. Vol. I. Tragicorum Romanorum fragmenta*, secundis curis rec. (Leipzig) (repr. Hildesheim 1962).

Ribbeck, O. (ed.) [R.²] (1873) *Scaenicae Romanorum poesis fragmenta. Vol. II. Comicorum Romanorum praeter Plautum et Terentium fragmenta*, secundis curis rec. (Leipzig).

Ribbeck, O. (ed.) [R.³] (1897) *Scaenicae Romanorum poesis fragmenta. Vol. I. Tragicorum Romanorum fragmenta*, tertiis curis rec. (Leipzig).

Ribbeck, O. (ed.) [R.³] (1898) *Scaenicae Romanorum poesis fragmenta. Vol. II. Comicorum Romanorum praeter Plautum et Syri quae feruntur sententias fragmenta*, tertiis curis rec. (Leipzig).

Romano, D. (ed.) (1953) *Atellana fabula* (Palermo) (Testi antichi e medievali per esercitazioni universitarie 7).

Warmington, E.H. (ed.) [W.] (1935) *Remains of Old Latin. Vol. I. Ennius and Caecilius* (London/Cambridge [MA]) (rev. and repr. 1967; several repr.) (LCL 294).

Warmington, E.H. (ed.) [W.] (1936) *Remains of Old Latin. Vol. II. Livius Andronicus, Naevius, Pacuvius and Accius* (London/Cambridge [MA]) (repr. 1957, with minor bibliographical additions; several repr.) (LCL 314).

(2) Livius Andronicus

Spaltenstein, F. (2008) *Commentaire des fragments dramatiques de Livius Androncius* (Brussels) (Collection Latomus 318).

(3) Naevius

Marmorale, E.V. (ed.) (1950) *Naevius poeta. Introduzione biobibliografica, testo dei frammenti e commento*, 2nd edn (Florence) (seconda tiratura 1953) (Biblioteca di studi superiori VIII).

(4) Ennius

Jocelyn, H.D. (ed.) (1967) *The Tragedies of Ennius. The Fragments.* Edited with an introduction and commentary (Cambridge) (repr. with corr. 1969) (Cambridge Classical Texts and Commentaries 10).

Vahlen, I. (ed.) [V.²] (1903) *Ennianae poesis reliquiae*, iteratis curis rec. (Leipzig) (= Leipzig ³1928; Amsterdam 1963, 1967).

(5) Pacuvius

Schierl, P. (2006) *Die Tragödien des Pacuvius. Ein Kommentar zu den Fragmenten mit Einleitung, Text und Übersetzung* (Berlin/New York) (TuK 28).

(6) Accius

Dangel, J. (ed.) (1995) *Accius: Oeuvres (fragments)* (Paris) (CUF lat.).

D'Antò, V. (ed.) (1980) *L. Accio: I frammenti delle tragedie* (Lecce).

(7) Plautus

Lindsay, W.M. (ed.) (1904/5) *T. Macci Plauti comoediae*, recognovit brevique adnotatione critica instruxit, 2 vols (Oxford) (repr.).

Christenson, D.M. (ed.) (2000) *Plautus. Amphitruo* (Cambridge) (Cambridge Greek and Latin Classics).

Hammond, M./Mack, A.M./Moskalew, W. (eds) (1963) *T. Macci Plauti Miles gloriosus*. Edited with an introduction and notes (Cambridge [MA]/London) (2nd edn, rev. M. Hammond, 1970).

Christenson, D.M. (tr.) (2008) *Plautus. Four Plays: Casina, Amphitruo, Captivi, Pseudolus* (Newburyport [MA]) (Focus Classical Library).

Nixon, P. (ed. and tr.) (1916-1938) *Plautus*. With an English translation, 5 vols (Cambridge [MA]/London) (repr.).

Segal, E. (tr.) (1996) *Plautus. Four Comedies: The Braggart Soldier, The Brothers Menaechmus, The Haunted House, The Pot of Gold*. Translated, with an introduction and notes (Oxford/New York) (Oxford World's Classics).

Smith, P.L. (tr.) (1991) *Plautus. Three Comedies: Miles gloriosus, Pseudolus, Rudens*. Translated with an introduction (Ithaca [NY]/London) (Masters of Latin Literature).

Watling, E.F. (tr.) (1964) *Plautus. The Rope, Amphitryo, The Ghost, A Three-Dollar Day* (Harmondsworth).

Wind, R. (tr.) (1995) *Plautus. Three Comedies: The Braggart Warrior, The Rope, Casina* (Lanham/New York/London).

(8) Caecilius Statius

Guardì, T. (1974) *Cecilio Stazio. I frammenti* (Palermo) (Hermes 9).

(9) Terence

Kauer, R./Lindsay, W.M. (eds) (1958) *P. Terenti Afri comoediae, recognoverunt brevique adnotatione critica instruxerunt R. K. et W. M. L. Supplementa apparatus curavit* O. Skutsch (Oxford).

Barsby, J. (ed.) (1999) *Terence. Eunuchus* (Cambridge) (Cambridge Greek and Latin Classics).

Brothers, A.J. (ed. and tr.) (2000) *Terence. The Eunuch*. Edited with translation and commentary (Warminster).

Gratwick, A.S. (1999) *Terence. The Brothers*. Edited with an introduction,translation and notes. 2nd edn (Warminster).

Martin, R.H. (ed.) (1976) *Terence. Adelphoe* (Cambridge/London/New York/Melbourne) (Cambridge Greek and Latin Classics).

Barsby, J. (ed. and tr.) (2001) *Terence*. Edited and translated, 2 vols (Cambridge [MA]/London) (LCL 22/23).

Brown, P. (tr.) (2006) *Terence. The Comedies*. Translated with introduction and notes (Oxford).

(10) Decimus Laberius

Panayotakis, C. (ed.) (2010) *Decimus Laberius. The Fragments* (Cambridge) (Cambridge Classical Texts and Commentaries 46).

(11) Seneca

Zwierlein, O. (ed.) (1986) *L. Annaei Senecae tragoediae, incertorum auctorum Hercules [Oetaeus] Octavia*, recogn. brevique adn. crit. instr. (Oxford) (repr. with corr. 1993).

Costa, C.D.N. (ed.) (1973) *Seneca. Medea*. Edited with introduction and commentary (Oxford) (repr. 1989).

Hine, H.M. (ed.) (2000) *Seneca. Medea*. With an introduction, translation and commentary (Warminster) (repr. 2007).

Fitch, J.G. (ed. and tr.) (2002) *Seneca. Hercules, Trojan Women, Phoenician Women, Medea, Phaedra*. Edited and translated (Cambridge [MA]/London) (LCL 62: Seneca VIII, Tragedies).

Fitch, J.G. (ed. and tr.) (2004) *Seneca. Oedipus, Agamemnon, Thyestes. [Seneca]. Hercules on Oeta, Octavia*. Edited and translated (Cambridge [MA]/London) (LCL 62: Seneca IX, Tragedies II).

Share, D. (ed.) (1998) *Seneca in English* (London) (Penguin Classics: Penguin Poets in Translation).

Boyle, A.J. (ed. and tr.) (2008) *Octavia. Attributed to Seneca*. Edited with introduction, translation and commentary (Oxford).

Ferri, R. (ed.) (2003) *Octavia. A Play Attributed to Seneca*. Edited with introduction and commentary (Cambridge) (Cambridge Classical Texts and Commentaries 41).

B 2. Secondary literature

(1) Greek drama

(a) General

Csapo, E./Slater, W.J. (1995) *The Context of Ancient Drama* (Ann Arbor). [brief introduction and collection of thematically grouped testimonia in translation, mainly on Greek drama]

Dugdale, E. (2008) *Greek Theatre in Context* (Cambridge) (Greece and Rome: Texts and Contexts). [accessible introduction to the background to Greek drama]

Pickard-Cambridge, A. (1968) *The Dramatic Festivals of Athens*. 2nd edn revised by J. Gould and D.M. Lewis (Oxford) (reissued with supplement and corrections 1988). [standard account of the organization of festivals and performances in Greece]

Storey, I.C./Allan, A. (2005) *A Guide to Ancient Greek Drama* (Oxford) (Blackwell Guides to Classical Literature).

(b) Tragedy and Euripides

Collard, C. (1981) *Euripides* (Oxford) (Greece & Rome, New Surveys in the Classics 14). [brief introduction to Euripides]

Easterling, P.E. (ed.) (1997) *The Cambridge Companion to Greek Tragedy* (Cambridge) (Cambridge Companions to Literature).

Ferguson, J. (1972) *A Companion to Greek Tragedy* (Austin [Texas]/London).

Goldhill, S. (1986) *Reading Greek Tragedy* (Cambridge/London/New York/New Rochelle/Melbourne/Sydney).

Gregory, N. (ed.) (2005) *A Companion to Greek Tragedy* (Oxford) (Blackwell Companions to the Ancient World).

Lesky, A. (1983) *Greek Tragic Poetry*. Translated by Matthew Dillon (New Haven/London) (German original: 1972).

Morwood, J. (2002) *The Plays of Euripides* (London) (Classical World Series). [brief overview of all plays]

Rabinowitz, N.S. (2008) *Greek Tragedy* (Malden [MA]/Oxford) (Blackwell Introductions to the Classical World).

Taplin, O. (1978) *Greek Tragedy in Action* (London) (repr. with rev. 1985, repr.).

Taplin, O. (1986) 'Fifth-century tragedy and comedy: a *synkrisis*', *JHS* 106: 163-74.

Taplin, O. (2007) *Pots and Plays. Interactions between Tragedy and Greek Vase-painting of the Fourth Century BC* (Los Angeles). [on vase-paintings as evidence for the spread and reception of Greek tragedy]

Webster, T.B.L. (1971) *Greek Tragedy* (Oxford) (Greece & Rome, New Surveys in the Classics No. 5).

(c) Comedy and Menander

Goldberg, S.M. (1980) *The Making of Menander's Comedy* (London).

Taplin, O. (1993) *Comic Angels and Other Approaches to Greek Drama through Vase-Paintings* (Oxford). [on vase-paintings as evidence for the spread and reception of Greek drama, esp. comedy]

Walton, J.M./Arnott, P.D. (1996) *Menander and the Making of Comedy* (Westport [CT]/London) (Lives of the Theatre).

Webster, T.B.L. (1970) *Studies in Later Greek Comedy* (Manchester) (1st edn: 1953).

Webster, T.B.L. (1974) *An Introduction to Menander* (Manchester/New York).

Zagagi, N. (1994) *The Comedy of Menander. Convention, Variation and Originality* (London).

(2) Historical and cultural context of Roman drama

Cornell, T.J. (1995) *The Beginnings of Rome. Italy and Rome from the Bronze Age to the Punic Wars (c. 1000-264 BC)* (London/New York) (Routledge History of the Ancient World).

Crawford, M. (1993) *The Roman Republic*. 2nd edn (Cambridge [MA]).

Dench, E. (1995) *From Barbarians to New Men. Greek, Roman, and Modern Perceptions of Peoples from the Central Apennines* (Oxford) (Oxford Classical Monographs). [studies the relationship between various peoples in Italy]

Feeney, D. (1998) *Literature and Religion at Rome. Cultures, Contexts, and Beliefs* (Cambridge) (Roman Literature and its Contexts). [discusses cultural processes]

Flower, H.I. (ed.) (2004) *The Cambridge Companion to the Roman Republic* (Cambridge).

Gruen, E.S. (1990) *Studies in Greek Culture and Roman Policy* (Leiden/New York/Copenhagen/Cologne) (Cincinnati Classical Studies. New Series. Vol. VII) (paperback edn: Berkeley/London 1996).

Gruen, E.S. (1992) *Culture and National Identity in Republican Rome* (Ithaca [NY]) (Cornell Studies in Classical Philology LII). [on the interaction between Hellenic culture and Roman values]

Nicolet, C. (1980) *The World of the Citizen in Republican Rome*. Translated by P.S. Falla (Berkeley/Los Angeles) (French original: *Le métier de citoyen dans la Rome républicaine*, Paris 1976).

Rosenstein, N./Morstein-Marx, R. (eds) (2006) *A Companion to the Roman Republic* (Oxford) (Blackwell Companions to the Ancient World).

Wiseman, T.P. (1994) *Historiography and Imagination. Eight Essays on Roman Culture* (Exeter) (Exeter Studies in History 33).

Wiseman, T.P. (1998) *Roman Drama and Roman History* (Exeter) (Exeter Studies in History). [on the possibility of a vibrant culture of lost Roman history plays]

(3) General treatments of Roman literary history

Conte, G.B. (1994) *Latin Literature. A History*. Translated by J.B. Solodow. Revised by D. Fowler and G.W. Most (Baltimore/London).

Harrison, S. (ed.) (2005) *A Companion to Latin Literature* (Oxford) (Blackwell Companions to the Ancient World) [esp. S.M. Goldberg, 'The Early Republic: the Beginnings to 90 BC', 15-30; E. Fantham, 'Roman Tragedy', 116-29; C. Panayotakis, 'Comedy, Atellane Farce and Mime', 130-47].

Kenney, E.J./Clausen, W.V. (eds) (1982) *The Cambridge History of Classical Literature. II. Latin Literature* (Cambridge/London/New York/New Rochelle/Melbourne/Sydney) [esp. A.S. Gratwick, '5. Drama', 77-137].

Suerbaum, W. (ed.) (2002) *Handbuch der Lateinischen Literatur der Antike. Erster Band. Die Archaische Literatur. Von den Anfängen bis Sullas Tod. Die vorliterarische Periode und die Zeit von 240 bis 78 v. Chr.*

(HLL 1) (Munich) (HbdA VIII.1). [provides brief portraits of all Republican writers and literary genres with testimonia and bibliography]

(4) Organization of festivals and dramatic productions

Bernstein, F. (1998) *Ludi publici. Untersuchungen zur Entstehung und Entwicklung der öffentlichen Spiele im republikanischen Rom* (Stuttgart) (Historia, Einzelschriften 119). [description of the history, structure and characteristics of all major festivals in the Republican period]

Easterling, P./Hall, E. (eds) (2002) *Greek and Roman Actors: Aspects of an Ancient Profession* (Cambridge). [overview of the different types of actors and their roles]

Garton, C. (1972) *Personal Aspects of the Roman Theatre* (Toronto). [essays on Roman actors, including a list of known Republican actors]

Goldberg, S.M. (1998) 'Plautus on the Palatine', *JRS* 88: 1-20. [discussion of the probable performance space of Plautus' *Stichus*, the size and layout of the venue]

Hanson, J.A. (1959) *Roman Theater-Temples*, Diss. Princeton University (Princeton [NJ]). [on the specific Roman structure of a combination of theatre and temple]

Kindermann, H. (1979) *Das Theaterpublikum der Antike* (Salzburg). [discussion of composition, education and background of theatre audiences in ancient Greece and Rome]

Sear, F. (2006) *Roman Theatres. An Architectural Study* (Oxford) (Oxford Monographs on Classical Archaeology). [up-to-date archaeological documentation of characteristics of Roman theatre buildings and all known sites]

Taylor, L.R. (1937) 'The opportunities for dramatic performances in the time of Plautus and Terence', *TAPhA* 68: 284-304. [calculation of the number of days available for dramatic performances in Republican Rome]

Wiles, D. (1991) *The Masks of Menander. Sign and Meaning in Greek and Roman Performance* (Cambridge/New York/Port Chester/Melbourne/Sydney). [on the use of masks in ancient theatre]

(5) Comprehensive treatments of drama

Beacham, R.C. (1991) *The Roman Theatre and its Audience* (London). [overview with emphasis on the phyiscal aspects of Roman theatre, especially the possible shape of early stages]

Beare, W. (1964) *The Roman Stage. A Short History of Latin Drama in the Time of the Republic*, 3rd edn (London). [standard account in English of the practicalities of the Roman stage as well as the various dramatic genres and poets]

Bieber, M. (1961) *The History of the Greek and Roman Theater*, 2nd edn, revised and enlarged (Princeton [NJ]) (4th print.: 1971; 1st edn: 1939). [illustrated account of practical, physical and literary aspects of the Greek and Roman theatre on the basis of a variety of sources; still provides useful material]

Dorey, T.A./Dudley, D.R. (eds) (1965) *Roman Drama* (New York) (Studies in Latin Literature and its Influence).

Lefèvre, E. (ed.) (1978) *Das römische Drama* (Darmstadt) (Grundriß der Literaturgeschichten nach Gattungen). [collection of survey essays on the individual dramatic genres]

Manuwald, G. (forthcoming) *Roman Republican Theatre* (Cambridge).

(6) Imperial theatre

Bartsch, S. (1994) *Actors in the Audience. Theatricality and Doublespeak from Nero to Hadrian* (Cambridge [MA]/London). [discusses aspects of theatricality and insincerity in the theatre and other areas of culture in the first century CE]

Beacham, R.C. (1999) *Spectacle Entertainments of Early Imperial Rome* (New Haven [CT]/London). [offers a 'theatrical history' of Rome from the last decades of the Republic to the death of Nero]

(7) Ancient reception and literary criticism

Gilula, D. (1989) 'Greek drama in Rome: some aspects of cultural transposition', in H. Scolnicov and P. Holland (eds) *The Play out of Context. Transferring Plays from Culture to Culture* (Cambridge/New York/New Rochelle/Melbourne/Sydney): 99-109.

Goldberg, S.M. (2005) *Constructing Literature in the Roman Republic. Poetry and its Reception* (Cambridge). [argues that 'early Republican literature' did not emerge in the middle Republic when the texts were written, but rather was a product of the late Republic, when texts were first systematically collected and studied]

Slater, N.W. (1992) 'Two Republican Poets on Drama: Terence and Accius', in B. Zimmermann (ed.) *Antike Dramentheorien und ihre Rezeption* (Stuttgart) (Drama 1): 85-103. [on the views on drama that emerge from Terence's prologues and Accius' treatises]

Wright, F.W. (1931) *Cicero and the Theater* (Northampton [MA]) (Smith College Classical Studies 11). [collection and discussion of passages in Cicero with references to plays and the theatre]

(8) Dramatic genres

(a) Tragedy

Boyle, A.J. (2006) *An Introduction to Roman Tragedy* (London/New York).

Erasmo, M. (2004) *Roman Tragedy. Theatre to Theatricality* (Austin [Texas]). [sketch of the development of Roman Tragedy from the beginnings until the imperial period with emphasis on theatrical and metatheatrical aspects]

Fantham, E. (2005) 'Roman Tragedy', in S. Harrison (ed.) *A Companion to Latin Literature* (Oxford) (Blackwell Companions to the Ancient World): 116-29.

Goldberg, S.M. (1996) 'The fall and rise of Roman tragedy', *TAPhA* 126: 265-86.

Goldberg, S.M. (2007) 'Research report: reading Roman tragedy', *IJCT* 13: 571-84.

Manuwald, G. (2001 [2004]) 'Römische Tragödien und Praetexten republikanischer Zeit: 1964-2002', *Lustrum* 43: 11-237. [bibliography]

Ribbeck, O. (1875) *Die Römische Tragödie im Zeitalter der Republik* (Leipzig) (repr. Hildesheim 1968, Mit einem Vorwort v. W.-H. Friedrich). [classic account of the possible content and plots of all fragmentary Republican tragedies]

Schiesaro, A. (2005) 'Roman tragedy', in R. Bushnell (ed.) *A Companion to Tragedy* (Oxford): 269-86.

(b) Praetexta

Flower, H.I. (1995) '*Fabulae Praetextae* in context: when were plays on contemporary subjects performed in Republican Rome?', *CQ* 45: 170-90.

Kragelund, P. (2002) 'SO debate: historical drama in ancient Rome: Republican flourishing and imperial decline?', *SO* 77: 5-105. [debate about characteristics, development and function of this dramatic genre with contributions by various scholars]

Manuwald, G. (2001) *Fabulae praetextae. Spuren einer literarischen Gattung der Römer* (Munich: Zetemata 108). [overview of this dramatic genre with texts, testimonia and bibliography]

(c) Comedy

Arnott, W.G. (1975) *Menander, Plautus, Terence* (Oxford) (Greece & Rome, New Surveys in the Classics No. 9). [brief introduction to the three major representatives of New Comedy]

Duckworth, G.E. (1994) *The Nature of Roman Comedy. A Study in Popular Entertainment.* 2nd edn. With a foreword and bibliographical appendix by R. Hunter (Norman/Bristol) (1st edn: Princeton [NJ] 1952). [classic account of characteristics and conventions of Roman Comedy]

Halporn, J. (1993) 'Roman comedy and Greek models', in R. Scodel (ed.) *Theater and Society in the Classical World* (Ann Arbor): 191-213.

Hunter, R.L. (1985) *The New Comedy of Greece and Rome* (Cambridge/London/New York/New Rochelle/Melbourne/Sydney).

Konstan, D. (1983) *Roman Comedy* (Ithaca [NY]/London).

Lefèvre, E. (ed.) (1973) *Die römische Komödie: Plautus und Terenz* (Darmstadt) (WdF CCXXXVI). [collection of important essays on Plautus and Terence]

Leigh, M. (2004) *Comedy and the Rise of Rome* (Oxford). [tries to place Roman Comedy into its context; studies the mutual relationship between Roman politics and society as well as the comic scripts]

Lowe, N.J. (2008) *Comedy* (Cambridge) (Greece & Rome, New Surveys in the Classics No. 37, 2007). [describes characteristics of comedy and its development from the beginnings in Greece to Terence]

Marshall, C.W. (2006) *The Stagecraft and Performance of Roman Comedy* (Cambridge). [discusses questions related to actually staging and performing a Roman comedy]

Moore, T.J. (1998) 'Music and structure in Roman comedy', *AJPh* 119: 245-73. [on the musical shape of Roman comedy as a structural element]

Moore, T.J. (1999) 'Facing the music: character and musical accompaniment in Roman comedy', in J. Porter, E. Csapo, C.W. Marshall and R.C. Ketterer (eds) *Crossing the Stages: The Production, Performance and Reception of Ancient Theater. Selected Papers Presented at a Conference Held in Saskatoon, Saskatchewan, on 22-25 October, 1997*, *SyllClass* 10: 130-53. [on patterns in the use of musical accompaniment in Roman comedy as a structural element]

Parker, H.N. (1996) 'Plautus v. Terence: audience and popularity re-examined', *AJPh* 117: 585-617. [discusses the respective popularity of Plautus and Terence]

Segal, E. (ed.) (2001) *Oxford Readings in Menander, Plautus, and Terence* (Oxford). [collection of reprints of important articles]

Wright, J. (1974) *Dancing in Chains: the Stylistic Unity of the Comoedia Palliata* (Rome) (Papers and Monographs of the American Academy in Rome XXV). [includes discussion of fragmentary comic poets and argues that Terence is the exception to an otherwise coherent palliata tradition]

(d) Other comic genres

Fantham, E. (1989) 'The earliest comic theatre at Rome: Atellan farce, comedy and mime as antecedents of the *commedia dell'arte*', in D. Pietropaolo (ed.) *The Science of Buffoonery. Theory and History of the Commedia dell'Arte* (Ottawa) (University of Toronto Italian Studies 3): 23-32.

Fantham, E. (1989) 'Mime: the missing link in Roman literary history', *CW* 82: 153-63.

Jory, E.J. (1981) 'The literary evidence for the beginnings of imperial pantomime', *BICS* 28: 147-61.

Jory, E.J. (1988) 'Publilius Syrus and the element of competition in the theatre of the Republic', in N. Horsfall (ed.) *Vir Bonus Discendi Peritus. Studies in Celebration of Otto Skutsch's Eightieth Birthday* (London) (BICS Suppl. 51): 73-81. [on competitions between actors and particularly on the contest between the mime writers Publilius Syrus and Decimus Laberius]

Jory, E.J. (1996) 'The drama of the dance: prolegomena to an iconography of imperial pantomime', in W.J. Slater (ed.) *Roman Theater and Society* (Ann Arbor) (E. Togo Salmon Papers I): 1-27.

Panayotakis, C. (2005) 'Comedy, Atellane Farce and Mime', in S. Harrison (ed.) *A Companion to Latin Literature* (Oxford) (Blackwell Companions to the Ancient World): 130-47.

(9) Dramatic poets

(a) Naevius

Suerbaum, W. (2000) 'Naevius comicus. Der Komödiendichter Naevius in der neueren Forschung', in E. Stärk and G. Vogt-Spira (eds) *Dramatische Wäldchen. Festschrift für Eckard Lefèvre zum 65. Geburtstag* (Hildesheim/Zurich/New York) (Spudasmata 80): 301-20. [concise overview of Naevius' comic output with bibliography]

(b) Ennius

Breed, B.W./Rossi, A. (eds) (2006) *Ennius and the Invention of Roman Epic*, *Arethusa* 39.3 (Baltimore). [special journal issue on Ennius' epic *Annales*, but discussing aspects that are also relevant for his dramatic works, on the basis of more recent theoretical approaches]

Classen, C.J. ([1992] 1993) 'Ennius: ein Fremder in Rom', *Gymnasium* 99: 121-45; repr. in C.J. Classen, *Die Welt der Römer. Studien zu ihrer Literatur, Geschichte und Religion.* Unter Mitwirkung v. H. Bernsdorff hg. v. M. Vielberg (Berlin/New York 1993) (UaLG 41): 62-83. [looks at Ennius' *Medea* and *Annals* and discusses the context of early literature in Rome]

Fitzgerald, W./Gowers, E. (eds) (2007) *Ennius perennis. The Annals and Beyond* (Oxford) (Cambridge Classical Journal, Proceedings of the Cambridge Philological Society, Suppl. Vol. 31). [on Ennius' epic *Annales*, but opening up perspectives also relevant for his dramatic output]

Prinzen, H. (1998) *Ennius im Urteil der Antike* (Stuttgart/Weimar) (Drama Beiheft 8). [on the reception of Ennius in antiquity]

Suerbaum, W. (2003) *Ennius in der Forschung des 20. Jahrhunderts. Eine kommentierte Bibliographie für 1900-1999 mit systematischen Hinweisen nebst einer Kurzdarstellung des Q. Ennius (239-169 v. Chr.)* (Hildesheim/Zurich/New York) (Bibliographien zur Klassischen Philologie 1). [comprehensive overview of 20th-century scholarship on Ennius]

(c) Pacuvius

Fantham, E. (2003) 'Pacuvius: melodrama, reversals and recognitions', in D. Braund and C. Gill (eds) *Myth, History and Culture in Republican Rome. Studies in Honour of T.P. Wiseman* (Exeter): 98-118. [on favoured structures and motifs in Pacuvius' tragedies]

Manuwald, G. (2003) *Pacuvius – summus tragicus poeta. Zum dramatischen Profil seiner Tragödien* (Munich/Leipzig) (BzA 191). [tries to establish characteristics of Pacuvius' dramatic output]

(d) Plautus

Anderson, W.S. (1993) *Barbarian Play. Plautus' Roman Comedy* (Toronto/Buffalo/London) (The Robson Classical Lectures).

Fraenkel, E. (2007) *Plautine Elements in Plautus (Plautinisches im Plautus)*. Translated by T. Drevikovsky and F. Muecke (Oxford) (German original: *Plautinisches im Plautus*, Berlin 1922 [Philologische Untersuchungen 28]; Italian translation [by F. Munari; with *Addenda* by the author]: *Elementi Plautini in Plauto (Plautinisches im Plautus)*, Florence 1960 [Il pensiero storico 41]).

Hughes, J.D. (1975) *A Bibliography of Scholarship on Plautus* (Amsterdam).

McCarthy, K. (2000) *Slaves, Masters, and the Art of Authority in Plautine Comedy* (Princeton [NJ]/Oxford) (repr. 2004).

Moore, T.J. (1995) 'How is it played? Tragicomedy as a running joke: Plautus' *Amphitruo* in performance', *Didaskalia* Suppl. 1 (www.didaskalia.net/issues/supplement1/moore.html).

Moore, T.J. (1998) *The Theater of Plautus. Playing to the Audience* (Austin [Texas]).

Segal, E. (1981) 'Scholarship on Plautus 1965-1976', *CW* 74: 353-433.

Segal, E. (1987) *Roman Laughter. The Comedy of Plautus* (Oxford) (1st edn: Cambridge [MA]) 1968).

Slater, N.W. (1990) '*Amphitruo, Bacchae*, and Metatheatre', *Lexis* 5-6: 101-25.

Slater, N.W. (2000) *Plautus in Performance. The Theatre of the Mind*. 2nd edn (Amsterdam) (Greek and Roman Theatre Archive 2) (1st edn: Princeton [NJ] 1985).

Wiles, D. (1988) 'Taking farce seriously: recent critical approaches to Plautus', in J. Redmond (ed.) *Farce* (Cambridge/New York/New Rochelle/ Melbourne/Sydney) (Themes in Drama 10): 261-71.

(e) Terence

Forehand, W.E. (1985) *Terence* (Boston) (Twayne's World Authors Series 745, Latin Literature).

Gilula, D. (1978) 'Where Did the Audience Go?', *SCI* 4: 45-9. [on the prologue to *Hecyra*]

Gilula, D. (1981) 'Who's afraid of rope-walkers and gladiators? (Ter. Hec. 1-57)', *Athenaeum* 59: 29-37. [on the prologue to *Hecyra*]

Goldberg, S.M. (1981) 'Scholarship on Terence and the fragments of Roman comedy (1959-1980)', *CW* 75: 77-115.

Goldberg, S.M. (1986) *Understanding Terence* (Princeton [NJ]).

Goldberg, S.M. (1993) 'Terence and the death of comedy', in C. Davidson, R. Johnson and J. H. Stroupe (eds) *Drama and the Classical Heritage. Comparative and Critical Essays* (New York) (AMS Ancient and Classical Studies 1): 52-64.

Kruschwitz, P./Ehlers, W.-W./Felgentreu, F. (eds) (2007) *Terentius Poeta.* (Munich) (Zetemata 127). [collection of essays]

Lentano, M. (1997) 'Quindici anni di studi terenziani. Parte prima: studi sulle commedie (1979-1993)', *BStudLat* 27: 497-564.

Lentano, M. (1998) 'Quindici anni di studi terenziani. Parte seconda: tradizione manoscritta ed esegesi antica (1979-1993)', *BStudLat* 28: 78-104. [bibliography]

(f) Seneca

Boyle, A.J. (ed.) (1983) *Seneca Tragicus. Ramus Essays on Senecan Drama* (Bendigo).

Boyle, A.J. (1997) *Tragic Seneca. An Essay in the Theatrical Tradition* (London).

Costa, C.D.N. (1974) 'The Tragedies', in C.D.N. Costa (ed.) *Seneca* (London/Boston) (Greek and Latin Studies, Classical Literature and its Influence): 96-115.

Davis, P.J. (1993) *Shifting Song. The Chorus in Seneca's Tragedies* (Hildesheim/Zurich/New York) (Altertumswissenschaftliche Texte und Studien 26).

Fitch, J.G. (ed.) (2008) *Oxford Readings in Classical Studies. Seneca* (Oxford). [collection of reprints of important articles]

Griffin, M.T. (1976) *Seneca. A Philosopher in Politics* (Oxford). [biography of Seneca]

Lefèvre, E. (ed.) (1972) *Senecas Tragödien* (Darmstadt) (WdF CCCX). [collection of essays on Seneca's tragedies]

Littlewood, C.A.J. (2004) *Self-Representation and Illusion in Senecan*

Tragedy (Oxford) (Oxford Classical Monographs).

Motto, A.L./Clark, R.J. (1989) *Seneca. A Critical Bibliography 1900-1980. Scholarship on his Life, Thought, Prose, and Influence* (Amsterdam). [bibliography on all works by Seneca, covering most of the twentieth century]

Pratt, N.T. (1983) *Seneca's Drama* (Chapel Hill/London).

Seidensticker, B./Armstrong, D. (1985) 'Seneca tragicus 1878-1978 (with Addenda 1979ff.)', *ANRW* II.32.2: 916-68. [bibliography on Seneca's tragic output]

Tarrant, R.J. (1978) 'Senecan drama and its antecedents', *HSPh* 82: 213-63. [on the relationship of Seneca's tragedies to earlier Greek and Roman tragedies in terms of style and structure]

Tarrant, R.J. (1995) 'Greek and Roman in Seneca's tragedies', *HSCP* 97: 215-30.

Wilson, M. (ed.) (2003) *The Tragedy of Nero's Wife. Studies on the Octavia Praetexta, Prudentia* 35.1. [collection of essays on the pseudo-Senecan *Octavia*]